Technolingualism

Technolingualism

The Mind and the Machine

JAMES PFREHM

BLOOMSBURY ACADEMIC
LONDON • NEW YORK • OXFORD • NEW DELHI • SYDNEY

BLOOMSBURY ACADEMIC
Bloomsbury Publishing Plc
50 Bedford Square, London, WC1B 3DP, UK
1385 Broadway, New York, NY 10018, USA

BLOOMSBURY, BLOOMSBURY ACADEMIC and the Diana logo are
trademarks of Bloomsbury Publishing Plc

First published 2018
Reprinted 2018

Cover design by Olivia D'Cruz
Cover images: Wiring © Shutterstock/takito.
Brain illustration © Shutterstock/shopplaywood

A catalogue record for this book is available from the British Library.

ISBN: HB: 978-1-4725-7835-8
PB: 978-1-4725-7833-4
ePDF: 978-1-4725-7836-5
ePub: 978-1-4725-7834-1

A catalog record for this book is available from the Library of Congress.

Typeset by Newgen KnowledgeWorks Pvt. Ltd., Chennai, India
Printed and bound in Great Britain

To find out more about our authors and books visit
www.bloomsbury.com and sign up for our newsletters.

Contents

List of Illustrations

Figures

Tables

Preface, or What This Book Is and Who It's for

Do you use language—spoken, written, or signed—to communicate? Do you use technology to communicate with language? If you can answer *yes* to one or both of these (admittedly rhetorical) questions—and we're guessing that you can—then this book is for you. More specifically, this is a book *about* you: both the language you use and the technology you use to communicate with language.

The 200-odd pages that lie before you explore the processes and products of a dynamic interaction between language and technology, a phenomenon we're calling *technolingualism*. And at the heart of this phenomenon, we'll see, lies the proposition that technology not only shapes but is also shaped *by* language. The flow of influence, in other words, runs both ways. On the one hand, technology can give rise to new linguistic structures, practices, and ideologies. Conversely—and this other half of the story often goes unacknowledged—language can also inspire technology, whether its physical shape or its operational design.

In short, technolingualism is the technological and linguistic consequences of the mutually influential relationship between language and technology.

What's more, it turns out that you, me, and all those who can at the least read the very words of this sentence bear the sociolinguistic marks of technolingualism. We are, to put it baldly, *technolinguals*. For this reason alone this book is both for and about you, Dear Reader.

Our exploration of technolingualism unfolds in six stages (aka chapters), in which we consider eight different communication technologies. In Chapter 1 we look at the *textualization of language*, a quantum leap for spoken language that occurred with the invention of writing, arguably the greatest communication technology. Chapter 2 covers the printing press and typewriter, which, we argue, resulted in a *mechanization of language*. In Chapter 3 we level our sights on the telegraph and telephone, making the case that these two technologies brought about an *abstraction of language*. In Chapter 4 we take a linguistic dive into the realm of ones and zeros, arguing that computer technology led to a *digitization of language*. Chapter 5 tackles the cell phone and canvasses the technolingualism that arises out of the *mobilization of language*. Our final chapter spotlights the cochlear implant, a game-changing technology that has impacted hundreds of thousands of speakers around the world and which, we argue, has amounted to a *regeneration of language*. At each stage along our investigative journey, and for each technology, we address how language both shaped and was shaped by the technology.

Ultimately, this book seeks answers to the following pair of questions:

- How do language and technology interact?

- What happens, to either or both, as a result of this interaction?

If these questions interest you, Dear Reader—if you want to learn more about yourself and your language, and the technology that has shaped and been shaped by them—please read on.

1

Textualization of Language: Writing

A Technology for Forgetting, or an Argument between Two Men in Tunics

Let's go back a few millennia, to the fifth century BCE.

Our setting is Athens. It's another sweltering afternoon in the intellectual capital of ancient Greece. Socrates ambles across a cobblestone street, where he bumps into an old friend, Phaedrus. Phaedrus is giddy with excitement; he has spent the morning listening to a speech by the famous rhetorician Lysias. Socrates is eager to hear more about the speech and accompanies Phaedrus into the countryside, where the two men cool their feet in a stream and settle beneath a tree.

"Please," Socrates begins, "repeat to me this speech which has stirred such excitement in you."

But Phaedrus balks. "My dear Socrates, surely you must know that such eloquence and wisdom, as is typical of Lysias's speeches, is impossible to 'repeat.'"

"Certainly, my sweet Phaedrus. I wouldn't want to tax your poor youthful memory more than it is used to." He extends a bony finger at Phaedrus's chest. "But since you have brought Lysias with you, perhaps you can produce him now."

Phaedrus frowns. "It would seem that the heat has gotten to you, my sweet, aged friend. It's only you and I here beneath this plane tree."

"Then what is that under your garb?"

Phaedrus reaches into his toga and pulls out a written copy of Lysias's speech.

"You've caught me," Phaedrus sighs. "It is not Lysias himself that I carry under my wrap, but his precious words."

Socrates takes the scroll and peers at the scribbled lines. "Would that you had brought Lysias instead. Tell me, sweet friend, if I ask this scroll a question, will it respond?"

"Surely you know that it will not."

"And should I need clarification of its arguments, or should I wish to challenge its wisdom, can I do so?"

Phaedrus only looks at the ground, deflated.

"Dear Phaedrus," Socrates continues, "this technology of yours has not only allowed you to forget the true speech, it has also cut you off from dialogue. These words that you now rely on are as silent as the stones upon the bed of this stream. Tell me, what good can come of such a discovery? What of memory, of verbal exchange, or of speaking from the heart? I tell you, sweet Phaedrus, this technology will be the end of man's intellect."

∞

Nearly 2,500 years ago Socrates critiqued the effect that writing, as a then-modern technology, would have on Athenian intellectual society. He recognized its transformative potential. And like many people in our own time, he was skeptical of how the new technology would change social behaviors and values. As we'll see in the pages ahead, writing has in fact led to many changes in the ways we think and act. This extends to our language, too—both in terms of how we actually use it and how we think about or evaluate it.

Yet Socrates failed to consider the other side of the coin: that the technology of writing has also been shaped by language itself. To this end, in the first part of this chapter we'll look at how linguistic structures, practices, and ideologies have acted on what Socrates, long ago, condemned as the "technology for forgetting."

Writing, we'll show, is a powerful technology that has both informed and been informed by human language. As such, it's a prime example of the nature and dynamics of technolingualism.

Writing as Technology

It might seem strange to think of writing as "technology." There's nothing electronic to it. No sophisticated assembly of mechanical parts. Yet every time you put pencil to paper, you're participating in one of humankind's grandest inventions—right up there with the wheel, the domestication of plants, and the computer.

Perhaps more than any other technology, writing fundamentally altered our relationship to ourselves and to others. It reconfigured our brains, both literally and figuratively.[1] And it allowed for new ways of conceptualizing time, space, and potentiality. Nobel Prize winner Hermann Hesse famously wrote that "among the many worlds which man did not receive as a gift of nature, but which he created with his own spirit, the world of books is the greatest. Without words, without writing, and without books there would be no history, there would be no concept of humanity."[2]

But writing also changed our relationship to language itself. It enabled us to overcome the fleeting, unruly nature of real-time speech; organize and document thought; and sculpt polished paragraphs from welters of words and ideas. Christian Vandendorpe notes that writing "introduced the possibility of order, continuity, and consistency where there had been fluidity and chaos."[3] Writing, in other words, was the yoke our ancestors strapped onto language to bring it under their control.

As we explore the many ways that writing and language have affected each other over the centuries, we'll occasionally return to this writing-as-a-yoke metaphor. It serves the larger point that, like other technologies, humans invented writing in order to master realities around them—in this case, language. But not just the words and sounds of language; the technology of writing afforded those who wielded it the power over language ideologies, too (i.e., the beliefs, judgments, and perceptions that speakers have about language, whether their own or the language of others).

But writing is not just *a* technology; it's a *language* technology, created from and for language. The two are inherently and inextricably linked. Thus we've chosen to begin our exploration of the interaction between language and technology—a mutually influential process we're calling technolingualism—with writing.

What Is Writing?

In the most basic sense, writing is a way of representing spoken language through symbols. These symbols can stand for a sound, a real or imaginary object, or an abstract concept. As a representative system, writing also displaces speech in time and space. Have you ever had something you wrote, or something you said that was written down and read by someone else, taken out of context? This was probably because of the displacing effect of writing. The symbols stripped your words of their immediate context and transported them to another time and place for reinterpretation.

Imagine that you take a picture of a person crying at a funeral, but you crop the picture down to only the person's tearful face. Then you send it to ten different friends and ask them to guess why the person is crying. You'll likely get different interpretations. Basically, the same thing happens to language when it gets textualized.

In fact this was one reason why Socrates took a skeptical stance on writing. He deemed it "inhuman" because, unlike speech, which is "alive" with sound and context, writing is a lifeless technology. It can neither defend itself when questioned nor respond to new questions. And as we saw in our chapter's opening scene, Socrates also argued that writing corrodes an individual's memory, essentially making the mind a slave to the page. Writing was, in his words, "an invented elixir not of memory, but of reminding."[4]

Granted, the tuniced sage had a point. Committing thoughts to paper means you don't have to commit them to memory. So yes, it seems plausible that writing might encourage some amount of "cognitive laziness." And it's also true that you can't "dialogue" with marks on a page—the corollary being that writing, then, discourages social interaction. (Is it just us, or do Socrates's criticisms of writing sound uncannily similar to modern-day criticisms of digital devices?)

But in all his cautioning and criticizing, Socrates failed to recognize the extraordinary benefits that the "technology for forgetting" might yield—especially for those who learned to wield it to their advantage. In his Pulitzer Prize–winning study of the inequities among the world's societies, Jared Diamond describes how writing benefitted Spanish conquistadors in their campaign against the preliterate Incan Empire. Commands, strategies, accounts of earlier expeditions, and field updates—these written documents provided the Spaniards with invaluable strategic knowledge. "While all those types of information," Diamond writes, "were also transmitted by other means in preliterate societies, writing made the transmission easier, more detailed, more accurate, and more persuasive.[5]" The argument here is that, as with weapons, microbes, and durable means of transportation, writing was a technology that afforded one smaller group of people (i.e., the conquistadores) an enormous, multifaceted advantage over a much larger group (i.e., the Aztecs). So much so that it helped several hundred Spaniards subdue an empire of millions.

Others have argued that the invention of writing changes the way a society thinks. Sociologists Jack Goody and Ian Watt make the case that the ability to physically record history encourages critical thinking, discussion, and solution finding.[6] Their argument goes something like this: Literate societies are more liable to deal with historical unpleasantries because these can be documented with writing. Oral societies, on the other hand, can selectively transmit across generations only what they wish to have remembered. Thus, Goody and Watt's conclusion goes, societies that have unsavory histories attested (or "captured," as it were) in written records are compelled to analyze, or even come to terms with, their pasts in order to explain their actions.

Some scholars have even considered whether the type of writing system a culture develops or adopts can affect the way its people think. In *The Alphabet Effect*, Robert Logan contends that the alphabet was the catalyst for intellectual thought and science in Western civilization. A phonetic alphabet, he argues, promotes abstraction, analysis, and the coding of information—cognitive skills that are used in philosophy, religion, law, social organization, and science. He sums up his thesis as follows: "Of all mankind's inventions, with the possible exception of language itself, nothing has proved more useful or led to more innovations than the alphabet.... It has influenced the development of our thought patterns, our social institutions, and our very sense of ourselves."[7]

A few years after Logan's book, William C. Hannas approached the same topic from another perspective. In *The Writing on the Wall*, he looks at the impact that non-alphabets might have on a society's capacity for creativity, in particular the Chinese and Japanese character-based writing systems. His theory goes like this: Non-alphabetic systems do not compel readers to parse language into individual sounds and abstract down to the smallest units of sound (i.e., phonemes); instead, they promote concrete, holistic and nonanalytical thought. Hannas furthermore claims that since abstract, analytical thought is the basis for ingenuity, the Asian orthographic systems "curb creativity" in nations like China and Japan. These societies are good at copying or adopting innovation, he argues, but it's the alphabet-using nations that are the trailblazers of originality in science, technology, and research.

To his credit, Hannas's evidence is wide ranging. He draws on linguistic data as well as history, science, commerce, sociology, and psychology. But his theory itself remains controversial, having been criticized as Eurocentric and for failing to consider deeper cultural practices that might discourage individualism and creativity. Nevertheless, most anthropologists today agree with the sociocultural precept that writing does, to various degrees, inform cultural practices, beliefs, values, and ideologies.[8]

Questions like this, about the relationship between writing and society, will no doubt continue to be discussed. Our main concern here, however, is the textualization of language—in particular, how language both affects and is affected by writing. But before we can start in on our technolingual argument, we need to take a quick look at where, when, and how writing came about.

How Writing Came About: A (Very) Short Primer

We'll start with some disappointing news: no one knows for certain when, where, why, how, or even by whom writing was invented. The reason is self-evident: before writing, there were no durable or material means of chronicling

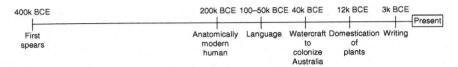

FIGURE 1.1 *Timeline of major innovations.*

its history. Most of what's been pieced together about the development of writing comes from archaeological finds, fragments of texts and documents from later periods, and stories passed down by word of mouth.[9] The consoling news, however, is that archaeologists, linguists, and historians have done an incredible job of reconstructing a likely narrative.

First, it's important to keep in mind how relatively "new" the technology of writing is in the grand scheme of human history. Figure 1.1 offers a simple timeline of mankind's major innovations. We can see that writing was invented anywhere from 47,000 to 97,000 years after the rise of human language, 37,000 years after people first crafted boats sturdy enough to travel to Australia from Southeast Asia, and 9,000 years following the first cultivation of crops in Mesopotamia.

Second, it's worth noting that writing *most likely* didn't come about through a onetime stroke of genius. A cavewoman, for instance, didn't kneel down by the fire one day and start scratching systematically recurring symbols in the dirt. It seems more likely that the symbolically representative concept behind writing—that one can "transport" and "capture" things in the real world with, say, scratches in the dirt—originated in artwork painted or engraved on cave walls, rocks, shells, and so on. The images there are indeed representations of things in the real world and can even be "read" as a picture story. Moreover, once the concept behind writing was hit upon, its subsequent evolution occurred in stages that appear to be common to the few independently developed writing systems: pictographs became ideographs, which became rebus, which became symbols with varying degrees of phonetic values.

Initial attempts to symbolize spoken language began with pictorial signs. No one paid attention to actual sounds. So a depiction of a "star" (★) represented the actual twinkling thing in the night sky and not a collective pronunciation of the s, t, and r sounds. These pictographs could also be put together to make a "sentence"; for instance, the string of pictographs ★ 人 ☉ could be interpreted, among countless other possibilities, as "the person gazes at the stars."

Then the pictographs grew up and left home, so to speak. They went from directly representing things in the world to representing the *idea* of these things. So ★ meant not just an actual star in the sky you can see twinkling, but the *idea* of that twinkling point of light. When this leap occurred, we say that the ★ pictograph became the ★ ideograph. One way to tell the two apart is by comparing the symbol's form and meaning. A pictograph generally has a clear visible relationship to what it represents (e.g., ☉ clearly resembles an eye), whereas the relationship between an ideograph and its meaning is often arbitrary (e.g., ▣ and ♌ might mean "cliff" and "remorse," respectively). Arabic numerals offer a more relatable example. The nonphonetic symbol "5" represents an idea (i.e., a countable amount, equal to the total number of fingers on one hand) and it doesn't resemble its meaning in either visual (e.g., ||||| or even, perhaps, ✋) or acoustic (i.e., *five* in English, *cinque* in French, *viisi* in Finnish, and so on) ways.

As far as we can tell, all writing systems, past and present, underwent this expansion from pictographic to ideographic symbolization. They then advanced to a third stage to varying degrees: the actual sounds of the language—whether for a single sound segment (e.g., "d") or a string of sounds (e.g., Japanese katakana カ, equivalent to the syllable *ka* in English)—were encoded into symbols.

But this giant step forward didn't happen suddenly. A crucial development occurred in between. At some point it was discovered that homophones—words that are pronounced the same—could lend their phonetic properties to signify an abstract word or idea that was difficult or impossible to render as a pictograph or ideograph. Linguists call this the rebus principle, and it's a stage common to all writing systems that were developed independently (i.e., without influence from an outside society's writing system).

Rebus works like this in English: The noun *bee* and the verb *be* are homophonous. The little buzzing insect isn't too hard to draw. But how would one go about drawing the verb *be*? Well, you draw a *bee* and make it stand for *be*. If we drew the numeral 4 followed by pictures of an eye, a tin can, and ocean waves, it wouldn't take you long, Dear Reader, to decipher *for I can see* from

Words like *be* and *can*, and most prepositions like *for, of, with*, and so on have a more abstract meaning than their homophonous comrades *bee, eye, can*, or *four*. Linguists call the former function words, and the latter content words. The function words of any language are nearly impossible to draw—unless you know of another content word that sounds the same and happens to be easy to draw. Moreover, these content pictographs can even represent parts of words. Try it: What would you draw if you wanted to write the abstract name *Jason*? A jaybird and a sun, right? Or consider the verbal suffix *-ize/-ise* (as in *fantasize* or *exercise*). You would draw a pair of "eyes."

All early attempts to textualize language made use of the rebus principle, in addition to pictographs and ideographs, before moving on to the final step of representing actual sounds—whether in the form of syllables (i.e., a syllabary)

or as individual sound segments (i.e., an alphabet). These stages originally took place in only a few places around the world. Nearly all other writing systems have been borrowed, adapted, or used as inspiration for creating a novel writing system.[10]

How Language Informed Writing

Now that we have a better idea of what writing is and how it developed, we can direct our attention to our central question: how have language and writing shaped each other? We'll start with the former. And by the end of our discussion we'll have shown how the basic properties of language itself shaped the thinking and inventiveness behind its textualization.

Language informed writing through its *inherent discreteness*

Among the many features that make spoken language unique as a system of communication, its *inherent discreteness* played the largest role in the invention of writing.

When we say that language is discrete, we mean that it comprises many pieces, which can also be combined, rearranged, and broken down.[11] These discrete pieces can be sounds (phonological units), parts of words (morphological units), words themselves (lexical units), strings of words (syntactic units), or the meanings that we attach to the pieces (semantic units).

Consider the utterance *we talked about the discreteness of language*. We can in fact break it down it into several separate, or discrete, units. *Talked* is an assemblage of four distinct sounds: *t – ah – k – t*.[12] What's more, *talked* is actually made up of two separate pieces, each bearing its own unit of meaning. *Talk* is a word with the unit of meaning "to use verbal language." The *-ed* appended to it is a widespread suffix in English with the grammatical unit of meaning "past tense." If you think about it, you can take the -ed suffix and stick it on a lot of verbs: *bake > baked, help > helped, test > tested*, and so on. It's a distinct unit, comprising sound and meaning, which can be detached from one word and stuck onto others.

Moving on to larger units within our sample utterance, we can see that individual words also combine into natural units: *we talked / about the discreteness / of language*. These are all smaller parts of the larger, complete utterance. Each is a discrete phrasal unit, made up of discrete word units, and so on.

We can use any number of metaphors to illustrate the inherent discreteness of language. Consider a suspension bridge. It's composed of foundations, towers, cables, and a deck. And each one of these pieces is made up of more parts. The deck is an assemblage of concrete, steel, nuts, and bolts. The support cables are an array of intertwined smaller steel cables. And so on. The point is that language is a system that, like many other structures in our world, is a composition of smaller, individual pieces. As early as the nineteenth century, the German philosopher and linguist William von Humboldt noted that language "makes infinite use of finite media." Although the earliest inventors of writing didn't directly address this remarkable feature of the phenomenon with which they were innovating, discreteness nevertheless framed the inventive routes they took.

As we've seen, whole words constitute discrete units. Writing systems that reflect this natural feature of language, at the word level, are called logographic systems. One symbol represents a single word or, more commonly, a single morpheme. In our discussion of the history of writing, we observed that the earliest experimentations with textualizing language involved pictographs or ideographs, which signified an entire word or concept. For instance, the Mayan glyph 🐢 meant "to arrive," and late Sumerian cuneiform ⤜ meant "god" or "heaven."

Modern languages also show the influence of language's word-level discreteness, though to varying degrees. To one extreme, Chinese and Japanese are written largely with logograms, though additional scripts have also been developed for both.[13] The Chinese call their traditional character-based script *hanzi* (汉字) and the Japanese call theirs *kanji* (漢字). Table 1.1 gives a few examples of the one-to-one relationship between sign and word in Chinese hanzi and Japanese kanji.

Most modern written languages fall on the other side of the spectrum; that is, they have relatively few logograms. The most common are logograms for special fields such as math (e.g., =, +, %), science (e.g., ♂, Δ, ☿), or economics (e.g., $, ¥, δ). Perhaps the most prevalent logograms in non-logographic systems are the numerals 0–9, borrowed from Arabic centuries ago.

But language's influence on writing wasn't limited to just word-level discreteness. Words are made up of syllables, and these units are also discrete.

TABLE 1.1 Logograms for Chinese and Japanese.

Chinese *Hanzi*	Japanese *Kanji*	English
爱	愛	'to love'
龙	竜	'dragon'
快	速	'quick'

TABLE 1.2 Syllabograms for Linear B, Japanese *katakana*, and Cherokee.

Syllabary	Syllabograms	Syllable Sounds
Linear B	𐂀 𐂃 𐂁	KO-NO-SO ('Knossos')
Japanese katakana	アメリカ	A-ME-RI-KA ('America')
Cherokee	Ꭷ Ꮑ Ꮎ Ꭷ	DI-NE-LO-DI ('play')

Consequently, discreteness at the syllable level also informed innovations in the technology of writing.

In fact, modern research in neurolinguistics (a field that studies the connections between language and the brain) indicates that the syllable is the most intuitive natural unit of language. To wit, it seems that we're born with an ear pre-tuned to pick out syllables.[14] So before we're able to "hear" *teddy* or *bottle*, we actually perceive something like *teh-dee* and *bah-tul*. A writing system that has been shaped by a language's syllable-level discreteness is known as a syllabary, and its written symbols are called syllabograms.

There have been numerous syllabaries in the history of writing, some of which survive today. In fourteenth century BCE, the Greeks of Mycenae used one. Dubbed Linear A, it wasn't deciphered until the 1950s. The Cherokee language was famously scripted into a syllabary in the early nineteenth century by a Cherokee silversmith named Sequoya. And two of the three scripts used to write modern Japanese are syllabaries, *hiragana* and *katakana* Table 1.2 gives a few examples of the syllabograms used for these languages, as well as their approximate phonetic value in English.

The Cherokee script offers a compelling illustration of how the discrete architecture of language informed the innovation of writing. In 1809, Sequoyah became inspired to create a system of writing for his native language. His trade brought him into regular contact with white settlers, and he grew fascinated with their written correspondences—which he reportedly called "talking leaves." Over a span of twelve years, Sequoyah created an inventory of eighty-six symbols, each corresponding to a syllable in Cherokee.

Taking the idea of discreteness yet further, notice that even syllables are made up of smaller, separate units. Take the trisyllabic word *friendliness*: each of its syllables comprises several sound segments, as we can see in Table 1.3.

The Phoenicians are generally regarded as the first to have figured this out. And it gave them the parameters for devising the earliest alphabet on

TABLE 1.3 Syllabic breakdown of *friendliness*.

Syllable	Consonant-Vowel Structure	Sound Segments
friend-	CCVCC	F-R-I-N-D
-li-	CV	L-E
-ness	CVC	N-E-S

TABLE 1.4 Sound/spelling correspondences in Finnish, Spanish, English, and Irish Gaelic.

Language	Spelling	Phonetic Pronunciation
Finnish	*kalastamisesta* ('hunting')	[kalastamisesta]
Spanish	*corazón* ('heart')	[kora θ on]
English	*knight*	[naɪt]
Irish Gaelic	*oíche shamhna* ('Halloween')	[ihjə] [haʊnə]

record. An alphabet is a writing system that captures the individual sound segments, or phonemes, of a language. The signs it uses to do this are technically called phonograms, but are better known to users of an alphabet as "letters."

Now, an ideal alphabet strives for a one-to-one correspondence between sound segment and letter. However, as we can see from our *friendliness* example, this is not always the case. Some alphabets, such as Finnish or Spanish, do a great job of upholding this ideal. We would say, then, that they have a "shallow" or "transparent" spelling system. Other languages are borderline maddening when it comes to spelling (read: English and Irish Gaelic). Their alphabets are notorious for a lack of correspondence between sign and sound. We can call their spelling systems "deep" or "opaque." Table 1.4 gives examples of sound/spelling correspondences in these four languages.

As we've seen, the natural discreteness of language influenced the various shapes that inventors gave their scripts. Spoken language can be broken up into increasingly smaller units, from words, to syllables, to single sound segments. And the various writing systems reflect this through their logographic, syllabic, or alphabetic forms.

But here comes the topper: if we take an even closer look, if we peer *within* the individual sound segments, we can find yet more evidence of language's influence on writing. In at least once instance, the innovators took cues from how the individual sounds of their language were produced in the mouth. The result was a "featural alphabet," a one-of-a-kind innovation in the history of writing, and largely the undertaking of one man.

Language Informed Writing through Its Articulatory Features

Have you ever pronounced a word very slowly and paid close to attention to what your lips, tongue, and teeth are doing? Try it on the word *finish*. You'll probably feel that, first, your upper row of front teeth come into contact with your bottom lip. Next, your lower lip springs free from your upper teeth while your tongue rises, contacting the hard ridge just behind your upper front teeth. As you complete the word, your tongue slides a tad farther back, but stays pressed against the roof of your mouth, and your lips pucker slightly. You can see in Figure 1.2 what this might look like if we took a cross-sectional picture of your mouth as you pronounced the consonants.

But it's not just your lips, tongue, and teeth that are active. Your lungs and throat also chip in. Say the word *finish* again, this time with your index and thumb gently pinching your throat. You'll notice that when you pronounce the *f* and *sh* sounds, there is no vibration in your throat. But when you pronounce the other sounds, there is indeed vibration. Now plug your nose and utter the word again. You'll feel sudden pressure when you get to the *n* sound. This is because you're blocking off the passageway, through the nasal cavity, needed to produce it. Finally, if you listen closely while you say *finish*, you might notice that you make a hissing sound when you pronounce the *f* and *sh*, and that the former is higher pitched than the latter. This is the friction that we generate with the air as it passes through our vocal tract and is pressed over, under, across, between, or around the articulators (e.g., throat, tongue, palate, teeth, and lips).

What you observed in the first paragraph above are the *places* of articulation: where, and with which articulators, sounds are produced in your oral tract. Your observations from the second paragraph refer to *manners* of articulation: the way our articulators manipulate the physical properties of sound. Among other things, we can use our oral tract to add nasality, friction, or aspiration (that is, an extra puff of air) to a sound. Examples of nasal, fricative, and aspirated sounds in English are given in Table 1.5.

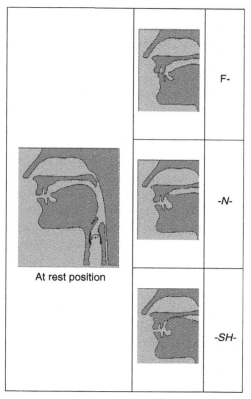

FIGURE 1.2 *Cross-sectional view of articulation of consonants in* finish. *(Images were created using "interactive sagittal articulation": http://homes.chass.utoronto. ca/~danhall/phonetics/sammy.html (accessed March 22, 2015).)*

TABLE 1.5 Nasal, fricative, and aspirated sounds in English.

Manner	Examples
Nasal	nut, mutt, sung
Fricative	hiss, his, fan, van
Aspirated	pet, take, cake

Incredibly, the place and manner of articulation of Korean actually shaped how it came to be written. Put another way, its spoken forms informed the design of its written forms. In the fifteenth century, King Sejong of Korea became increasingly concerned with how few of his people could read and write. The king, we should add, was an enlightened ruler ahead of his time. He assembled a royal Academy of Worthies and, with their help, brought about advancements in the areas of law, agriculture, music, science, medicine, and printing. These achievements were written down and disseminated throughout his lands. King Sejong quickly realized, however, that without literacy his subjects were limited as to how much they could benefit from these advancements. This inspired him to devise a script for the Korean language that his people could learn quickly and easily.

Writing had been around in Korea since the early fifth century. But the Koreans hadn't invented their own system; like many of the societies in Mesopotamia 2,000 years prior, they borrowed the technology from the literate group nearest to them—in this case, the Chinese.

As we've seen, Chinese uses logograms to encode entire words. The actual sounds of the language are largely ignored. Now, a logographic system can work just fine for multiple languages if those languages have similar grammatical structures. Cantonese and Mandarin, for example, resemble each other to an extent that allows for an uncomplicated use of the same character-based writing system.

But Chinese and Korean are very different languages, especially as concerns their grammatical structures. Korean nouns and verbs have a lot of different forms, mostly through added endings (suffixes); it's what we call an agglutinative language. Chinese words, on the other hand, lack any such suffixes; each word has one form, what we call an isolating language.

Now, this difference between agglutinative and isolating languages is crucial if you are thinking of adopting a foreign script. First of all, Chinese was developed to encode full words, as opposed to pieces of them, like grammatical endings. Second, its signs represented real and abstract concepts as opposed to actual sounds. In short: Chinese logograms were not a good fit for Korean. So Koreans essentially had to learn to read and write in a foreign language (i.e., Chinese) instead of in their mother tongue.

Which brings us back to the problem facing King Sejong. His subjects not only had to learn another language if they wanted to read and write; they also had to memorize hundreds, if not thousands, of characters. Moreover, the characters didn't represent the actual sounds of the foreign language they had to learn. (Imagine trying to learn French or Spanish by memorizing arbitrary symbols like $\oslash$, $\otimes$, ∞, or $\$$.) To become literate in Korea, from the fifth century through the early fifteenth century, was no small undertaking. Only the very wealthy and aristocratic of the population had the time and resources to do it.

King Sejong's solution was to create a writing system tailored to the Korean language, whose symbols not only encoded for sound, but also had phonetically intuitive shapes. In a remarkable stroke of genius, he incorporated the articulatory features of Korean into the actual design of the letters he invented. In other words, he based the shapes of his symbols on where (the place) and how (the manner) the sounds of Korean originated in the mouth. King Sejong dubbed his achievement *Hunminjeongeum*, meaning "the correct sounds for the instruction of the people." The modern term for it, Hangul ("great script" or "Korean script"), came into use in 1912.

Earlier we saw how the first attempts to textualize language were pictorially iconic: the symbol for "eye" looked like an actual eye, and so on. The brilliance of King Sejong's script was that its symbols are *articulatorily* iconic. Their shapes literally resemble the position or state of the lips and tongue, and how these interact with the teeth, palate, and throat. Figure 1.3 shows how this works, by example of the Hangul symbols for [k], [n], [s], and [m], and [ʕ].

Hangul Symbol	Sound	Depiction of Articulation	Iconicity
ㄱ	[k]	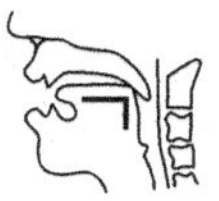	Outline of the root of tongue, positioned at the back of the mouth near the molars.
ㄴ	[n]	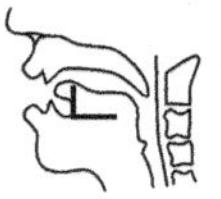	Outline of the tongue touching the hard palate just behind the teeth.
ㅅ	[s]		Outline of an incisor.
ㅁ	[m]		Outline of the mouth.
ㅇ	[ʕ]		Outline of the open throat.

FIGURE 1.3 *Articulatory iconicity of Hangul. (Images from http://www.wright-house.com/korean/korean-linguistics-origins.html (accessed March 23, 2015).)*

In 1940 the original supplement to the king's *Hunminjeongeum* surfaced, after being lost for nearly six centuries. From its sixty-five pages of commentary, written by scholars in the Academy of Worthies, we learn the background of the Hangul script, in particular King Sejong's process for developing its characters.

The sound generally written in English as a *k* or *c* the king labeled "molar sound." Accordingly, the Hangul symbol depicts the tongue drawn back toward the throat (close to the molars). He called *n* a "tongue sound," and its symbol indicates the blade of the tongue pulled upward and touching the alveolar ridge (i.e., the hard palate area that spans the upper canine teeth). The *s* sound was dubbed an "incisor sound"; its pointy shape outlines the bottom front row of teeth. And in fact, if you look in a mirror and enunciate a word starting with *s*, you'll observe that your lips part and curl back just enough to reveal your teeth. Turning to the sound English denotes with the symbol *m*, the king categorized it as a "lips sound"; as such, its rectangular shape outlines the lips in a closed position. Finally, the sound in the middle of the word *uh-oh*, which isn't actually written in English,[15] was termed a "throat sound." Its round shape depicts the throat, like the hole of a pipe connecting to the lungs.

The manner of articulation also played a role in how King Sejong constructed Hangul letters. He was particularly keen on incorporating the features of aspiration and double consonant length into their design.

In Korean, the sounds generally written in English as *p, t, k*, and *ch* also had aspirated counterparts. Basically, this means that the sounds were pronounced with an extra puff of air.[16] The king indicated this puff of air by adding a stroke to the symbol for the unaspirated sound. Thus, ㄱ (*k*) became ㅋ (*kh*), and from ㄷ (*t*) was derived ㅌ (*th*), as examples.

The Korean language of the fifteenth century also had a phonetically longer variant to its incisor sound (or alphabetic *s*). The fancy term for this is "geminate consonant" and means, basically, that the sound is pronounced longer than normal. English doesn't have geminate consonants, but you can get a sense of how it works by saying the word *lesser* and holding the *s* for twice as long as you would naturally. King Sejong worked this feature into his script in a wholly logical fashion: he wrote the symbol twice. So the geminate version of ㅅ was ... you guessed it: ㅆ.

In her historical treatment of writing, *The Writing Revolution: From Cuneiform to the Internet*, Amalia E. Gnanadesikan calls the Korean system of writing "the paragon of scripts." She goes on to praise it for "match[ing] the phonology of the Korean language perfectly" and "encod[ing] a large range of linguistic insights." She concludes with the observation that "[s]imilar phonemes are given predictably similar shapes; this property not only reflects the linguistic insight that phonemes are composed of smaller distinctive features, but is a crucial factor in making the han'gŭl alphabet so easy to learn."[17]

Indeed, the distinctive features in any given language are yet another dem-onstration of language's discreteness in general: each segment is a compil-ation of traits, expressed through both articulation and manner; each syllable is a concatenation of segments; each word an assembly of syllables; and each utterance an assembly of words. The natural, discrete design of language directly informed the various approaches and shapes for its textualization. Consequently, writing is perhaps the quintessential invention for illustrating the interplay between language and technology.

But so far we've only considered half the argument. Recall that one of our driving arguments in this exploration of the relationship between lan-guage and technology is that the relationship is reciprocal; language, in other words, both shapes and is shaped by technology. Let's now look at the other side of the coin: the various ways that writing has influenced language.

How Writing Influences Language

Language is more than the concrete sounds, words, and grammatical struc-tures that come out of our mouths. The ideas that we have of language—whether our own language or the language of others—can also be considered part of our linguistic inventory. Take the unfortunate word *ain't*. Even as I just typed it, Microsoft Word underlined it in red, indicating that the word is "incor-rect." Of course, millions of people say *ain't* every day. And the many millions who hear it can surely understand it.

In fact *ain't* has a documented history going back centuries. (In the eight-eenth century it was a contracted form of *am not*, alongside *an't* and other variants.[18]) The only thing divesting *ain't* of its credibility as a "word" is the idea or perception that "*ain't* ain't a word." At some point in its history, one or more speakers took up undesirable opinions of it and started passing this idea on to more and more speakers. But there never was, nor has there ever been, anything intrinsically or phonetically "bad" or "word-unworthy" about *ain't*. It became stigmatized for ideological reasons.[19]

Language ideologies are not limited to words. Sounds are also subject to value judgments, whether a single sound segment like the *h* in certain British regional dialects, or a person's accent as a whole. Even grammatical forms aren't beyond the reach of language ideologies. Consider how you would react to the following sentence if it appeared naturally in this paragraph, that is, sans quotation marks or non-italic: *We don't have no control over language ideologies*. You'd cringe over the word *no*, because you've been inculcated with the belief that it's "incorrect" or "illogical" to use double negatives. Yet countless languages around the world have double negatives. In French, for example, it's actually considered "incorrect" or "nonstandard" if you don't insert the second negation word, the adverb *ne*, in sentences like *je ne sais rien* ('I don't know nothing').

The point here: When we reflect on how a given technology has influenced language, we need to think beyond the sounds, words, and grammar of a linguistic system. We need to also consider that technology's effect on our beliefs, judgments, and perceptions of language. The technology of writing is no different. It has had a tremendous impact on the way we ideologically relate to language.

Writing Influences Languages through Ideologies

If you've received enough schooling in letters to be reading this sentence, chances are your perceptual basis for comparing and evaluating language—especially spoken language—is, literally, this very sentence.

That is to say, part of your education in literacy included not just learning the letters themselves, but also the *idea* that the language you make with those letters is the epitome of "real language." And the way you talked with your friends on the playground or at the party Friday night—well, that's just some "derivative" or "deviation" from "real" or "correct" language. And while descriptive linguists—i.e., mesmerizing, sexy academics who study language from a judgment-free perspective—cringe at such scenarios, it's apparent that when we learn to read and write we ingest ideas and attitudes along the way. Written language, we come to believe, is "true" and "good." It's the filet mignon, while spoken language is just chopped liver.

In a sense, the culprit for this perceptual injustice against spoken language is writing itself. Writing, you see, tends to lend language a degree of prestige, formality, correctness, and authenticity.

Now, it's important to note that long before the invention of writing there were various styles or registers of spoken language. Every language has the means to express things in more or less formal ways, whether through different words, sounds, or grammatical structures. Japanese and Korean, for instance, have entire sets of endings (also known as honorific suffixes) that you attach to nouns to convey formality. Most languages of the world have different pronouns to address someone you know versus someone you don't know (e.g., German *Sie ~ du*, French *vous ~ tu*, or Spanish *usted ~ tu*). In English we can substitute words to sound more prestigious (e.g., *I will hazard a conjecture* versus *I'll take a guess*). Moreover, only about half of the languages spoken in the world today are written.[20] Surely their speakers communicate with each other in contexts that call for various styles of linguistic expression.

All this to say: it's safe to assume that language encoded into its words, sounds, and grammatical structures these and other attitudes *before* it became written.

However, it's also the case that with the invention of writing came a new context to which values and beliefs about language could be extended. Consider the notion of "intelligence." What do you associate with the concept of "an intelligent person"? Quick-wittedness. Street smarts, perhaps. But most likely you associate education, and the literacy that it entails, with "intelligence." Put another (though less flattering) way: how likely are you, at first blush, to judge someone who can't read or write as "intelligent"?

History tells us that the people who first learned to read and write were also those who occupied privileged positions within their societies: Egyptian and Mayan priests, Sumerian administrators, Chinese noblemen, Frankish chancelleries, to name a few. The ability to write was prized. It meant that you didn't have to toil in the fields to eke out a living; rather, you had the time and money to get an education. So writing became associated with privilege and learnedness. Moreover, what the privileged and educated wrote also served as a model for others; hence, writing became associated with correctness and formality. In short, the textualization of language contributed to the repertoire of ideas, beliefs, and attitudes that we have vis-à-vis our own language and the language of others.

Writing affects our perception of language in many ways. It can even play a role in whether or not, and to what extent, we recognize actual similarities or differences between languages. This is most evident in the Balkans and in China, although in opposite ways.

In the Balkan nations of Serbia and Croatia, the people speak what are essentially dialects of a single language, Serbo-Croatian. Naturally there are regional and stylistic differences within and between the countries, but for the most part native speakers in Serbia and Croatia have little difficulty understanding each other. Nevertheless, the official website of the government of the Republic of Serbia, states that "[t]he official language of Serbia is Serbian"—not Serbo-Croatian, mind you, *just* Serbian. And in 2013, when Croatia was admitted into the European Union (EU), its official language immediately became one of the twenty-four official languages of the EU as well. Take a guess what that language was? Here's a hint: it was neither Serbian nor Serbo-Croatian.

Now, there are a host of explanations for why Serbia and Croatia have declared separate official languages. Politics, social identity, and religion certainly weigh heavy in the equation. Serbia has traditionally identified more with the eastern Slavic nations, in particular Russia, and its denizens are predominately Eastern Orthodox Christians. Croatia has a long history of involvement in Western European politics and culture (it was part of the Austrian

Habsburg monarchy for several centuries), and most of its people are Catholic. But would these sociocultural factors suffice to convince the people of Serbia and Croatia that they speak "different languages," when in fact they can understand each other in most circumstances? It's certainly possible. But another powerful factor might be that Serbian and Croatian are written with different scripts: the Cyrillic alphabet for Serbian and the Roman alphabet for Croatian. It's possible that this orthographic differentiation plays a role in how native speakers view their own linguistic identity, particularly the classification of their language. Beginning in early childhood, Serbians and Croatians attend school and learn how to write "their language." And when confronted with the writing system of what they are instructed is "another language"—even if the sounds, words, and grammatical structures of this "other language" are surprisingly familiar—it's understandable that they would believe the written evidence over the spoken.

Then there's the case of Chinese. To say that Chinese is spoken in China is somewhat misleading. Strictly speaking, there is no single Chinese language; what many in China view as dialects of a single language are, from a comparative linguistic standpoint, separate languages. For instance, a person from Hong Kong speaks Cantonese (also known as Yue) but cannot understand his compatriots from Beijing, who speak Mandarin; from Shanghai, who speak Wu; or from Taiwan, who speak Hokkien (also known as Min). These spoken varieties of Chinese differ to such an extent, in vocabulary and tonal grammar, that they are not mutually intelligible.

Nevertheless, the government of the People's Republic of China promotes a unified language ideology. Its official terms for the spoken and written forms of Chinese are, respectively, *hànyǔ* (汉语 "spoken languages of the Han people") and *zhōngwén* (中文 "main writing"). Now, as we saw in our discussion above, a Chinese character signifies an entire word or concept, and not the sounds of the language. So our hypothetical speakers from Hong Kong, Beijing, Shanghai, and Taiwan would all write the character 我 ("I") but would pronounce it alternately as *ngǒ, wǒ, ngu,* and *gùá.* But the fact remains that the sounds are represented by one and the same symbol. This perhaps motivates the perception that Chinese is one "language," despite the multiple—and often widely incomprehensible—differences in vocabulary and grammar.

Writing Influences Language through **Lexical Enlargement**

The technology of writing also allowed language to grow as never before. You see, when a language gets textualized, it then becomes possible to physically catalog—preserve, as it were—its vocabulary. Think of writing as a deep freezer into which you can place words you know and use now, and keep them there for years—for so long, even, that when later speakers open it up they won't recognize some of the words anymore.

Try this: Flip open a girthy English language dictionary to a random page and read all the entries. Chances are you'll encounter one or more words you've never heard of. Some may be technical terms or obscure borrowings from other languages. Others, however, might include some form of notation indicating that the word is "archaic" or "obsolete." Ever heard of a *cordwainer*? (For the record, neither has this version of Microsoft Word, as indicated by the squiggly red underline.) The *Oxford English Dictionary* (*OED*) entry for it reads:

> A worker in cordwain or cordovan leather; a shoemaker. Now obs. [obsolete] as the ordinary name, but often persisting as the name of the trade-guild or company of shoemakers, and sometimes used by modern trades unions to include all branches of the trade.[21]

Or how about a *cruse*? The *OED* defines it as "a small earthen vessel for liquids."[22] Both *cordwainer* and *cruse* are marked as "arch." The list of "arch"-words could go on and on.[23] The last printed edition of the *OED*, in 1999, comprised twenty volumes and 22,000 pages. According to the official Oxford dictionaries website, the dictionary contained 171,476 full entries of words in current use, and 47,156 entries for obsolete words.[24] Put another way: more than one out of every four words contained within its covers was no longer in use!

In fact, words come and go all the time, though we're generally more liable to notice an addition to a language's lexicon (e.g., *google* or *twerk*) than a loss (e.g., *charabanc* or *wittol*). But were it not for writing, these and many more words would be lost forever.

The argument here is that writing leads to quantitative changes in the lexicon of a language. It allows us to record words that don't survive in a context of pure oral transmission. Writing is one reason that the latest online edition of the OED can tout itself as the "unsurpassed guide to the meaning, history, and pronunciation of 600,000 words."

Writing Influences Language through Syntactic Complexity

Writing also allows us to craft longer and more syntactically complex sentences than is generally the case in off-the-cuff speech. We've already seen that, in many ways, writing has become an idealized model for speech. And if writing enables us to string words together in more complicated ways, it's reasonable to assume that this bleeds over into the way we speak in *some* contexts.

Note the emphasis on *some*. We adjust our speech to various degrees in nearly every context, and writing plays a larger or lesser role in only some. For instance, it seems unlikely that during a phone conversation with your best friend you would model your speech on the last autobiography you read. Still, there are many contexts that call for a more formal or standard use of spoken language: addressing an unfamiliar audience in a professional setting; conferencing with a prestigious individual; or participating in a religious ceremony.

In situations like these we might find ourselves using a style of speech more typical of the printed page. Our sentences get longer and contain more imbedded clauses (e.g., *Meeting with clients is the kind of work which I believe I would enjoy most* vs. *I'd most enjoy meeting with clients*). We tend to avoid contractions (*It is* and *there are* vs. *it's* and *they're*). We use extended verb-plus-noun phrases like "take into consideration" or "have an influence on" in lieu of "consider" and "influence."

These are examples of how the technology of writing—and our perceptions of a more "formal" or "correct" style of language based on a written model—can affect language, in particular the syntax of our speech.

Writing Influences Language through Etymologized Pronunciation

Etymology is a fancy term for word history. The word *wise*, for instance, is historically related to the Latin word *videre* ('to see'). If you have seen something, it implies that you have firsthand experience or knowledge of whatever you saw. Hence, the meaning of "to see" morphed into something expressing "having knowledge." This is a very simplified etymology of the word *wise*.

Etymology is also a field of study. Its practitioners search for the origins of words and phrases. So, you might be asking: what does etymology have to do with writing's influence on language? In some instances, a word's history motivated the respelling of that word, which in turn altered its pronunciation.

The words *perfect*, *advise*, and *fault* are good examples of this. Borrowed into English from French between the twelfth and fifteenth centuries, *perfect* was originally pronounced without a *k*; *advise* had no *d*; and *fault* was bereft of any *el* sound whatsoever. However, each of these words underwent changes in its pronunciation because, at some point between the fifteenth and seventeenth centuries, their spellings were changed from *parfet*, *aveys*, and *foute* (among other forms) to more clearly resemble their Latin roots of *perfectus*, *advisere*, and *fallita*. Today we pronounce the *t*, *d*, and *l* because the words were re-etymologized through the written medium.

Writing Influences Language through Hypercorrection

Another way that writing affects language is through "orthographic hypercorrection." This is a highfaluting way of saying that speakers pronounce a word by referring to its exact spelling, even if this writing-based pronunciation is incorrect.

In German, for instance, the verb *sehen* ('to see') is spelled with an *h*, but its pronunciation is ZAY-EN. There is no breathy *h* sound at the start of the second syllable, and 99 percent of the time a native speaker will pronounce it this way. Children, before they learn to read and write, will generally only say ZAY-EN. Now, on a rare occasion they might hear a literate adult pronounce the verb as ZAY-HEN. However, that adult is hypercorrecting their speech; they know that ZAY-EN is written with an *h*, and they want to serve as a good linguistic model for the child, so they base their pronunciation on what they believe to be the model of "proper language": the written form *sehen*.

A similar process governs the hypercorrect articulation of *honest* as HAW-NEST in Britain. The *h* sound at the beginning of a word is already troublesome for some speakers of certain varieties of British English. Add to this the fact that a lot of words spelled with *h* are pronounced in British English with the *h* sound (e.g., *herbs, hand*), while others are not (e.g., *honour, hour*), and you get a context ripe with uncertainty over what, exactly, the "correct" pronunciation is of words like *honest* or *honour*. When in doubt, go by how it's spelled, right? The result is a hypercorrected form based on writing.

Like the syntactic effects of writing, this hypercorrective effect is linked to perceptions of what constitutes "more correct or formal" spoken language. A speaker models their pronunciation after a textualized form of language because they believe their own pronunciation is wrong, and the textualized form is "right."

Writing Influences Language through Internationalization

Which of these languages have you heard of: Simeku, Guajá, Suundi?

Most likely, none of them.

These languages are spoken in remote areas of the world and by relatively few people. Around 3,000 people speak Simeku, in the mountains of the autonomous Bougainville Province of Papua New Guinea. Only three hundred or so people in Amazonian Brazil speak Guajá. And Suundi has more than 100,000 native speakers in the Republic of Congo. What these languages have in common, however, is that they are not written. They therefore lack a powerful and efficient instrument for making them known outside of their immediate region of use.

This is another effect that the technology of writing has on language: it exports it to other parts of the world. A textualized language can be packaged into instructional resources that reach a broad audience. Nowadays you can familiarize yourself with Zulu or Xhosa by going online and buying a textbook. Imagine trying to learn these languages without any written manuals. Both have dozens of complicated sounds totally foreign to speakers of Indo-European languages. (Ever heard of clicks, ejectives, or implosives?) Very few of us would consider trying to "pick up" these tongues on our own. This is one reason that unwritten languages are more likely to remain obscure to the outside world, even if a large population speaks them. When, in the nineteenth century, Christian missionaries adapted the Latin alphabet to Zulu and Xhosa—and published Bibles and instructional guides to help fellow missionaries learn the languages—they laid the groundwork for the exportation of these languages.[25]

Ethnologue: Languages of the World bills itself as "a comprehensive reference work cataloguing all of the world's known living languages."[26] Its online statistics go back to 1951 and are regularly updated. As of this writing, *Ethnologue* reports that just over half of the world's languages fall into a "language status" category that accounts for the presence of a system of writing. If you were to scroll through the roughly 3,500 languages in this category, you would recognize many of them. Browse the other 3,500, and you're basically left scratching your head.

Granted, writing neither inevitably nor automatically makes a language more international. Take Cree, for instance. It's an indigenous language in eastern Canada, and it has not one, but *two* standardized writing systems (a syllabary and a Latin-based alphabet). Yet it's rarely known outside of Canada.

Our argument here is not that once a language becomes written it automatically becomes international; rather, we're saying that writing is a powerful tool that gives language a chance at, and medium for, internationalization.

Writing Influences Language throug Preservation

Today we can capture and store spoken language with digital recording devices. Nearly 150 years ago, the phonograph captured live speech through etchings in small cylinders. Prior to the phonograph, however, the only way to capture and "preserve" ephemeral speech was to write it down. In many ways, this has been writing's greatest lingual effect: it allowed language to be catalogued for posterity.

Let's take Gothic as an example. It was an East Germanic language that, for the most part, had died out by the sixth or seventh century CE. If not for

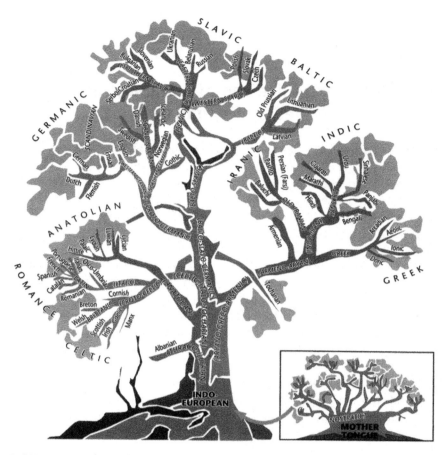

FIGURE 1.4 *The Indo-European language family tree. (Image from http://phae-selis.wikia.com/wiki/File:Indoeuropean_language_family_tree.jpg (accessed January 26, 2017).)*

writing, and the translation of the New Testament prepared by the Visigothic bishop Wulfila in the fourth century, the Gothic language would have joined the countless other languages lost to history.

Moreover, the language that Wulfila preserved in text has allowed linguists to piece together a "family tree" of the Germanic languages. With Gothic as their base for comparison, linguists have reconstructed the probable parent language of all Germanic languages, known as Proto-Germanic. In fact, linguists have accomplished similar reconstructions and classifications for many languages of the world. Figure 1.4 shows an example of the "language family trees" that linguists have constructed using script-preserved evidence of now-extinct languages.[27]

Think of writing as the aspic medium in which language of the past has been preserved for the present.

The Textualization of Language and Technolingualism

Writing is an exemplary place to begin our exploration of the dynamic interplay between language and technology. On the one hand, the bedrock features of language offered inventors a template for devising various writing systems—in particular, language's inherent discreteness and articulatory features.

On the other hand, the technology of writing—what we've called the textualization of language—has left its mark on language in several ways: how we think about and perceive language; how we pronounce certain words; the forms we use in certain contexts of live speech; the size of a language's lexicon; the geographic spread of language; and the preservation of language.

What's more, we have shown that writing was an incredibly transformative invention. It transformed our social, psychological, and even cognitive worlds. For our linguistic worlds, writing has been especially transformative: it created a new type or variety of language, complete with its own forms, ideologies, and rules.[28]

With the textualization of language, and the new linguistic variety it spawned, the stage was set for another historic development in the dialogue between language and technology: the mechanization of language. In Chapter 2 we'll see how this played out.

First Interlude

How Writing Doesn't Affect Language

The preceding section argued for various ways that writing affects language—whether our attitudes and perceptions of language, or the actual sounds, words, and structures we use in speech. Here, though, we offer the following caveat: there are limits on writing's influence on language.

In this short interlude we'd like to note two effects, in particular, that writing does *not* have on language.

Writing Doesn't Make Language "Better"

The first thing we want to caution against is the idea that writing somehow makes language "better."

Recall that writing is a manufactured (in the true, original Latin meaning of "handmade") technology. Strictly speaking, language was never "meant" to be written. We come into this world preprogrammed to speak. Writing, then, is biologically unnatural. It requires extrinsic, postnatal training. When spoken language is committed to paper, there are those who then label the printed forms as "proper," "good," or "correct" in terms of spelling, punctuation, and style. But these evaluative terms are psychosocial fabrications. There is nothing intrinsically "proper," "good," or "correct" about the language of a native speaker.

Sure, uttering *goddammit* in church is a social no-no (what some might call "blasphemous"). Writing *ain't* on a college exam is "incorrect." But only because someone (or a group of someones) has given these words their negative connotations for those particular contexts.

For the sake of comparison, imagine that you have a Japanese pen pal who writes: *Next year I the United States to come.* Three things are intrinsically incorrect about your pen pal's language: the preposition and verb are in the wrong place, and it needs the future markers *will* or *am coming.* These are three mistakes that no native speaker would make, regardless of their judgments of "incorrect" or "proper" language. They're language-system errors, as opposed to language-ideological missteps.

Our point: "improper" and "bad" elements of language existed long before writing was invented. Writing just provided a more concrete way to label, regulate, and prescribe spoken language—to ideologize it, as it were.

Recall our metaphor of writing as the harness that humans strapped onto language so as to control discourse and social relations. This metaphor applies to *ideas* about language, too. When the sounds of speech become textualized and then standardized in this textualized form, speakers often come to view this instantiation of language as "better" than the spoken mode.

From a linguistic standpoint, however, writing does not necessarily a "better" language make.

Writing Doesn't Affect Grammar Systems

We've seen that writing can motivate a speaker to pronounce a word "hypercorrectly"; that etymologically informed respellings of certain words led to changes in these words' pronunciations; and that speakers often model their formal styles of speech on written language.

In the grand scheme of things, however, these are examples of "shallow" language variation. "Deep" variation involves changes in a language's grammatical structures: its word order, sound system, function words, and word forms. And these linguistic domains are generally immune to writing's influence.

Let's say, for instance, that a classroom of kindergartners hears their teacher regularly pronounce the word *raspberry* as RASP-BERRY. Those kids might start saying RASP-BERRY to each other on the playground, but are corrected once they get home and ask mom for RASP-BERRY ice cream. This we can call shallow language variation: the sounds of an isolated word were altered, and only temporarily. Shallow language variation usually doesn't persist long enough to spread within or between speech communities, and it doesn't seep into a language's grammar.

On the other hand, imagine a horde of eighth-century Vikings ransacking a village on the coast of England. After the dust settles, many of the plunderers decide to take a local woman as a wife and settle down. The Vikings speak Old Norse, their wives Old English. Their children grow up hearing three varieties of language: native Old Norse from their father and the other Vikings in the village; Old English from their mother at home and from the English villagers; and a nonnative, grammatically underdeveloped form of Old English from the Vikings trying to learn it in order to assimilate.

And now imagine that one day this child says *I must take a bath* instead of the at-that-time-correct Old English *I must a bath take*, because the former is how you'd say it in Old Norse. And there is no such thing as organized public education (school, that is). Hence there's no native speaker teacher who daily corrects the children's grammatical mistakes. So the child continues to say *I must take a bath*, and his friends also say *I must take a bath*.

But the child doesn't stop there, with just that one utterance. They also say *I must eat a pie* and *I must have food*. (It's a clean and hungry child.) Furthermore, because there are so many other children with a nonnative speaker parent, and so many Viking nonnative speakers of English in the village, other children produce similar utterances. And voila: the underlying word order of your language has changed from subject-object-verb (SOV) to subject-verb-object (SVO).

Now, for reasons of space and time, we have presented a somewhat over-simplified explanation of the complicated and multifaceted phenomenon of language change.[1] The point here, though, is that sociocultural forces more powerful than writing cause "deep" language variation.

Don't Believe Everything You Read about Writing and Language

There have been arguments to the contrary (i.e., that writing does and has affected spoken language). For instance, one previous explanation for the emergence of the present perfect tense in English (e.g., *I have done, I have said, I have gone*, etc.) held that it was an emulation of the present perfect in written Latin. More recently, William C. Hannas claimed that the character-based Chinese writing system affected the language's syllable structure: "The monosyllabism of Chinese morphology is an artifact of character-based writing, which imposes a one-to-one relationship on the language's sound, script, and meaningful units.[2]" He also argued that the same writing system extensively promoted homophones in Chinese. In his words:

> Another effect characters have had on Chinese and the Sinitic parts of other Asian languages is a high incidence of homophony. Since Chinese

characters convey a great deal of visual information compared to the phonetic information associated with them, there is no incentive for writers take a word's sound into account when introducing new vocabulary.[3]

As enticing as such arguments might be, the likelihood that writing had these kinds of effects on English and Chinese (or any other language) is miniscule. A much more probable explanation would take into consideration the types of interaction between native and nonnative speakers, and the sociocultural contexts for these interactions.

2

Mechanization of Language: The Printing Press and the Typewriter

Mechanical Thoughts, or How a Nearly Blind Philosopher Explained His New Writing Style to His Publisher

Hunched over and eyes shut, the German moves his fingers slowly but knowingly across the orb of keys.

CLACK. CLACK. CLACK. PING.
He lifts up the hinged keypad, unfastens the brass fixture, and hands the sheet of paper to his guest.

```
Herr Ernst Schmeitzner, Proprietor
Ernst Schmeitzner Publishing House
Chemnitz, Germany


Winter, 1882                              Genoa, Italy

Esteemed Herr Schmeitzner:

    God is dead.

Respectfully,
Friedrich W. Nietzsche
```

"Fascinating," Ernst remarks.
"It took a week to learn the layout of the keys," Nietzsche says.

FIGURE 2.1 *Hansen's "writing ball" from 1878. (http://commons.wikimedia.org/ wiki/File%3ASkrivekugle.jpg (accessed December 12, 2014).)*

"And you say you got it from a Dane?"

"From Mr. Hansen, yes. At the Royal Institute for the Deaf, in Copenhagen."

"It's not like the American invention at all," Ernst says, bending over to inspect the machine more closely.

"He calls it the 'writing ball.'"

"A rather odd-looking contraption," Ernst remarks.

Nietzsche clears his throat. "Yes, well—it's helped me to write again."

"So this is where your recent musings—the material you've been sending me of late—this is where it's been coming from. This ball . . ." Ernst strokes his moustache, eyes still studying the cactus-like machine.

There's an uneasy pause. A draft whistles its way through a windowsill. Nietzsche shivers. Groping out a path over to the window, he removes his scarf and crams it between the glass and the porous frame. "I suspect I know what you're going to say," he utters.

"Please know that I mean no offense," Ernst starts. "It's just that this . . . change in style, it's rather sudden. Your manuscripts from earlier: the language there, it was rich. The arguments were full. But the last texts you sent me, the ones you've drafted with this machine . . . They were . . . different. Many of them read more like a . . ."

"Yes . . .?"

"Telegram."

Nietzsche shuffles back across the room and plops down in his chair.

"I hope I haven't offended you, Friedrich. You know how much I admire your work."

"It's okay, Ernst," he murmurs. "In fact, I agree with you."

"You do?"

"I've been pondering it for weeks. And I believe I have an explanation."

"Go on."

Nietzsche leans forward in his chair, props his elbows on his knees. "I believe," he begins, "that the devices we use to write with, these same tools imprint our minds as much as they imprint the paper." Nietzsche takes the typed sheet of paper from the table and holds it up demonstrably. "CLACK CLACK CLACK . . . Up and down, up and down . . . Don't you see? It molds our thoughts."

Ernst lets out a long exhale. Had it really come this far? Had the doddering philosopher finally lost his tenuous grip on sanity? "Well, let's not make too much of it," he says halfheartedly.

"I'm telling you, Ernst. This device has mechanized my language."

∞

In Chapter 1 we saw how the technology of writing both shaped and was shaped by language. We considered, for instance, how writing functions as a representative system. For hundreds of years this system was exploited only by human hand; as such, writing was a strictly manual endeavor. To wit: words were wedged into clay by stylus, etched into wood by knife, scratched onto parchment by quill, or painted onto papyrus by brush. Consequently, there was a close, palpable connection between the writer of the symbol and the written symbol itself.

And then two technologies came around that changed this relationship. First, the printing press replaced the flowing quill with inert type. Instead of a supple hand, a hard metallic plane embossed the paper with symbols. And the relationship between writer and written became more indirect and detached.

Second, until the late nineteenth century, authors submitted only hand-written manuscripts to their publishers. And then came the typewriter. It made writing more legible, consistent, and—after some practice—faster. (Friedrich Kittler calls the typewriter a "discursive machine-gun."[1]) Most radically, though, the typewriter made every office or study into a small-scale printing house. And the detachment between symbol writer and written symbol became more widespread.

In *The Writing Revolution,* Amalia Gnanadesikan argues that, "[t]he use of type not only revolutionized the scale of book production, but marked a significant conceptual change in the way writing was done. The original process of writing by the *creation* of letters became a process of writing by a *selection* from a preformed set of letters."[2] This conceptual shift, from creator to selector, was a product of the physical distancing between writer and written. And in the following pages it will become clear that both this distancing and the conceptual change in the writing process were products of what we're calling the *mechanization* of language.

In this chapter we take a closer look at two technologies associated with this mechanization of language: the printing press and the typewriter. Keeping in line with our overarching argument—that there's a dynamic interplay between language and technology, an interaction we've dubbed *technolingualism*—we explore how language informed the development of these technologies and, alternatively, how these technologies affected language. Our goal, by chapter's end, is to offer a compelling picture of how and why the mechanization of language was an important milestone in our emergent technolingual landscape.

Part 1: The Printing Press

It's impossible to convey in just a few sentences the extent of the printing press's influence within the context of European history. When Elizabeth Eisenstein researched this in the 1970s, she needed more than 700 pages and two volumes to present her findings.[3] Through extensive documentation, she argues that the printing press had a lasting impact on the religious, political, economic, and social spheres of Western Europe. "As an agent of change," she writes, "printing altered methods of data collection, storage and retrieval systems and communication networks used by learned communities throughout Europe."[4] She ultimately associates several key sociocultural and intellectual movements with the printing press: the Reformation, Enlightenment, Scientific Revolution, capitalism, language standardization, the spread of literacy, and the rise of silent reading, among others.

Now, Eisenstein's arguments were superbly researched and couched in polished prose—but they weren't novel. Almost two decades earlier, Marshall McLuhan published *The Gutenberg Galaxy: The Making of Typographic Man.*[5] In this seminal work, he contends that the printing press led to a "visual homogenizing of experience in Europe."[6] That is to say, McLuhan argues that the press replaced a culture that was based mostly on the oral transmission of information, with a culture that focused on—one might even say fetishized—visual material. "Printing from movable type," he writes in the book's preface, "created a quite unexpected new environment—it created the PUBLIC. The unique character of the 'public' created by the printed word was an intense and visually oriented self-consciousness, both of the individual and the group."

The scholarship of Eisenstein, McLuhan, and others leaves little doubt as to the extent of the printing press's impact on Western European civilization. What about the role of language, though? How did language inform the development of printing technology, both mechanically and procedurally? And, alternatively, in what ways did this new technology affect language?

Writing Systems: How Language Informed the Technology of Printing

In Chapter 1 we saw how a language's sound and word patterns inspired certain kinds of writing systems. The Chinese language, for example, abounds with single-syllable words. This may have encouraged the development of a writing system in which an entire word—and not the discrete sounds of that word—is represented by a single character. Linguists call such writing systems logographic.

As it turns out, a language's writing system also influenced the design of its printing technology. Think of it like this: Say you want to print a language that's written with logographs, like Chinese. There aren't twenty or thirty symbols that you would combine to spell a word; instead, there are tens of thousands of distinct characters. And (generally) one character = one word. This means, then, that you'd have to make multiple copies of tens of thousands of symbols. (Because words tend to reoccur within and between paragraphs in any document.) Thus, we're talking about, potentially, hundreds of thousands of little characters that you'd need to whittle from wood or bake out of clay or whatever. (Talk about sore fingers!)

Now here's the twist: this quaint thought experiment only works if you are thinking in terms of *movable* type. In fact, the Chinese writing system, with its thousands of characters each signifying a different word, did not—at first, anyway—encourage printing technology that used movable pieces. (This makes more sense if you return to our thought experiment. Think how dissuasive it must have been, the realization that you'd need to hand-fashion an amount of characters that, when lined up side by side, would compete with the Great Wall.) Instead, the logographic writing system framed Chinese

FIGURE 2.2 *Woodblock used for printing Chinese. ("Yangzhou Museum—woodblock for printing—CIMG2878" by User:Vmenkov – Own work. Licensed under Creative Commons Attribution-Share Alike 3.0-2.5-2.0–1.0 via Wikimedia Commons. http://commons.wikimedia.org/wiki/File:Yangzhou_Museum_-_woodblock_for_printing_-_CIMG2878.JPG#mediaviewer/File:Yangzhou_Museum_-_woodblock_for_printing_-_CIMG2878.JPG (accessed December 18, 2014).)*

inventors' approach to printing in a more holistic manner. For them, it was more linguistically intuitive to approach the technology from a *word*-centered, as opposed to a *sound*-centered, perspective. And a word-centered piece of writing, one that comprises a bunch of mostly dissimilar characters, would be easier to copy if you thought in terms of a single, non-movable template. Like ... a block of wood.

And in fact, as early as the third century the Chinese began carving characters into woodblocks. Figure 2.2 is an example of what these blocks looked like, in the Yangzhou region of China during the Tang Dynasty (seventh–tenth century CE). The blocks were besmeared with ink and pressed against a strip of cloth. As we've seen, unlike an alphabet, which has many recurring letters within and between words, Chinese characters (mostly) only need repeating if the entire word itself also recurs. In this sense, woodblock printing was a logical outgrowth of the Chinese logographic system: you etched into a block precisely those characters needed for that text, and then started on a new block.

But as much as this holistic technique seemed to suit the Chinese writing system, it was physically laborious and spatially inefficient. After you finished printing your text, the blocks that had taken hours of painstaking carving were either discarded or had to be stored somewhere. And this was followed by more hours dedicated to whittling a new block, which would also be scrapped or banished to a printer's basement. (Imagine the frustration!)

And so, after nearly a thousand years of block printing, a commoner named Bi Sheng came up with the idea of making individual and reusable Chinese characters out of hard-baked clay (in a process similar to, but much more sophisticated than, making holiday-shaped cookies with rolled-out dough).

Bi Sheng's ceramic movable type was integral to the further development of printing, in both the East and West, and even caught the attention of eminent scholars of his day. The great Chinese polymath Shen Kuo, for instance, dedicated an essay to Bi Sheng's invention in his *Dream Pool Essays* from 1088 CE:

> For printing hundreds or thousands of copies, it was marvelously quick. As a rule [Bi Sheng] kept two forms going. While the impression was being made from the one form, the type was being put in place on the other. When the printing of the one form was finished, the other was then ready. In this way the two forms alternated and the printing was done with great rapidity.

In the centuries that followed, others would improve upon Bi Sheng's movable type, replacing the ceramic with wooden and metal types.

But still—even with each improvement of Bi Sheng's invention, the technological and ergonomic challenges of printing a language written with characters became more glaring. Remember (just one more time, if you will) that a logographic system assigns a one-to-one relationship between written symbol and spoken word. Just as our thought experiment above illustrated, this meant that Bi Sheng and his successors still had to make *a lot* of characters. And don't just think about how much time and work this would take—consider, too, how much space you would need to store x-thousands of clay-cast characters![7]

Now let's consider printing technology from the perspective of an inventor whose language is written with an alphabet. In this case, instead of approaching the design from a context teeming with thousands of different characters,

FIGURE 2.3 *Chinese movable type cases. (http://news.xinhuanet.com/english2010/ photo/2010–11/17/c_13610642_2.htm (accessed December 18, 2014).)*

your conceptual context is circumscribed by a much more practical set of twenty-six symbols. So you, the printer, know that you'll need—at a minimum, because there are numbers and punctuation marks, too—multiple copies of twenty-six letter types, instead of multiple copies of thousands of characters.

Enter one Johann Gutenberg, in Mainz, Germany. In the fifteenth century he began deliberating the design of an apparatus that would allow him to duplicate long texts more efficiently and in greater quantities than scribes could by hand. Since he was working with a fraction of the number of symbols that a printer of Chinese or Japanese had to manage, Gutenberg struck on the following conceit: instead of stenciling an entire text onto a single surface, it makes more sense to cast a bunch of movable letters and to arrange these, on a flat surface, as needed for each text. And the bonus: all of these movable metallic letters—called sorts—could fit into a single wooden case with a few dozen cubbyholes, called a type case.

To limn a clearer picture of Gutenberg's alphabetic leg up in the realm of printing technology, compare Figures 2.3 and 2.4. Figure 2.3 shows the layout of Chinese character type cases, as the ancient art is still practiced today in the Museum of Wooden Movable Type Printing (located in Dongyuan County, in northeastern China). Notice the rows of type cases needed to house the thousands of characters. Figures 2.4 is a sketching of an eighteenth-century type case for printing German.

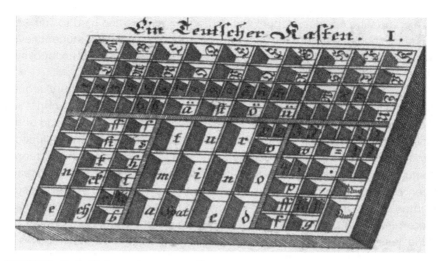

FIGURE 2.4 *Eighteenth-century German type case. (Image captured from p. 357 of digitized version of* Die so nöthig als nützliche Buchdruckerkunst und Schriftgiesserey: mit ihren Schriften, Formaten und allen dazu gehörigen Instrumenten abgebildet auch klärlich beschrieben, und nebst einer kurzgefassten Erzählung vom Ursprung und Fortgang der Buchdruckerkunst, *by Christian Friedrich Geßner, 1740. http://google.com/books?id=eLkBHPDIUvkC (accessed December 19, 2014).)*

Standards, Literacy, and the Written Word as Property: How the Printing Press Affected Language

Not since the invention of writing was language so affected by a technology than with the advent of printing. One explanation for this has to do with quantities—specifically, how much written material reached how many people. From the fifteenth through the nineteenth centuries, European printers duplicated and distributed more written material—whether in the form of books, newspapers, or pamphlets—than had ever been imaginable in the age of handwritten manuscripts. Imagine, for a moment, that the sum of all written language were an ivy plant. The Manuscript Age would be a single vine, with only a few people there to water its tiny rooted bed. It would grow slowly, slithering up the side of a single wall of a Gothic church. The Printing Age, on the other hand, would be a viny jungle, with countless names and faces watering its maze of roots. And its sprawling outgrowths would envelop the entire church.

Before printing, manuscripts in the Western world had to be copied by hand, letter by letter, on precious vellum. And even if you were among the slim group who could read, books were both expensive and hard to come by. So much so that, well into the sixteenth century, few university students even owned textbooks. (They would actually have to make their own textbooks by copying down what the professor read from his sole copy.)

A few statistics illustrate this point. In the early sixteenth century, around 400 books (not individual printed copies, but book titles) were in print, and these were mostly Bibles or otherwise religious in content. By the end of the nineteenth century, this number had grown to about 60,000 and included a few thousand novels.[8] Naomi Baron reports that by the middle of the sixteenth century, a million copies of Martin Luther's translation of the Bible had already been printed in Germany.[9] And according to the renowned Harry Ransom Center, at the University of Texas in Austin, "it has been estimated that there were perhaps 30,000 books in all of Europe before Gutenberg printed his Bible; less than 50 years later, there were as many as 10 to 12 million books."[10]

The takeaway here is that printing technology raised written language to a level of visibility and popularity that it had never before experienced. The printing press, you could say, made an international rock star out of the written word.

Now, when a technology makes use of such a vast amount of language, for such a large community of people, you can bet that that technology puts its stamp on both. Let's consider more closely the printing press's impact on language. Specifically, we see that the printing press:

- accelerated and spread language standardization efforts begun in the Manuscript Age;

- contributed to a rise in literacy and metalinguistic awareness; and

- helped reshape perceptions of who "owns" written language.

Standardization

Earlier scholarship tends toward overgeneralized conclusions as to the printing press's role in language standardization. Elizabeth Eisenstein, for instance, did reveal a number of fresh points, and instigate many new ideas, about printing technology's impact on the Western world. But her arguments about standardization, specifically, leave the reader with the impression that this development happened more quickly, and with more consistency, than was the case. "Typography," she writes, "arrested linguistic drift, enriched as well as standardized vernaculars, and paved the way for the more deliberate purification and codification of all major European languages."[11] And in *A History of Writing*, linguist Steven R. Fischer asserts that the printing press spawned a new "anonymous literate public," which "[i]n turn forced printers to standardize their texts to ensure widest comprehension." Ultimately, he argues, "this standardization led to the 'written languages' of Europe, which become more influential and prescriptive."[12]

Both Eisenstein's and Fischer's arguments are accurate in the grand scheme of things. The printing press *did* speed up and circulate written standards that—as we saw in Chapter 1—scribes had begun to develop in chanceries in pre-Gutenberg times. But their arguments are also misleading. They seem to suggest that the early printers single-handedly, swiftly, and cleanly concocted standard languages. That they simply "whipped up" a homogeneous, regularized variety of German and English—languages with such a density of regional and social variation that, often, a speaker needed only to travel to the neighboring village to hear a different word or accent.

It's hard to deny that printers played a decisive role in matters of spelling and stylistic appropriateness. And, certainly, their linguistic choices were copied and circulated to a wide audience. However, we shouldn't overstate the nature of their role. Language standardization in Western Europe—even with the printing press—was a gradual, multifaceted, and multiparty development. "It would be mistaken," Baron cautions, "to assume that the moment English began to appear in print, the written language was suddenly standardized."[13] In actuality, it took hundreds of years before printed works showed consistent uniformity in spelling.

Take, as a case in point, William Caxton, considered the original entrepreneur of printing in England in the fifteenth century. A survey of the scholarship on Caxton reveals that he alternatively spelled "book" as *boke* and *booke*, and "had" as *had, hadd,* or *hadde*. But his orthographic promiscuity for the word "fellow" takes the cake: it appears as *fellow, felow, felowe, fallow,* and *fallowe*. An online search of the *Oxford English Dictionary* shows that between the fifteenth and seventeenth centuries printers circulated more than twenty different spellings of "busy."[14] Baron sums it up well:

> Standardization of texts wasn't a high priority in the early centuries of printing. Spelling showed considerable variety, and punctuation and grammar weren't much more consistent. Copies of the "same" edition were rarely identical. There are no two copies of the first folio of Shakespeare's works (of which probably a thousand "copies" were printed in 1623). And it's been estimated that 24,000 variations of the King James Bible came into being between 1611 and 1830.[15]

In fact, the first widely circulated dictionaries and style guides for the English language didn't appear until the seventeenth and eighteenth centuries. So if a sixteenth-century typesetter or print master was uncertain about spelling this or that word, there wasn't any reference book to turn to. What's more, it wasn't until the late seventeenth century, with Joseph's Maxon's *Mechanick Exercises on the Whole Art of Printing*, that British printers had their own manual of typography to consult. In 1608, the German copyeditor Hieronymus Hornschuch crafted the very first technical manual for printers, *Orthotypographia*. Originally in Latin, it was translated into German and printed in 1638. And the first French-language printer's manual, *La science pratique de l'imprimerie*, by Martin-Dominique Fertels, didn't come out until 1723.

Nevertheless—and this point is key to our argument in this section—the printing press *did* contribute to the gradual and multiparty effort to standardize language in (though not all the languages of) Western Europe. Since texts could now be duplicated and distributed en masse, it was in a printer's best interest—for their purse and reputation—to strive for uniformity in their publications. Eisenstein, for example, shows that as early as the sixteenth-century publishing houses were putting out correction lists. "The very act of publishing errata," she concludes, "demonstrated a new capacity to locate textual errors with precision and to transmit this information simultaneously to scattered readers."[16]

Moreover, linguists have studied the early publications of the most influential authors and printers. Their conclusion: yes, the works of these individuals helped shape their language's standard variety. Gnanadesikan, for instance, summarizes Luther's role in the standardization of German:

> He did much to set the standards for written High German. Others before him had written in German, both High and Low [dialects], and they had attempted to write in as dialectically neutral a way as possible, so as to reach a wider audience. Luther [. . .] continued this trend. On the one hand he strove to avoid regionalisms (even those of his own native Lower Saxon dialect), while on the other he used words from a wide variety of dialects, searching for those that would most precisely translate biblical concepts. His use of language decisively shaped the standard German language.

As for Caxton, even Baron—who we've seen tends to be skeptical of sweeping conclusions—concedes:

> It's often said that Caxton was responsible for the initial step towards standardizing written English. This is, in the main, true. His use of the Southeast Midlands dialect for his texts (such as using *I* instead of *ich, home* instead of *hame*) helped guarantee that this would be the dialect later standardized.

Figures such as Caxton, Gutenberg, and Luther influenced the written standards of their native languages because they had at their disposal a powerful new technology, the printing press. As we've seen, this new technology alone didn't account for the standardization of the most widely written languages in Western Europe. But the printing press did accelerate and spread regularized forms and ideologies that had started to arise centuries before, in the Manuscript Age. Consequently, the technology of printing left an indelible mark on many languages as they are written and read today.

Upward Trends: Literacy and Metalinguistic Awareness

Another way that the printing press affected language has to do with how an individual speaker related to the printed word on a personal level. Assuming, of course, that the speaker was socially advantaged enough to learn how to read, the printing press enabled them, more than ever before in recorded human history, to form personal, one-to-one relationships with the written word. "Europeans became readers on a large scale," Fischer concludes in *A History of Writing*, "only after the printing press appeared in the mid-1400s."[17] Within a span of 300 years following the introduction of printing in Europe, the literacy rate of the general population rose from about 8 percent to 30 percent.[18]

Now, the more you read, the more exposure to language you get. And the more exposure you have to all this printed linguistic material, the more you notice differences in spelling or punctuation. Or you notice that, while one author describes a character as *being of keen wit,* another author writes that his character *possesses an acute intellect*. Moreover, the second author, you realize, crafts longer sentences than the first. His are littered with dependent clauses and hard to understand, while the first writer's sentences are shorter, with mostly main clauses. Furthermore, you read in the first author's book that, "Anyone who uses inkhorn words like *acute* and *possess* instead of *sharp* and *have* is just compensating for shortcomings in their own wit."

The point here is that, as you go from book to book, you begin to note differences, both in language structures and ideologies. Consuming language with your eyes leads you to become more mindful of it; you develop a metalinguistic awareness.

Education was a key factor in the rise of literacy and, consequently, this metalinguistic awareness. The printing press made books more affordable, plentiful, and portable—particularly for students. As you can imagine (especially if you've ever tried your hand at teaching) printed books made educating youth easier by light years.

Imagine you're a university student in Paris in the thirteenth century. And you have to sit at a desk for hours on end, five or six days a week, and write down your professor's words verbatim, just so you can have your own reference materials to study. Why? Because a personal copy of that thickly bound book your professor reads aloud in the lecture hall costs more than your parents make in a year.

Bearing this scenario in mind, you can understand the immense convenience that a compact assemblage of paper meant. McLuhan calls the printed book "a new visual aid available to all students [that] rendered the older education obsolete."[19] It was, he concludes, "literally a teaching machine where the manuscript was a crude teaching tool only."[20]

With printed books, teachers could spend more time discussing texts instead of dictating them. Students' homework changed from post-lecture to pre-lecture assigned readings. Even more importantly, the trend of silent reading exploded, as eager pupils could now tote their books around freely and form private relationships with the bound pages. Gone was the lecturing mediator that once stood between them and the prized written word. It was now just student and book, alone at long last, destined to change the intellectual world . . .

Noting the power of this new, liberated relationship between reader and written word, Eisenstein remarks that a "serious student could now endeavor to cover a larger body of material by private reading than a student or even a mature scholar needed to master or could hope to master before printing made books cheap and plentiful."[21] Indeed, one of the printing press's most lasting effects was the liberation it brought about in the relationship between individuals and language. It gave more people than ever before access to the written word and, as a result, revolutionized their habits and perceptions associated with it.

The Written Word: From Communal Resource to Individual Property

The printing press didn't just revolutionize the relationship between the written word and the pupil; it also transformed the way that authors related to their work in terms of ownership. In the Gutenberg Galaxy, ideas about literary creativity—in particular, the right to claim this type of creativity as exclusively one's own—began to change. It took a few hundred years for the ideological shift to happen, but by the nineteenth century the words and ideas contained within printed volumes had come to be viewed as individual and intellectual property, protectable by law.

In the age of the manuscript, a text was considered a communal, physical resource. Its words and ideas were there to be copied. For many a monk, for example, the "literary skill" or "artwork" lay in the actual copying endeavor. Scribes took pride in sprucing up a text with colorful ornamentation and stylish calligraphy. "For writers at least up through Ben Jonson and John Dryden," Baron writes, "the role of the writer was to embellish or translate (literally or figuratively) the works of previous authors."[22] Even poets and troubadours— word artists of the highest order!—didn't think twice about "borrowing" phrases, characters, and plots from fellow bards.

And why should they? There were no laws against it. And even society didn't look upon copying with the kind of shameful condemnation that we do today. Baron claims that "Chaucer and even Shakespeare would have been horrified"[23] at our present-day pedagogical crusades against plagiarism. And the French literary scholar Michael B. Kline tells us that "the terms plagiarism and copyright did not exist for the minstrel. It was only after printing that they began to hold significance for the author."[24]

With the capability to reproduce texts on a large scale, and the potential for monetary returns associated with wide circulation of one's work, authors— only too understandably—became protective of their literary creations. Printed words ceased to be communal resources; they were now the individual property of their authors. "Printing," Eisenstein writes, "forced legal definition of what belonged in the public domain. A literary 'common' became subject to 'enclosure movements,' and possessive individualism began to characterize the attitude of writers to their work."[25] This attitudinal shift led to the first copyright laws in England—though it took "only" a few hundred years.

As early as 1557 the British Crown granted a guild of printers, binders, and booksellers (aka The Stationers) the exclusive right to print and sell books. But guess who wasn't included in that guild? The authors. In fact, there is no mention of authors at all, in any of the English legal documents related to printing, until 1641. There, in an "Order made by the House of Commons" on Saturday, the 29th of January, it was proclaimed that, "the printers doe neither print nor reprint anything without the name and consent of the author."[26]

However, this was still a long way from ensuring an author's claim to intellectual property. Significant headway wasn't made until 1710, with the passing of the Statute of Anne, shown in Figure 2.5. The first sentence in its preamble—though somewhat of a rambling affair—should give you an idea of whose side its proponents were on:

Whereas Printers, Booksellers, and other Persons, have of late frequently taken the Liberty of Printing, Reprinting, and Publishing, or causing to be Printed, Reprinted, and Published Books, and other Writings, without the Consent of the Authors or Proprietors of such Books and Writings, to their very great Detriment, and too often to the Ruin of them and their Families.[27]

Essentially, the Statute of Anne took away the publishers' monopolistic grip on the reproduction of texts and, for the first time, vested copyright in the

(261)

Cup 19

Anno Octavo

Annæ Reginæ.

An Act for the Encouragement of Learning, by Vesting the Copies of Printed Books in the Authors or Purchasers of such Copies, during the Times therein mentioned.

Whereas Printers, Booksellers, and other Persons have of late frequently taken the Liberty of Printing, Reprinting, and Publishing, or causing to be Printed, Reprinted, and Published Books, and other Writings, without the Consent of the Authors or Proprietors of such Books and Writings, to their very great Detriment, and too often to the Ruin of them and their Families: For Preventing therefore such Practices for the future, and for the Encouragement of Learned Men to Compose and Write useful Books; May it please Your Majesty, that it may be Enacted, and be it Enacted by the Queens most Excellent Majesty, by and with the Advice and Consent of the Lords Spiritual and Temporal, and Commons in this present Parliament Assembled, and by the Authority of the same, That from and after the

FIGURE 2.5 *The Statute of Anne. (http://commons.wikimedia.org/wiki/File:Statute_of_anne.jpg#mediaviewer/File:Statute_of_anne.jpg (accessed December 19, 2014).)*

authors—though not indefinitely. It gave the authors "sole right and liberty" to their work for a term of fourteen years. But hey, it was a start!

Meanwhile, in eighteenth century Germany a new generation of writers was emerging, and they held impassioned views on the value of their craft. For authors like Fichte, Lessing, Schiller, and Goethe, writing was the linchpin of their livelihood. The words and ideas they put into books were no different than the barrels fashioned by a cooper, or the horseshoes wrought by a blacksmith. For them, it was self-evident that they should own, and be able to sell at their discretion, the finished product of their toil—no different from a vintner selling bottles of their wine. "These writers," notes Martha Woodmansee, "set about redefining the nature of writing. Their reflections on this subject are what, by and large, gave the concept of authorship its modern form."[28]

A case in point is Fichte's essay from 1793, *Proof of the Illegality of Printing*. In it he describes three ways that the concept of ownership applies to a printed book: physically, materially, and formally. When you buy a book, that mass of paper (or as is today more often the case, digital data) becomes your *physical* property; you can give it to a friend or even sell it to a used bookstore for money.

And the knowledge or information you take away from that book you read? According to Fichte, this *material* content is also yours to keep. It's the third aspect of property that Fichte was most fervent about protecting: the linguistic *form* in which the author couches his ideas. "Each writer," he argues, "must give his thoughts a certain form. But neither can he be willing to hand over this form in making his thoughts public, for no one can appropriate his thoughts without thereby altering them. This latter thus remains forever his property."[29]

The printing press changed the way that users of language—in this case, authors—viewed the written products of their creativity. The hand-written words in the Manuscript Age had been seen as something like an open communal resource for those lucky few who could read and write. But in the Gutenberg Galaxy, an author's printed words became a protectable, intellectual commodity. "In the span of roughly 300 years," Baron concludes, "the legal notion of authorship was transformed from that of a writer whose thinking reflected the ideas of others and who had little financial stake in the fruits of his labor, to a creator of original works that were his property."[30]

Part 2: The Typewriter

For centuries the only way to write was with a hand-wielded utensil. Consequently, many a writer had to deal with hand cramping and ink-blotted fingertips. And readers had to decipher half-smeared scrawls. In the late nineteenth century, however, one invention changed this. An invention that used individual metallic letter pieces (attached, as we'll see, to the ends of iron rods called typebars) to punch out a text, in much the same way that a printer worked with movable type. Reported to have been invented more than fifty times,[31] the machine went by various names—the *typographer, pterotype, scribe harpsichord, literary piano, phonetic writer*, and *Caligraph*, to name a few—before the now-familiar term was introduced in 1873. In that year, the Remington company marketed the first commercially successful machine as "The Sholes and Glidden Type-Writer." Figure 2.6 shows an early advertisement for the machine.

In this second part of our treatment of the mechanization of language, we won't address the history of the typewriter per se—though it's certainly an interesting one, full of inventive tinkering and financial disputes.[32] Here, as

FIGURE 2.6 *Advertisement for first commercially successful "type-writer" machine. (http://www.loc.gov/exhibits/british/images/vc151.jpg (accessed December 20, 2014).)*

before, we're more concerned with the ways that language itself shaped and was shaped by the new technology. And once again we won't limit our discussion to the sounds, words, and grammar of spoken and written expression; we also consider language ideologies. That is, we look at how the typewriter influenced attitudes, beliefs, and opinions of language.

First, however, let's go back to the earliest days of the typewriter and consider the role that language played in its creation. We see that, not surprisingly, language informed the construction of the typewriter in many of the same ways as the printing press: through its writing systems and sound/letter patterns.

Writing Systems and Letter Patterns: How Language Shaped the Typewriter

In the first part of this chapter we saw how a language's system of writing influenced the development of printing technology. The combinatorial, discrete nature of the alphabet inclined European printers toward movable pieces, which they could then arrange in endlessly combinatorial ways. They didn't inscribe texts into a single mass, like a wooden block, stone slab, or copper plate, and use that as a template. However, this latter technique did arise in ancient China, where writing had developed along an ideographic route, involving thousands of symbols that each stood for a different word. We argued that this character-based writing system likely dissuaded Chinese inventors from creating text-reduplicating technologies grounded in movable type. As we see in this latter part of our chapter on the mechanization of language, the question of what kind of writing system an inventor used also played a role in the development of the typewriter.

Let's start by putting ourselves in the shoes of the man whom history has dubbed the "father of the typewriter," Christopher Latham Sholes.[33] (It's a lesser-known fact that Sholes became inspired to construct his own typewriting machine only after reading an editorial in an 1867 issue of *Scientific American* about a contraption built by one John Pratt, an Alabama lawyer who had immigrated to England.)

But regardless of who was "the first" to "think up" the machine itself, what's important for our discussion here—and, ultimately, our overarching exploration of the relationship between language and technology—is how language influenced the way that Sholes conceived of his *own* typing machine. Here we argue that, after reading the article in 1867, when Sholes began brainstorming the form that his own contraption might take, his own language's writing system molded his conceptual framework. That is, he knew that he would need mechanical pieces to accommodate twenty-six letters (and numbers and punctuation marks, of course), which could be combined in an infinite number of ways to produce any text.

Like several typewriter inventors before him, Sholes's first designs drew on the familiar layout of a piano keyboard. A C-note key, for example, might be the first letter of the alphabet; C-sharp would be the letter *b*, and so on. Figure 2.7 shows what this looked like in one of Sholes's early patents.

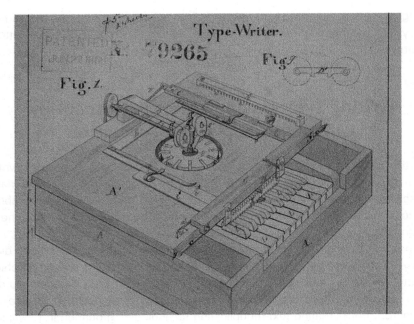

FIGURE 2.7 *Sholes's early patent for the typewriter with a piano-based keyboard layout. (http://cosahoimparatooggi.files.wordpress.com/2014/06/typewriter.jpg (accessed December 22, 2014).)*

As we now know, it wasn't in the cards for this piano-inspired layout. Typing with it was cumbersome and slow, the keys jammed easily, and the apparatus itself was too big and unwieldy. But the point here is that the alphabet, with its (generally) one-to-one relationship between sound and symbol, was not unlike a piano's one-key-to-one-note association. So it's understandable that Sholes would experiment with a piano-esque blueprint for a machine that needed to type letters. His writing system predisposed him to this conceptualization.

Now let's consider how Kyota Sugimoto, the inventor of the first practical Japanese typewriter, would have conceptually approached his machine. Recall that Japanese kanji is a character-based system of writing, much like Chinese. A symbol stands for an entire word. You don't combine a small set of recurring units into larger ones; rather, you're dealing with thousands of distinct symbols. Sugimoto knew, then, as he began brainstorming what his machine might look like, in the early 1900s, that his contraption would need to accommodate thousands of dissimilar inputs. A piano-like arrangement was clearly out of the question—its keyboard would run the length of a football field!

Even the QWERTY setup of American typewriters, which by Sugimoto's time was well on its way to establishing itself as *the* standard keyboard, couldn't serve Sugimoto as an appropriate model. The Remington No. 10 from

1910, for instance, had forty-six keys—far too few for the kanji system.[34] Thus Sugimoto's creative thinking was framed by his language's character-based writing system; that is, he had to start with the question of how his typewriter would contain so many characters.

The Japanese government's patent office website gives the following explanation of Sugimoto's efforts:

> In order to adapt typewriters to kanji, which has a large number of characters, Kyota Sugimoto carefully considered the nature of this writing system, including the frequency of use of characters used in public documents. The 2,400 characters chosen as a result were arranged by classification on a character carriage, and the chosen character was raised by a type bar that could move forward and backward and left and right. The character was then typed against a cylindrical paper supporter.[35]

Figure 2.8 shows how complex the machine's design was. And while other writing machines were eventually produced in Japan and China—among them an incredible contraption known as the Ming Kwai typewriter, designed by Dr. Lin Yutang in the 1940s—Richard Sproat notes that "when it came to languages with really large character sets such as Chinese or Japanese, typewriting broke down. Unlike typewriters for English and many other languages, Chinese and Japanese typewriters never became household items."[36]

In addition to its alphabetic writing system, the sound patterns of the English language played a role in the development of the typewriter. As we'll see, the frequencies and combinations of English's sounds, as these are expressed through its spelling conventions, contributed to the layout of the machine's keys. What's more, this layout has remained nearly unchanged since Sholes patented his Remington No. 2 in 1878. Figure 2.9 depicts the keyboard from his early patent.

Perhaps you're thinking to yourself: why not just arrange the keys alphabetically? And this was indeed what Sholes is reported to have done in his early prototypes[37]—which would make a lot of sense, since every literate speaker of English is familiar with the alphabet. But Sholes quickly ran up against the mechanical shortcomings of this keyboard arrangement: the faster the typist cranked out a text, poking at the keys with their two index fingers (touch typing, which involved the use of ten fingers, wasn't introduced until the late 1880s), the more the typebars jammed up.

Mind you, this wasn't just a minor design glitch. The Remington Company had couched their marketing strategy in the guarantee that, with this revolutionary typing machine, its customers would be able to write more cleanly, comfortably, and—especially—faster. When, for example, Mark Twain considered purchasing Remington's first model, he was sold by the salesman's

FIGURE 2.8 *An early Japanese typewriter. (http://www.jpo.go.jp/seido_e/rekishi_e/ kyota_sugimoto.htm (accessed March 10, 2015).)*

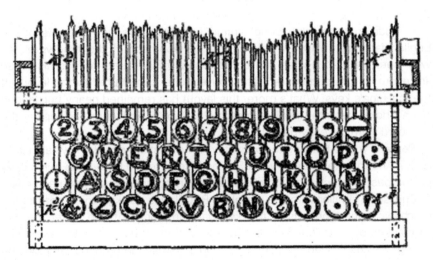

FIGURE 2.9 *Layout of keyboard for Sholes's 1878 typewriter patent. (C. L. Sholes U.S. Patent No. 207,559, via Wikimedia Commons. http://commons.wikimedia.org/ wiki/File%3AQWERTY_1878.png (accessed March 20, 2015).)*

demonstration of how *fast* the machine allowed its operator to write. (We return to this topic, the speed factor associated with the typewriter, later on.) The key-jamming issue, in other words, was critical. Before Sholes's investors could confidently market the device, this mechanical hiccup had to be stilled.

To really understand this early mechanical shortcoming, and how Sholes solved it, we need look more closely at both the inner workings of Sholes's typewriter and the letter patterns of English—and consider how the two interacted. More importantly, we will see how the English language itself, in particular the combinations and frequencies of its letters, steered Sholes's construction of the keyboard and typebar mechanics.

Today's collectors call Sholes's early machines "understrike" or "blind" typewriters. When you pressed the keys, the typebars didn't hit the paper against the platen where you could see it.[38] (A platen, by the way, is the roller of a typewriter. You twist it to scroll the paper up or down, or to load or unload paper.) Instead, the forty-four typebars of Shole's early models were located beneath the carriage and struck upward. The typist couldn't actually see what they were writing until they unhinged and raised the carriage. The typebars themselves were arranged in a single circular row, in what's known as a typebar basket. Both the understrike mechanics and typebar basket construction are depicted in Figure 2.10.

FIGURE 2.10 *Typebar machinery of Sholes's early typewriters. (http://type-writer. org/wp-content/uploads/2013/10/1888-Scientific-American-on-Remington-Fig.- 05.jpg (accessed June 21, 2015).)*

Here's where the English language's sound and letter patterns come into play. As Sholes tested the machine more thoroughly, he discovered a hang-up: whenever his typing picked up in speed, the more frequently operated typebars would get in each other's way and the machinery would jam up. The problem, he realized, was how he had arranged the typebars in the basket relative to each other. Letters that often occurred in combination with each other would collide.

Sholes realized that if he wanted to market a mechanically reliable machine, he needed to understand more about sound and spelling patterns of English. Specifically, he needed to know which letter pairs (or bigrams) occurred most frequently. Then he could fashion a keyboard that would maximize typebar distance between these jam-causing bigrams. And so the story goes:

> QWERTY was a direct result of the key jamming problem. Sholes's motivation for QWERTY was actually to enable typing that was as rapid as possible given the capabilities of the early machines. The design of QWERTY was rather clever, and depended upon corpus statistics, namely the relative frequency of letter pairs in English. Sholes's financial backer James Densmore had a brother Amos Densmore, who was a schoolteacher. Sholes asked Amos Densmore to compile a list of common English letter pairs.[39]

Unfortunately, the corpus that Amos Densmore used to compile these bigrams was never committed to the historical record. If he used the King James Bible, according to Sproat he would have arrived at the following top ten bigrams:[40]

TH
HE
AN
ND
IN
ER
HA
RE
OF
OR

Interestingly, Peter Norvig, director of research at Google, ran an n-gram analysis of English bigrams, based on millions of scanned books, and came up with the following hierarchy:[41]

TH
HE

IN
ER
AN
RE
ON
AT
EN
ND

Let's synthesize the lists and propose the following twelve as the most common bigrams in English:

TH
HE
IN
ER/RE
AN
HA
ON
OR
OF
AT
EN
ND

Sholes likely took into account high-frequency bigrams, such as these twelve, when he configured the mechanical relationships between the lettered keys on the keyboard and the typebars in the basket. The typebars for the T and H keys, for instance, would need to be arranged distantly from each other, since those keys would regularly be punched in succession. And remember: the farther apart the typebars are located in the basket, the less likely they would be to collide and jam. Figure 2.11 shows the key-to-typebar mapping in the Remington No. 2's typebar basket.

Now let's consider this typebar-to-letter relationship. If you look closely, you'll see that Sholes placed the typebars for T and H (the most frequently occurring bigram in English) diametrically across from each other. There are twenty-one typebars between them. And it turns out that one way of gauging the unlikelihood of any two typebars colliding is to examine their distance from each other, that is, to count the intervening typebars. The more intervening typebars, the less likely that that pair of letters will cause the machine to jam up. Therefore, if Sholes was indeed intent on reducing typebar snarl ups, he would have engineered a typebar basket that left a lot of typebars between the most frequently occurring bigrams, as he did for the T and H. Table 2.1

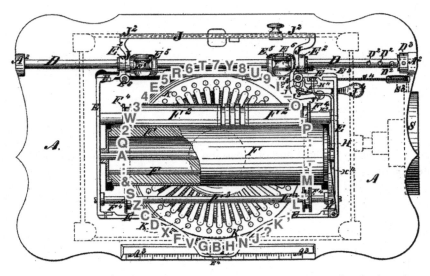

FIGURE 2.11 *Arrangement of typebars in Remington No. 2 typebar basket. (http://yasuoka.blogspot.com (accessed June 23, 2015).)*

TABLE 2.1 Number of intervening typebars for most frequently occurring bigrams in English.

Bigram	# InterveningTypebars	DegreeApart
TH	21	180
HE	17	147
AN	12	106
ND	6	57
EN	18	155
IN	14	123
HA	11	98
ON	12	106
OR	9	82
OF	17	147
AT	9	82
RE / ER	1	16

displays the number of typebars, and the distance in degrees, between each of the twelve most common English bigrams.

Looking at this table, it would appear that Sholes made decisions about typebar placement—and therefore the layout of his machine's keyboard—based on how often certain letter combinations occur in English. The two most common bigrams, TH and HE, were spaced especially far apart, to avoid jams. Sproat notes that "this in itself speaks to the cleverness of Sholes's design: the most common letter bigram in English has the keys close together for easy access, yet the chance of jamming is minimal since the typebars are maximally far apart."[42] The same goes for the other common bigrams—with the notable exception of RE/ER. Only one typebar separated them.

Which should strike us as odd. How could Sholes have overlooked this? Some diligent digging into the historical archive provides a possible explanation. Figure 2.12 shows one of the earliest known drawings of Sholes's prototype, which appeared on the cover of *Scientific American* in August 1872.

If you look closely, you'll notice that the E and R keys were *not* next to each other. The "." key was in R's place. This means that Sholes's original layout had eighteen typebars between the R and E keys, or a distance of 155 degrees. Somewhat inexplicably, though, when the first Remington machines rolled off the production lines a year later, the keyboard had been changed to its QWERTY form.

One hundred and twenty years on, Sholes's keyboard has remained largely unchanged and has become "universal in every English-speaking country, indeed practically universal (with minor local variations) in all countries where

FIGURE 2.12 *Illustration of Sholes's prototype keyboard from August 1872.* (*http://yasuoka.blogspot.com (accessed June 23, 2015).*)

the Latin alphabet is used."[43] And as we have seen, Sholes's inventive process took cues from the sound and spelling patterns of English. The phonology of the English language, and the letters used to encode it, shaped the typewriter keyboard—and indeed all modern-day alphabet boards.

Mechanized Thoughts, the Spoken Text Effect, Language Ideologies, and Writing Rapidity: How the Typewriter Impacted Language

Let's now consider the other side of the technolingual equation: the type-writer's effect on language. We begin with the titillating suggestion that the typewriter can influence its operator's mental landscape; specifically, that the physical, mechanical operation of the machine bleeds over into a writer's lin-guistic thoughts and, in effect, bootstraps their textual style. We then turn to the spoken text effect of the typewriter; in particular, we consider how type-writer dictation superimposed a distinctly spoken language character onto typewritten texts. Next, we discuss the various ways that the typewriter insti-gated new ideas and attitudes about language usage, language etiquette, and the people who used typewriter-mediated language. And we conclude our chapter on the mechanization of language with a look at how the typewriter sped up the physical process of writing.

Nietzsche's Mechanized Thoughts and James's Mechanical Mind

The philosopher Martin Heidegger was not a friend of the typewriter. At the University of Freiburg in 1942–43 he argued that the machine "tears writ-ing from the essential realm of the hand, i.e., the realm of the word."[44] In Heidegger's view, this was a dire development for the existential state of mankind. Because, to him, the human hand also "holds the essence of man."[45] And any machine that severed the connection between the human hand and the "realm of the word" would render man into something existentially and linguistically mechanical. "In the typewriter," he concluded, "we find the irrup-tion of the mechanism in the realm of the word."[46]

Perhaps it was this "mechanical irruption" that made Nietzsche aware of the toll that his Danish-made writing ball was taking on his linguistic mind. As we saw in our fictionalized—though based on factual circumstances—introduction to this chapter, Nietzsche felt that his writing machine was affecting his mind: shap-ing the thoughts he framed in language and put onto the page. The typewriter's staccato sounds and movements, he suspected, were encroaching on his brain and decomposing his once-fluid thoughts into clipped cognitive morsels.

But let's look to Nietzsche's own words on this. In a letter to composer Paul Gast in the winter of 1882, he suggested that "our writing tools are also working on our thoughts."[47] The mechanics of his writing ball, he believed, had rubbed off on his linguistic mind. The repetitive motion of the keystrokes (down-up, down-up, down up . . .) and the cold, hypnotizing rhythm of the type striking the paper (clack, clack, clack . . .) had begun to sculpt his language. Friedrich Kittler, for example, notes in his *Gramophone, Film, Typewriter* that Nietzsche's writing "changed from arguments to aphorisms, from thoughts to puns, from rhetoric to telegram style."[48] The typewriter, he concludes, "made Nietzsche into a laconic."[49]

There are other reports of the typewriter influencing a writer's thoughts and language—though, to be clear, they are no less anecdotal than the "evidence" above. Take Henry James, the heralded nineteenth-century American novelist. In 1907 he hired Theodora Bosanquet as his personal secretary and typist. For seven years, until his death, James dictated massive amounts of narrative to her. As luck would have it, Bosanquet was an author in her own right, and in 1924 she published the memoir *Henry James at Work*. In her memoir, "Bosanquet relates not only the particulars of her working relationship with James, but the effects that the typewriter had on James's writing."[50] According to Bosanquet, the introduction of the typewriter into James's writing process led to more words and longer sentences. Sholes's machine, she believed, made his writing more diffuse.

But was this really the case? Did the typewriter "make" James more prolix, more wandering with his prose? Did it really affect his language? In an article from 2013—aptly entitled *Typewriter Psyche: Henry James's Mechanical Mind*—Matthew Schillemann argues the following:

> The mental model found in Henry James's late works derives from his switch to typewritten dictation. . . . Through careful investigation, it can be demonstrated that the properties of typewritten dictation play a crucial role in forming the dynamic system of drives, compulsions, repetitions, and displacements for which James's late works are famous.[51]

As such, it would seem that the typewriter's linguistic effect on James was quite the opposite as that on Nietzsche. Apparently it was the sounds of the typewriter that influenced James's language output. According to Bosanquet, "the click of a Remington acted as a positive spur" for his writing.[52] That is, the mechanical workings of the typewriter ushered James into a linguistically productive mindset.

Think this sounds iffy? Well, it turns out that Henry James isn't the only case of an author reported to have experienced this particular effect of the "discursive machine-gun."[53] Richard N. Current, for instance, describes how Florine Thayer McCray, a nineteenth-century journalist and novelist, "testified that while she was operating her machine she felt her thoughts 'flowing easily, called forth and led on by the monotonous and isolating click of the rapidly forming words.' "[54]

Even today, as the typewriter tends more and more toward the proverbial fate of the dodo, there are contemporary accounts of this phenomenon (i.e., that a typewriter's sound can affect a writer's productivity). "Typewriters make me a more focused and disciplined writer," the freelance writer Matthew Solan proclaims in a piece for the literary magazine *Poets and Writers*. "Sometimes when I'm on a roll, and the clicking reaches a steady rhythm, like a train in the open country, I can't grab the return lever fast enough. The sound fuels me to keep going."[55] Such statements from typewriter devotees suggest that there's something linguistically conducive about the technology's machinery. The tactility and acoustics of its operation combine to coax out sentences. In his review of Wershler-Henry's *The Iron Whim,* literary critic Thierry Guitard concluded: "Typewriters made writers feel they were being dictated to."[56] Can we say the same thing about our computers?

Dictating to the Machine: The Spoken Text Effect

In the preceding section we noted that the typewriter influenced Henry James's writing through its repetitive, mechanical sounds, that it sparked his linguistic output and led to a more diffuse, verbose character in his prose. Note, however, that, unlike Nietzsche and the other authors we mentioned, James himself was not producing language on the typewriter. He was *dictating* to his secretary, Theodora Bosanquet. This detail is crucial for our consideration of how the typewriter impacted language. Because when you use a typewriter in this way to create text—a process we'll call *dictational authorship*—it bears linguistic consequences for said text; specifically, it imprints the writing with a spoken-language quality.

Dictation, of course, had been around long before the typewriter. In ancient Rome everybody who was anybody employed their own personal scribe—known as an *amanuensis*—to whom they would dictate all kinds of correspondences and documents. Philosophers dictated epicurean musings, as did senators their statutes, and attorneys their legal claptrap. To have to write your own material was considered plebeian.

After the fall of the Roman Empire, dictation largely passed out of vogue. And then, some 1,500 years later ... Enter the typewriter. This machine ushered in a renaissance of dictational authorship.

Slowly but surely—once the technology was thought to be as efficient and reliable as the hand—businesses began hiring typists (or "typewriters," as they were ambiguously referred to at first). In 1870 there were 154 stenographers and typists in the United States. By 1900 this number had bal-looned to 112,364.[57] Typists (predominately female, by the way) were woven into the fabric of American office life. In law firms, banks, insurance compan-ies, advertising and sales outfits, typists became a priori personnel fixtures.

Not to mention government agencies. By the turn of the century, it was common for a newly elected official to arrive on Capitol Hill with a nimble-fingered typist in tow. In a piece from a 1904 issue of *The Atlantic Monthly*, the author observed that "[i]t is no uncommon thing in the typewriting booths at the Capitol in Washington to see Congressmen in dictating letters use the most vigorous gestures as if the oratorical methods of persuasion could be transmitted to the printed page."[58] Even well-known writers joined the dicta-tional bandwagon. Figure 2.13 shows a sepia photo of Leo Tolstoy dictating to his daughter, Alexandra, in 1909.

The linguistic upshot of all this dictational authorship was that typewritten text began to reflect oral elements of language. Sentences were long. They ran on and into each other, in a multi-clausal cobwebbed mess. Bosanquet writes that Henry James himself was aware of the unfocused, sprawling form that his prose took on when he composed aloud: " 'I know,' he once said to me, 'that I'm too diffuse when I'm dictating.' "[59] This spoken text effect was another way that typewriting technology shaped language. Baron also con-cludes as much: "To the extent that typewriters are used either for composing

FIGURE 2.13 *Leo Tolstoy dictating to his daughter. (Mark Adams, "Ephemera: Remington Notes," 2, no. 11 (1912). http://type-writer.org/wp-content/uploads/2014/03/Tolstoy-and-his-typewriter.jpg (accessed June 28, 2015).)*

at the keyboard or dictating to a typist, the gap between speech and writing is reduced."[60] Baron ultimately interprets Sholes's invention as an early catalyst in the "growingly oral character of writing."[61]

But Baron was hardly the first to bring attention to this instance of typewriter-induced technolingualism. In the same *Atlantic Monthly* article mentioned above, Robert Lincoln O'Brien remarks:

> The invention of the typewriter has given a tremendous impetus to the dictating habit. This means not only greater diffuseness, inevitable with any lessening of the tax on words which the labor of writing imposes, *but it also brings forward the point of view of the one who speaks.*[62] (Italics mine.)

If we were to rephrase the italicized bit of O'Brien's argument, it might go something like this: dictating to a typewriter leads to writing that smacks of spoken language.

Ideologies and Etiquette: The Social Aspects of Typewritten Language

In Chapter 1, "The Textualization of Language," we saw that the invention of writing also spawned new ideas, beliefs, and perceptions of language. Speakers developed new opinions of, and assigned varying social and ideological values to: a) the written symbols themselves; b) the use of the symbols; and c) the users of the symbols.

Earlier in the current chapter, we saw that this was also the case with the invention of the printing press. New perceptions of language emerged, which led to the recognition of written texts as personal and intellectual property. We've referred to these ideas, beliefs, and perceptions of language as *ideologies*. And like writing and the printing press, the typewriter also resulted in new language ideologies: about the nature of typewritten language as a medium of communication, of who should use the typewriter, and even of the personal character of those who use the typewriter.

Let's explore this with a relatable example: writing someone a letter. Letter writing, in fact, is both a linguistically and socially regulated act. You're supposed to use particular wording for salutations and valedictions. When addressing the intended recipient, you're supposed to insert specific titles, because these titles should reflect the social relationship between you and said recipient (close friend? erstwhile acquaintance? loan officer? courted fiancée?). Your handwriting should be disciplined enough as not to offend the reader. And don't forget the importance of stationary—you wouldn't think of sending your loan officer a communiqué on purple, filigreed paper; nor would you dispatch a gooey love note to your betrothed on corporate letter-head. In short: whether we author or receive a letter from someone, we have expectations and ideas about what that letter should look and sound like. We know what constitutes appropriate etiquette for that particular use of language.

And it seems that early on the typewriter flew in the face of this established letter writing etiquette. Why? Well, keep in mind that for hundreds of years the only printed form of language that people encountered was in books and newspapers (i.e., written material that was copied and circulated in spades). And this writing felt cold, mechanical, and impersonal. That is to say, a press-printed page evoked the opposite social effect of a handwritten letter. So when the first typewritten letters—whether from businesses or acquaintances—began landing in nineteenth-century mailboxes, they were often met with consternation. "The print-like quality of the typewriter," Baron relates, "caused some recipients of typewritten messages to find the means of production to be socially inappropriate."[63] And in Margery Davies' fascinating *Women's Place Is At the Typewriter*, one learns that "it was considered rude or disrespectful for a firm to type its correspondence, and some dictation was at first transcribed in a fine longhand."[64]

This unfortunate sociolinguistic side effect even had commercial consequences for the typewriter. Sales of the first Sholes & Glidden Type-Writer remained stagnate for a good decade after Remington put it on the market. "Fewer than a thousand a year were sold during the 1870s," writes technology critic Edward Tenner, adding that "the machines were far more popular with court reporters than with businessmen, whose customers often suspected typewritten letters of being printed handbills intended for the semiliterate."[65]

Such is the might of language ideologies. The typewriter was a cutting-edge specimen of American innovation and engineering. And, yes, it had the potential to alleviate the arduous process of writing by making it faster, more uniform, easier to read, and user-friendlier for the visually impaired. But Sholes's "Wonderful Type-Writing Machine" was no match for the social propriety associated with good ol' handwriting. As Tenner puts it: "The technique of penmanship was still esteemed. Sears, Roebuck and Company sent handwritten correspondences to its rural customers, and the U.S. government did not start to authorize typewriter use until the end of the century."[66]

Along with language ideologies connected to social etiquette, the typewriter also prompted new ideas about what kind of person should use it. Early advertisements for the typewriter touted the machine as an essential tool for a slew of professionals. "Editors, authors, clergymen—all who are obliged to undergo the drudgery of the pen, will find in the type-writer the greatest possible relief," vowed one advertisement for the Remington No. 1, shown in Figure 2.6. The same poster claimed that "hundreds [of typewriters] have come into use in the last few months in banking, insurance, law, and business offices, in the Government departments in Washington, and in private families." What the ad didn't specify, though, was *who* in those offices actually operated the machine. Here's a hint: neither the bigwig businessman nor the big-shot attorney pecked away at the keys himself.

Fact was, as the typewriter made its way into these professional domains, it became a sign of prestige to *not* do your own typing. That's what a secretary or hired typist was for. By the turn of the century, it had become a sign of workplace status to dictate your typewritten letters. Certain communities of language users started perceiving typing as a form of manual labor, something only those lower on the social totem pole did. Baron writes:

> Up through the 1960s, typing classes in public schools were generally reserved for students pursuing a business track. College students rarely knew how to type well, generally relying on the hunt-and-peck method or hiring someone with the requisite skills. Similarly, in the legal world, up through the 1970s, the more prestigious law firms frowned upon lawyers having typewriters in their own offices. (You were supposed to write texts out in longhand and submit them to a secretary, or use a dictaphone.)[67]

This linguistic belief, which prescribed who should and shouldn't use the typewriter in a professional setting, was a distinct and powerful language ideology that emerged as the typewriter migrated into the business world. And it persisted all the way until the advent of desktop computing and word processing in the latter half of the twentieth century.

Rapid Writing, Typewriter Style

We end our discussion of the typewriter's effect on language with a look at the speed factor. Sholes and others designed their machines with a mind toward making writing neater, more forgiving on the hand and fingers, and faster. As we've already mentioned, early vendors emphasized the speed factor in particular. One ad, in an April 1904 issue of *Scientific American*, boasted that "Remington typewriters work with the highest speed." Another ad from 1929 grandstanded the "Speed with Ease" of the Royal typewriter and assured buyers that "[t]he Easy-Writing Royal is known throughout the world for its exclusive principles of smooth, precise operation ... factors that speed production, promote accuracy, lessen human effort." These ads are shown in Figures 2.14 and 2.15.

Mark Twain, it's said, got a hankering for a typewriter shortly after it came onto the consumer market. He believed the contraption would quicken his writing. In his autobiography he relates his first encounter with Sholes's model. It was 1874, and Twain and his friend Nasby were strolling the streets of Boston when they happened upon a shop window displaying the Remington No. 1. The machine had been on the market for only a few months and—as we've reviewed in some detail—still had a few kinks.[68] But a young typist's demonstration of its capabilities so impressed Twain that he snapped one up for $125—equivalent to more than $2,500 today! (Twain recounts that he and Nasby "timed her [the type-girl] by the watch" and that "she actually did fifty-seven [words] in sixty seconds."[69]) Clearly, if he was willing to spend that much money on what he later referred to as a "curiosity-breeding little joker,"[70] he must have been convinced that it would benefit his writing. A couple of months later in a typewritten letter to his brother, Twain explained that he was "trying to get the hang of this new fangled writing machine.... I believe it will print faster than I can write."[71]

And sure enough, future iterations of the typewriter would prove him right. Writing with it can be much faster than by hand. In Twain's time, a trained and dexterous hand could crank out an estimated 30 words per minute (wpm).[72] This is in fact the same statistic one finds in the latest printing of *Linguistics for Dummies*.[73] A quick search on Wikipedia informs you that "[t]he average human being hand-writes at 31 words per minute for memorized text and 22 words per minute while copying."[74] And a study from 2001 tested handwriting speeds of 300 adults and showed that their rates ranged from 26 to 113 letters per minute. That's 6.5 to 28 wpm, if one assumes an average word length (in English) of four letters.[75]

The point here is that none of these numbers comes close to the wpm speeds that even the earliest typists achieved. In 1888, for instance, the publishing outfit D. Appleton & Co. staged one of the first known typing competitions; the winner was clocked at around 100 wpm. The victors of the annual World's Typewriting Championship Contest, held annually from 1906 to 1930, consistently turned out speeds of 130+ wpm. As for the all-time speed record for writing on a typewriter, Stella Pajunas achieved this in 1946. She managed a mindboggling 216 wpm on an IBM electric machine.[76] Accomplishments such as these give credence to Kittler's turn of phrase: the typewriter really is a "discursive machine-gun." It brought a rapidity to writing that penmen, with their quills and ballpoints, could have never imagined.

FIGURES 2.14 AND 2.15 *Early ads promoting speed factor of typewriter. (Image 18: http://blog.modernmechanix.com/remington-typewriters (accessed July 1, 2015). Image 19: http://www.vintageadbrowser.com/office-ads-1920s (accessed July 1, 2015).)*

The Mechanization of Language as an Example of Technolingualism

The printing press and typewriter are examples of technologies that introduced a mechanical interface between language and language user. The printer no longer copied manuscripts by hand. The typist no longer composed prose by pen. Neither felt palm nor wrist chafe against grainy paper. Instead, an assembly of mechanisms became the mediator between them and their language. The printer arranged thousands of tinny morsels on a tray, laid a sheet of paper atop it, and pulled down on a lever. The typist twisted knobs, yanked on return levers, slid back carriages, and hammered away at plastic keys attached to steel typebars. In the galaxies of Gutenberg and Sholes, the production of written language became mechanized.

In this chapter we explored the technolingual side of this mechanization—namely, how language both shaped and was shaped by the printing press and typewriter. We saw how properties of language framed an inventor's conceptual thinking—specifically, that a language's writing system and sound symbol patterns disposed the innovator to approach their design in certain ways.

The character-based system for writing Chinese or Japanese, for instance, was an ergonomic nightmare in terms of movable type and keyboard arrangement. As a result, the first Chinese printers thought in terms of carving characters into wooden blocks, and reusing these blocks. Moreover, the typewriter posed a much greater challenge to Japanese and Chinese inventors, as their keyboard design needed to accommodate tens of thousands of character-labeled keys.

On the other hand, most European languages were written with an alphabet. As we've seen, this writing system breaks down the spoken form of languages, such as German and English, into individual sounds that can be combined and rearranged. As such, when Gutenberg and Sholes brainstormed the designs for their inventions, they benefited from having a smaller, more feasible set of values to guide them (i.e., a couple dozen letters, as opposed to tens of thousands of characters).

We also considered the flipside of the technolingual effect: how these language-mechanizing technologies shaped language, in terms of structures and ideologies. We saw that the printing press played a role in the standardization of languages in Europe; that it was an instrument in the rise of literacy, and helped more people become attentive to language itself (metalinguistic awareness); and that it contributed to the reconceptualization of written language as individual and intellectual property, protectable by laws, as opposed to an "open-source" communal resource.

As for the impact of the "discursive machine-gun" on language, we considered how its mechanical-ness influenced its user's thoughts, writing style, and total linguistic output. We also looked at the dictation trend that it spawned, and how this resulted in typewritten texts that resembled spoken language. Next, we looked at how speakers negotiated the typewriter's appearance in the sociolinguistic landscape; that new opinions arose about the etiquette of typewritten letters; and about who uses a typewriter in the workplace. Last, we saw how the typewriter made the process of writing faster than ever before.

In Chapter 3 we take on two more technologies that, like the printing press and typewriter, illustrate the concept of technolingualism: the telegraph and telephone. Our argument will be that, essentially, these inventions resulted in an *abstraction of language*—in time (e.g., from gradual to near instantaneous), place (e.g., from immediate to distant), and material (e.g., from sound waves to electric pulses). And of course we'll stick to our technolingual agenda, spotlighting both the role that language played in the conceptualization and construction of these technologies, and how the technologies affected language structures and ideologies.

3

Abstraction of Language: The Telegraph and Telephone

How a Dead Man's Ear Inspired the Telephone

At first glance it looks like an ordinary microscope stand—except that, where the scope would normally be mounted, this contraption holds a chunk of skull and three tiny bones excised from the ear of a human corpse.

The year is 1874. It's a cloudless July afternoon in Brandtford, Ontario—though the young man hovering giddily around the wooden chassis and inspecting each part for a possible flaw pays it no mind. As usual, he's been shut up in the stuffy carriage house on his parents' estate since early morning.

Satisfied with his inspections, he positions the charred pane of glass on the chassis's stage and winds the clockwork mechanism. He takes his place in front of the cone, reaches over, and trips the spring. The glass begins its timed horizontal crawl, and he brings his lips close to the mouthpiece:

"WEEE sEEE shEEEp."

At once the wisp of straw jumps into action. Ever so slightly—barely visible to the naked eye—it twitches back and forth, tracing a serrated pattern across the soot-smeared glass.

He removes the glass from the stage and holds it up to the light. *Excellent,* he thinks. *Dr. Blake will be pleased.*

Two sharp wooden knocks cut through the stifling air.

"Aleck? Are you in there presently?"

His father. The voice is unmistakable. Alexander Melville Bell's vowels and consonants are carefully polished, each syllable the result of years of elocutionary study.

Twenty-seven-year-old Alexander—known to his family as Aleck—takes a handkerchief from his pocket and mops the sweat from his forehead. (*Had it been this hot in here all morning?*)

"One moment, Father."

He jostles boxes, books, papers, and random hardware out of the way, creating a crude but traversable path to the door.

"Why have you the door locked?"

Aleck unbolts the door and opens it. "I prefer not to be disturbed while I conduct my experiments."

Without invitation the elder enters and begins surveying the room. *The boy has built himself quite a workshop*, he thinks. His gaze halts on something that looks like a microscope stand.

"I take it you're feeling better?" he asks his son.

"Yes, thank you. Much better. One cannot even begin to compare the air here with that in Boston." Aleck follows his father's stare, still anchored on the contraption. "My experiments are also going splendidly."

"It seems that some folks in town have been talking, Aleck . . ." the elder Bell announces. "Your mother has fielded more than one query from the neighbors, since your return. Consequently, I thought that I might—"

And it occurs to him: that's not a microscope.

"May I inquire into the nature of this particular instrument?"

Aleck's eyes brighten. In fact, he'd been waiting for the right moment to invite his father into the workshop.

"That, Father, is the ingenious instrument about which I wrote you and Mother in May. It's called a phonautograph."

"I see." He clears his throat. "May I have a closer inspection?"

Aleck jumps to attention. "Certainly."

The two men walk over to the contraption.

"May I ask what the townspeople are saying?" Aleck inquires. It's takes all he can muster to keep from smirking.

"Some of them have come into the notion that you've taken to experiment-ing with . . ."

"Yes?"

"The auricular portions of deceased animals."

This time Aleck can't help himself; the chuckles spill forth.

"Your mother," the elder Bell interjects, "is rather less amused by these rumors."

"My apologies, Father." He clears his throat and straightens up his torso. "You and Mother shall be happy to learn that there is no truth to this scuttle-butt. My work does not involve the auricular portions of deceased animals."

"Well. Mother will indeed be pleased to hear this."

"My phonautograph contains the tympanic membrane and ossicles of a human."

The older Bell's right eyebrow rises.

"For the sake of accuracy, that is," Aleck adds.

His father stares at him. *A human ear? Here? Transported all the way from Boston? No wonder the townspeople are astir with chatter!*

Although ... He himself had always inspired the children—especially Aleck and his older brother Melville, may he rest in peace—to experiment with the sounds of speech. Indeed, the more he considered it, the more he realized that this carriage house workshop—yes, even this contraption with the human ear—was a result of his encouragement.

Alexander Melville inhales long and slowly. "Please do enlighten me."

Aleck starts from the top. He tells his father of his acquaintance with Dr. Clarence Blake, an otologist in Boston. How he had sought out Dr. Blake in hopes of learning more about the mechanics behind the ear's processing of speech sounds, especially vowels. How Dr. Blake had assisted another doctor in Vienna on the construction of an instrument, directly modeled after the anatomy of the middle ear, that funneled the vibrations of speech down into a stylus that sketched out these vibrations on smoked panes of glass. And how, ultimately, he and Dr. Blake had decided to attempt their own human ear phonautograph. (It was Dr. Blake who, through his connections at Harvard Medical School, had procured the cadavers and actually excised the temporal bone, eardrum, and ossicles.) For several weeks now they had been capturing tracings of their speech, taking photographs of their results and comparing them.

"Imagine this, Father!" he beams. "An instrument that produces a concrete account of the ephemeral sounds of speech. Imagine the possible applications of such a device!"

The aging elocutionist bends down and inspects the phonautograph more closely. He gets it now. The conical mouthpiece. The straw stylus. The darkened glass surface. The squiggly pattern in the smudge. And all at once it hits him.

This is visible speech.

"Extraordinary," he utters. He stands up straight, turns away from the apparatus, and faces his son. For the second time Aleck nearly flinches. "Congratulations, son." He extends a hand. "This shall be a grand milestone for visible speech."

As their hands embrace, and the elder Bell's mind swells with sanguine thoughts of the future, Aleck considers also telling his father of his latest idea. It had come to him just yesterday, on a late-afternoon stroll along the banks of the Grand River.

What if, he'd thought, the eardrum and trio of bones channeled the pulsations of my voice into a stylus made of iron instead of straw? And what if this piece of iron were magnetized? And instead of gathering the vibrations and conveying them onto a sheet of glass, what if this magnetized iron reed were arranged to create a fluctuation in current against an electromagnetic coil? Might it be possible to use one phonautograph as a transmitter of these

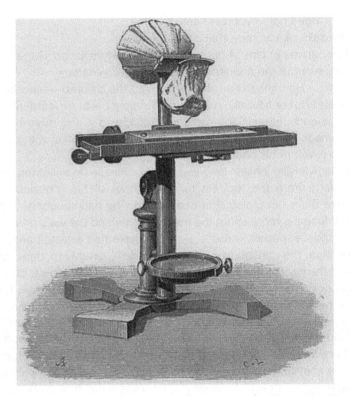

FIGURE 3.1 *Bell and Blake's human ear phonautograph. (Count Du Moncel*, The Telephone, the Microphone and the Phonograph *(New York: Harper & Brothers, 1879), 45. https://archive.org/details/telephonemicrop00moncgoog (accessed January 20, 2015).)*

fluctuations in current, and then simply reverse the mechanics on the other end, with another phonautograph as a receiver?

Imagine the possible applications . . .

But just as quickly as the impulse to share had come over him, he decides to ignore it. Right now, it's enough to enjoy his father's praise. This other new and exciting idea—which, Aleck had to admit, was still in its infancy and would only come across as far-flung—would have to wait.

Still . . . The idea was there. Embossed in his mind. And with the last twenty-seven years as an indication of how his mind works, young Aleck senses that this idea won't be going away easily, far-flung or not.

∞

In Chapter 2 we explained how the printing press and typewriter amounted to a "mechanization" of language. We argued that these technologies introduced a mechanical interface between language per se and the use of language, effectively disrupting the corporal connection between them. Writing, we showed, could now be done with cold, mechanical apparatuses, replacing the human hand and putting physical and emotional distance between writer and written word.

Most importantly, though, we showed how this mechanization of language offers a compelling illustration of the sociolinguistic phenomenon we've been calling *technolingualism*; namely, that technology both shapes and is shaped by language.

In this chapter we consider a further step in the dislocation of language and user, a process that began as far back as 3000 BCE with the technology of writing (i.e., the textualization of language) and progressed with the language-mechanizing technologies. Here, we concern ourselves with two technologies that disassociated speaker and language even more radically, resulting in what we're calling the *abstraction* of language.

In what follows we argue that the telegraph and telephone—inventions that revolutionized nineteenth- and twentieth-century life in many parts of the world— abstracted language in time, place, and substance. Put more specifically, the devices that we deal with in this chapter freed language, spoken or written, from the bonds of:

a) time—in terms of how fast a speaker can transmit linguistic content from one point to another;

b) location—in terms of the distance between the producer and receiver of linguistic content; and

c) physicality—in terms of the form that the linguistic content takes (e.g., concrete or immaterial, visible or imperceptible).

With the telegraph, writing was, for the first time in human history, abstracted from visible marks on a page to invisible electric pulses created by breaks and completions of a circuit. This electric abstraction of language progressed with the telephone: it transduced concrete undulations of air pressure (aka sound waves) into fluctuations of electric current, which were instantaneously transmitted to a receiver that converted these back into sound.

Sticking to Our Technolingual Guns

As always, our discussion unfolds within the larger theoretical framework we've termed *technolingualism*—the sociolinguistic waltz that technology and language have engaged in for millennia. Our goal, by chapter's end, is to have demonstrated how two language-abstracting technologies both shaped and were shaped by language. And of course we continue our practice of including both linguistic structures and language ideologies in our definition of "language."

In this vein we start with the telegraph. We see how a language's writing system, and the frequency distribution of letters in English, guided the development of codes for communicating via telegraph. Conversely, we explore the new language forms and ideologies that the telegraph inspired: from abbreviations, journalistic styles, and jargon, to a new conceptualization of what it means to "communicate."

Then we shift to the telephone. As should be clear from our opening narrative, the conceptualization of the telephone owed much to the physical and physiological processes behind the production and perception of speech sounds. In fact, we make the argument that, although several creative minds had already experimented with devices for transmitting speech over a wire, it was Alexander Graham Bell's unique background in the articulatory, acoustic, and auditory properties of spoken language that lent him the ultimate advantage, enabling him to construct the first practical telephonic device. But even more importantly, we see that Bell understood the physiological components involved in how the human ear perceives sounds.

This anatomical insight was crucial; it informed the mental models that Bell used to develop his diaphragm membrane telephone. One particular compelling entry in his notebook from 1867, for example, reads: "Make transmitting instrument after the model of the human ear. Make armature the shape of the ossicles. Follow out the analogy of nature."[1] In short, the physical nature of speech sounds and the anatomy involved in their perception guided Bell in his inventive approach. "Thus," Carlson and Gorman conclude, "Bell saw his telephone as a kind of electro-mechanical ear."[2]

On the other hand, the telephone also affected how speakers used and thought about language. The phone bereaved discourse of its age-old face-to-face context, opening the door for new linguistic strategies to handle things like opening conversation, changing topics, turn taking, and closing a conversation. And, as always, there were those who felt a need to conventionalize these linguistic strategies by prescribing a litany of conventions for the "proper" use of the telephone.

Part 1: The Telegraph

The early brainchild of what, years later, evolved into the telegraph popped into the mind of one Samuel B. Morse in October 1832, onboard an American-bound ship out of France. The New England painter-by-trade was listening intently as Dr. Charles Jackson, a well-regarded Boston physician, enlightened fellow passengers on the latest scientific insights into electromagnetism. And when Dr. Jackson noted that electricity could be made to pass through even miles of wire at the speed of lightning, and therefore instantly, Morse reportedly interrupted him. "If this be so," he announced, "and the presence of electricity can be made visible in any desired part of the circuit, I see no reason why intelligence might not be instantaneously transmitted by electricity to any distance."[3]

By intelligence, of course, Morse had in mind *language*. And after this conversation he became obsessed with the idea of transmitting linguistic intelligence—instantly and across great distances. One reason for this, perhaps, was his own devastating experience with the slowness of communication in his day. Before the telegraph—and this is a key point to which we will return—*communication was synonymous with transportation*. A letter took as much time to arrive at its destination as was needed by the courier, horse, or ship to transfer it. The transmission of information was dependent on the manner of transportation. But the "singing wire" (as it was popularly referred to) changed this. In terms of speed and geography, the telegraph was a watershed in communication: it freed the transfer of information from the bondage of physical conveyance.[4]

But first to Morse's devastating experience. One day in 1825, while Morse was in Washington, DC, on a painting assignment, he received a letter from his father. Samuel's wife, his father wrote, had taken ill but was now convalescing. The next day, however, Samuel got another message informing him that his wife had died. Morse would soon learn that, weeks earlier on the same day that she had died, he had sent her an ebullient letter describing his experiences and new acquaintances in Washington. But because communication was so slow, he hadn't known that that whole while she was actually lying on her deathbed. And when he finally did arrive home, he discovered that his wife had already been buried, weeks earlier, in fact. So much had occurred, yet he'd been out of the loop for all of it.

This unsavory experience had a lasting effect on Morse. Several sources suggest that it inspired him early on to seek a means of sending information at faster speeds and over greater distances, lest someone else have to go through what he did.

And so when, on that maritime vessel headed for the United States, he heard Dr. Jackson speak about the wonders of electromagnetism, something in Morse's mind clicked: here, at last, was the solution. Ultimately it would take more than a decade of tireless work before Morse—aided by a young engineering whiz named Alfred Vail—could bring his dream to fruition. But by the turn of the century, millions of messages in the form of electric pulses were zipping nearly instantaneously along the "singing wire" between cities as far apart as New York and San Francisco. In Chicago in 1900, for instance, the Western Union relay office alone was handling more than 2 million messages per month.[5]

Letter Frequencies and Telegraphic Code: How Language Shaped Telegraph Technology

Although it bears Morse's name, it appears that the historical record is less certain about exactly whose genius was behind the dot-and-dash code for communicating over the telegraph.[6] Whether it was Morse himself or one of his assistants, here we'll stick with terminological convention and call it "Morse code." (And anyway, what concerns us most is the role that *language* played in its conception and development.)

Interestingly, in this section we see parallels to our discussion in Chapter 2, where we looked at language's influence on the conception and development of the printing press and typewriter. It appears that letter frequency (in this case, the alphabetic system for writing English) also informed Morse code's dot-and-dash communication design. Moreover, we see that logographic writing systems—such as those for writing Chinese—compelled telegraphers to come up with a different code for communicating via pulses of electricity—one based on numerals instead of letters.

Morse began mulling over a code as early as 1832. The challenge, he realized, lay in devising an elaborate code with only two inputs at his disposal: the opening and closing of a circuit. He knew, in other words, that he'd need to formulate a binary-based combinatorial system that could be used to transmit words, numbers, and even punctuation. But where to begin?

As it happened, during his travels through France, Morse had seen the semaphore system developed half a century earlier by Claude Chappe. This ingenious system conveyed information across distances by using large wooden poles. The varying position of each pole signified either a letter or a number. Figure 3.2 gives an idea of what Chappe's contraption looked like. And by the time Morse was touring Europe, France had erected hundreds of them.

As you can see, the code for Chappe's semaphore was ternary based, that is, it used three values to encode information: the position of the main horizontal crossbar and the position of the vertical poles fastened, like wings, to each end of the crossbar.

The point here is that Morse knew, as early as 1832, that at least one semiotic code had already been developed to communicate across distances. And

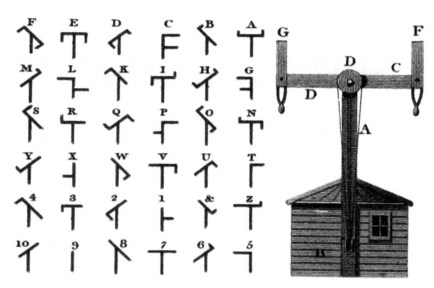

FIGURE 3.2 *Chappe's semaphore system. (Image available within the public domain. Courtesy of John Farey Jr., Rees's Cyclopædia, Plates Vol. IV, "TELEGRAPH," Fig. 4; from a digital scan at http://archive.org/details/cyclopaediaplates04rees (accessed February 20, 2015).)*

he knew that this code transmitted information letter by letter.[7] Thus, in many ways it's surprising that it took Morse several years to finally decide upon an alphabetic form for his own code. Both his journal entries and sketches in his notebooks suggest that his earliest brainstorms involved *numbers*. The numerals 1–5, for instance, were to be conveyed with a corresponding number of quick completions of the circuit (dots); the numerals 6–0 added drawn-out circuit completions (dashes) to the dots. Table 3.1 illustrates this simple, numerically based code.

The next step was to assign each word its own number. Thus, 45 might be "tree," 322 "happy," and so on. Interestingly, Morse also gave each individual letter a number, so that proper names, foreign words, or any other words not in the dictionary could be spelled out. In fact, he spent several years compiling a numbered dictionary for the transmission of English words. Years later, he reflected back on this original approach:

In the earlier period of the invention it was a matter which experience alone could determine whether the numerical system, by means of a numbered dictionary, or the alphabetic mode, by spelling of the words, was the better. While I perceived some advantages in the alphabetic system, especially in the writing of proper names, I at that time leaned rather towards the

TABLE 3.1 Morse's earliest idea for telegraph code, based on numbers.

Numeral	Circuit Completion	Numeral	Circuit Completion
1	.	6	. __
2	..	7	.. __
3	...	8	... __
4	....	9	.... __
5	.....	0	..... __

numerical mode under the impression that it would, on the whole, be the more rapid. A very short experience, however, showed the superiority of the alphabetic mode, and the big leaves of the numbered dictionary, which cost me a world of labor, and which you, perhaps, remember, were discarded and the alphabetic installed in its stead.[8]

Key to our discussion here—and for language's influence on telegraph technology—is Morse's remark about an "experience" that "showed the superiority of the alphabetic mode." Early experiments with the telegraph showed how cumbersome and memory taxing it would be, for both sender and receiver, to communicate with tens of thousands of numbers. Thus the decision was made to pursue an alphabetic code. (Though, as we alluded to above, exactly *when* and *who* decided on going alphabetic, is still unclear.)

Which brings us to our technolingual highlight: when Morse and his associates set about devising the dot-and-dash code for the English alphabet, they realized that a letter's frequency of occurrence would influence the speed and efficiency of communication with the code. In other words, they understood that more commonly occurring letters should have the shortest, easiest-to-transmit codes. And, alternatively, those letters that were less regularly used should be encoded with longer dot-and-dash sequences.

Now you might be asking yourself: how did they figure out which letters were used more and less often? The answer: they visited a local printer. And a quick examination of his type case, and the quantity of sorts it contained for each letter, gave them the answer they were looking for. William Baxter, who served as an assistant to Vail and Morse, would later recall the following:

After going through a computation, in order to ascertain the relative frequency of the occurrence of different letters in the English alphabet, Alfred [Vail] was seized with sudden inspiration, and visited the office of the

Morristown local newspaper, where be found the whole problem worked out for him in the type cases of the compositor.[9]

Figure 3.3 shows a page from one of Morse's notebooks, on which he tallied the quantity of sorts for each letter, as found in the compositor's type case.

As you can see, Morse and his associates learned that their local printing office used the sorts *e, t, i, s,* and *a* most often, and the sorts *z, x, j,* and *q* most seldom. As a result, they assigned simpler configurations to the former and longer codes to the latter. Tables 3.2 and 3.3 offer a breakdown of Morse code according to letter and sort quantity, as noted in Morse's journal. Table 3.2 presents the five letters with the greatest number of sorts in the type case; Table 3.3 shows the five letters with the least number of sorts.

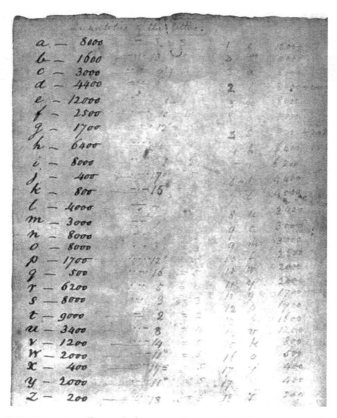

FIGURE 3.3 *Morse's tallies of the sorts in a printer's type case for each let-ter. (Image from Edward L. Morse, "The Dot and Dash Alphabet," The Century Illustrated Monthly Magazine 83, 1912: 695. https://books.google.com/ books?id=jl1NAQAAIAAJ (accessed February 21, 2015).)*

TABLE 3.2 Breakdown of Morse code by letter and quantity of sort (five highest quantities).

Letter	Type Case Sort Tally	Code
E	12,000	·
T	9,000	–
I	8,000	· ·
S	8,000	· · ·
A	8,000	· –

TABLE 3.3 Breakdown of Morse code by letter and quantity of sort (five lowest quantities).

Letter	Type Case Sort Tally	Code
K	800	– · –
Q	500	– – · –
X	400	– · · –
j	400	· – – –
z	200	– – · ·

In this way language affected telegraph technology: the creators of its dot-and-dash code were guided by how frequently letters were used in their language's writing system.

Beyond English, the dot-and-dash code could be easily adapted—provided that the language was written with an alphabet or syllabary. Naturally, adopters expanded the code to include letters specific to their respective alphabets. In 1848, for instance, the German telegraphy pioneer Friedrich Gerke introduced codes for the umlauted vowels *ä* (· – · –), *ö* (– – – ·), and *ü* (· · – –). For Japanese, a protocol was created based on the kana syllabary. Dubbed the Wabun code, each dot-and-dash combination represented a syllable character. A few examples: カ ('ka') had the code · – · ·, and チ ('chi') was transmitted with · · – ·.

But languages written with logographs, like Chinese, required a different approach. As we've seen in earlier chapters, logographic writing systems use symbols (aka characters) to represent entire words, instead of the individual sounds within the words. Thus, to communicate telegraphically in Chinese, you'd have to devise a particular dot-and-dash sequence for each word. Moreover, because we're dealing with many thousands of distinct codes, the dot-and-dash sequences would need to be longer and more complex to accommodate all of them. (A common word like *the* might be, say, "· ", and a rarer word like *sable* might be "— — · · · — — · · ".) Both sender and receiver of the telegram would need to know all of these long, complex dot-and-dash codes!

This, assigning each word its own code, was one possible approach, if you were creating a telegraphic code for Chinese. But there was another way, too. Ironically, the solution to the challenge that non-alphabetic languages posed for telegraphic communication went back to Morse's original efforts to formulate his code: numerals.

Each Chinese character was assigned a distinct four-digit number 0000– 9999. So, for example, to send the four-character message 中文信息 ("information in Chinese"), you would transmit the numerical sequences 0022 2429 0207 1873.[10] These digits also indicated where the character was located in the official codebook: the first two numbers gave the page, the third number the row, and the fourth number the column. So, the character 中 ('zhōng') was listed in row 2 of column 2 on page 00 of the codebook, 文 ('wén') in row 2 of column 9 on page 24, and so on. Figure 3.4 shows the codebook developed in 1881 by Zhèng Guānyīng.

It was an ingenious solution, and this numerical code was used effectively in China for several decades (though it posed a greater challenge to operators than the alphabetic code).

Let's now look at the telegraph from the opposite technolingual perspective: how it impacted language, both in terms of concrete forms and abstract ideas.

Of Morse Speak, Jargon, Journalistic Style, and a New Conceptualization of "Communication": The Telegraph's Effects on Language

The telegraph sent significant, lasting ripples of influence across the nineteenth- and early-twentieth-century linguistic landscape. But lest you rush to conclusions and take this (shamelessly metaphor-laden) statement to mean that the telegraph triggered fundamental changes in a language's sound, word, and grammatical system, let us clarify: the telegraph did not have *that* kind of impact on any language. What it *did* do to language, however, was just as fascinating and indelible. It created a new context for speakers to use language in, and in which they could fashion new ideas about communicating

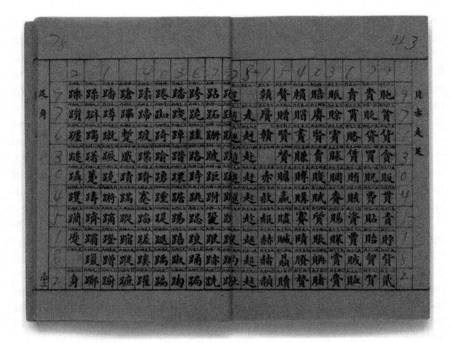

FIGURE 3.4 *Zhèng Guānyíng's Chinese codebook. (http://www.bonhams.com/ auctions/21070/lot/1/ (accessed February 22, 2015).)*

with language. In other words, it led to the expansion of a speaker's *linguistic repertoire*.

By linguistic repertoire we mean the entirety of what a speaker can do with their own language, and how they perceive of and regulate both their own language and the language of others. A speaker's repertoire includes the systematic parts of language (e.g., sounds, words, grammatical rules), but also extends to what a speaker knows about the social and attitudinal negotiation of language. Speakers know, for instance, when and with whom to use which language, dialect, or style. And they sense how to judge a certain language or dialect or style, and the speakers of these. All of us have a linguistic repertoire that is both unique and shared.

When the telegraph was introduced, it swung open the proverbial door of many a linguistic repertoire. "New technologies," Crystal declares, always increase a language's stylistic range."[11] Thus speakers developed a host of structural and perceptual additions to their repertoire:

- a new language variety that we'll call *Morse Speak*;

- an elaborate, abbreviation-loaded telegraphic jargon;

- a clipped journalistic style that inclined newsmen to more objectivity; and

- a new conceptualization of "communication" per se.

After we look at each of these points in turn, we think you'll agree with our larger message; namely, that this expansion of the linguistic repertoire was yet another testament to the awesome adaptability and creativity of human language.

Morse Speak

Interestingly, the actual sounds that the telegraph's machinery made, when transmitting and receiving code, gave rise to a novel form of aural/oral communication—"Morse Speak," if you will.

Morse and Vail's original design proposed an instrument that both sent and recorded information via electrical pulses. On one end of the line sat an operator who tapped out the code, while on the other end was a receiving device, complete with an armature to which a sharp stylus was affixed. Each time the transmitting party completed the circuit, an electromagnet activated the armature, which then pressed the stylus against a strip of paper and left indentations. Figure 3.5 gives an idea of what the receiving device looked like.

Short and quick spurts of current sent across the wire left a "dotted" imprint on the paper tape. A series of longer-held circuit completions left a "dashed" imprint. The point here is that Morse and Vail first envisioned the code as a written form of communication between operators. (Indeed, even

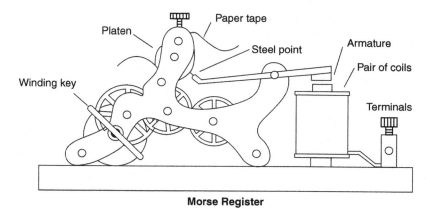

Morse Register

FIGURE 3.5 *Morse and Vail's receiving device for recording transmitted code. (Image from J. B. Calvert's "The Electromagnetic Telegraph." http://mysite.du.edu/ ~jcalvert/tel/morse/morse.htm (accessed February 23, 2015).)*

the terms used to describe the code's features—"dots" and "dashes"—were borrowed from the domain of writing.) The receiving device imprinted a strip of paper with dots and dashes, which the telegraph operator could then read, decipher, and transcribe.

But soon after the telegraph came into more widespread use, and proficiency in the code grew, operators realized that they didn't have to wait for the paper tape. Remarkably, they found they could "understand" the sequences of clicks that the armature made as it tapped against the electromagnetic coil. Thus emerged the practice of "sound reading"; operators switched to deciphering and transcribing the clicking sounds in real time, and the stylus and paper were largely done away with.

Not long after operators discovered they could understand Morse code by sound alone, some of them even began to vocalize it. A dash was rendered into speech as *dah*, while a dot was pronounced as *dit*. Furthermore, if the *dit* wasn't the last segment in the word, it was spoken as *di*. The word *send* for example, was transmitted telegraphically as · · · · · — — · · , but could also be spoken as *di-di-dit dit di-dah dah-di-dit.* Essentially, those proficient in Morse code could sit down and have an entire conversation using this telegraphic phonology.

For decades after the telegraph was introduced, the number of people with command of its code remained small. Ergo, you could be fairly certain that your conversation in Morse Speak would be private. So imagine, if you will, two nineteenth-century American telegraph operators meeting in a saloon for a happy-hour ale. Their conversation might have gone something like this:[12]

> OPERATOR ONE: dit–di-dit, di-di-dah, dah-di-di-dit di-di-dah di-dit–di-dit dah-dit
> OPERATOR TWO: dah-dit, di-di-dah, dit–di-dit
> OPERATOR ONE: dit–dit dah-di-dah
> OPERATOR TWO: dah di-di-di-dit dah-di-dah, dah-di-di-dah di-di-dah-di-dit, di-di-di-di-dit daah di-di-dit.
> (*Both laugh at the joke.*[13])

Granted, our Morse Speak spoken dialogue is fictional. But coded convo of this ilk *was* possible. The telegraph and its click-based mode of transmitting intelligence allowed for speakers to create a new coded language to communicate with, expanding their linguistic repertoire.

Morse Jargon

If you consulted the endnotes for the translation of our fictionalized saloon chat in Morse Speak, you noticed something curious yet familiar (especially if you're old enough to remember the pioneering days of text messaging on "dumb" phones)—the abundance of abbreviations. You also figured out that the reason our hypothetical operators share a laugh at the end of the exchange has to do with Operator Two's use of the digits 9 and 2, which was insider number jargon for "deliver promptly." Both of these features of telegraphic communication—abbreviations and numeric ciphers—are examples of the jargon that the telegraph inspired. "After sound reception became common in the early 1850s," David Hochfelder writes, "abbreviations and codes became staples of operators' work culture.[14]

One telegrapher even made this his life's work. In 1879 Walter Phillips published a sixty-four-page booklet containing hundreds of abbreviations for words and phrases that journalists commonly used in telegraphic dispatches. Eventually his work came to be known as—brace yourself!—the Phillips code. It was, as the booklet's subtitle suggests, "a thoroughly tested method of shorthand arranged for telegraphic purposes, and contemplating the rapid transmission of press reports." It soon became a staple for the industry. Richard Harnett, in his book *Wirespeak: Codes and Jargon of the News Business*, tells us that "[Phillips's] method became the standard in telegraphy and then in journalism. It was in every telegrapher's pocket and was learned by heart."[15]

But the artistry of encipherment operated along schemes more complicated than populating your telegram with a bunch of abbreviations and number codes. "Wire service employees also learned to use 'cablese.' This was a method of shortening messages and dispatches by combining words."[16] Why shorten and combine? Because telegraph companies charged by the word. But you couldn't just cleave a bunch of words together and pass it off as one. Inamannerjustlikethis. Telegraph outfits, you see, were smart, often restricting the maximum length of a single word to fifteen characters. After that, you were charged for another word. Thus emerged a unique written variety of language that was maximally cost-efficient yet thoroughly expressive.

To become skilled in cablese required linguistic intuition and steady practice. There were a few strategies, though, that the greenhorn could lean on for guidance.[17] First, words that weren't essential to a message's content were left out; this included articles (*the, a, an*), demonstrative pronouns (*these, those, this, that*), auxiliary verbs (conjugated forms of *be* and *have*), and even prepositions (*to, of, etc.*). Second, verbs with a fixed preposition and written as two words, like "check out" or "hold down," were reversed and written as one: *outcheck* and *downhold*. Third, prefixes and suffixes were used in abundance, and augmented by drawing from existing prepositions in English and other languages. The prefix un-, for example, did a lot of heavy lifting. Essentially, you could stick it onto any verb or adjective and it would mean "not." So, *unsend, unsaw,* and *unupblown* were to be read, respectively, as "do not send," "did not see," and "not blown up." The Latin prepositions *cum* ("with") and *ex* ("out of" or "from") were fused to any noun: *cumluggage*, for example, meant "with luggage," while *exParis* signified that something or someone was "from Paris." French found its way into the mix, too: the prepositions *dans* ("in") and *sur* ("on") showed up in chimeras like "danshouse" ("in the house") and "surplains" ("on the plains"). Suffixes were also slung around profligately. English -ed, -ing, and -ly made appearances all over the place. If you got a telegram with the words *Olivered, efforting*, and *otherhandedly*, you were supposed to interpret them as "Oliver had," "making an effort," and "on the other hand."

These are a few examples of the cablese jargon that developed among speakers who frequently communicated by telegraph. No one ever wrote an official manual or dictionary for cablese, like Phillips did for his code; rather, cablese came about from the bottom up. It was a grassroots phenomenon that emerged out of an econo-linguistic tug-of-war between telegraph companies and telegraph customers: the former bent on maximizing profit and regulating word usage, the latter on sending messages that were fast, inexpensive, and maximally expressive. In *The Telegraph in America, 1932–1920*, Hochfelder concludes:

> From a linguistic perspective, these canned messages [i.e., containing cablese jargon] were the logical culmination and fullest extent of compression driven by telegraph industry technology and economics. From the beginning of the telegraph industry, therefore, company managers sought to compress messages in order to reduce costs. Customers, charged by the word, likewise condensed their dispatches as much as possible.[18]

Harnett offers the following nineteenth-century telegram as an illustration of cablese jargon's efficient yet elaborate expressiveness:

HB BAIRESWARDING EXNXCUMFDRPAPER UTMOSTING ARRIVE PRECONFAB A CUMGAINZA.[19]

Did you get that? The initiated newsman would read it as follows: "Hugh Baillie [then-president of United Press International] is traveling to Buenos Aires from New York with the President Franklin D. Roosevelt documents and is trying to get there before the conference between the president and Gainza Paz [a well-known publisher in Buenos Aires]."

By now you've probably asked yourself: Why all the fuss, just for jargon? Why did the telegraph motivate people to encode what was already an encoded system of communication? In his charming *The Victorian Internet*, Tom Standage suggests that customers were concerned about the confidentially and privacy of their telegrams: "There was certainly a demand for codes and ciphers; telegrams were generally, though unfairly, regarded as less secure than letters, since you never knew who might see them as they were transmitted, retransmitted, and retranscribed on their way from sender to receiver."[20]

Another motivation boils down to basic finance. Recall from above that telegraph companies charged customers according to word count. In general, prices were steep. According to one source: "The cost varied depending on the location of the station, but it was normally calculated at twenty-five cents per hundred miles for ten words or less in the early 1850s."[21] Another source indicates that in 1869 the flat rate for a standard telegram (i.e., of ten words or fewer) from Chicago to New York was $2.05.[22] What's more, for each word beyond ten you got slapped with a 15-to-30-cent per-word fee. (Bear in mind that, in the 1850s, $1 was worth around $30 today.[23]) Companies did offer the press a special rate, but dispatches that ran over a hundred words still incurred a hefty fee. Thus, it was in the sender's interest to use as little language as possible to get the point across. Recall from above Hochfelder's argument that "[from] the beginning of the industry the economics of telegraphy acted to condense written language."[24]

A final reason was speed. Until the 1870s, when Joseph Stearns engineered the duplex and Thomas Edison the quadruplex telegraph technology, it was only possible to send one message at a time in each direction across the wire. Consequently, in the telegraph's early days every minute that an operator spent tapping out a message meant that other customers had to wait. A single transaction might tie up the line for a while—which, for the company, translated into potential dollars lost, and, for the newsman, that he might lose out to the competition on breaking a big story. Thus, the abbreviations and cablese went a long way toward speeding up the telegraphic transaction for both parties. Within minutes, an operator could transmit a detailed news report and get on to the next customer, while the nail-biting stringer could delight in getting his scoop submitted before the competition.

A New Journalistic Style

In terms of communication and discourse, Morse seems to have conceived of the telegraph, at first, as a quasi-household item that would allow for "synchronous two-way communication between two people."[25] In other words, he envisioned people having a "chat" in Morse code across a wire, much as we exchange instant messages over the internet today. Baron recounts how "as a form of publicity, Morse's assistants arranged chess tournaments between clubs in Washington and Baltimore to demonstrate the interactive potential of the new technology."[26] Similarly, the communications theorist and historian Menahem Blondheim writes that Morse initially designed his telegraph to "encourage social intercourse through space ... linking wives with their distant husbands, allowing children to communicate with their parents, and encouraging lovers to exchange sentiments over the wires."[27] And this early vision of the telegraph—i.e., as a quotidian, accessible tool for socializing across distances—remained a pipe dream for most of its history. "Statistics from the nineteenth century amply demonstrate," Hochfelder writes, "that the vast majority of Americans rarely sent or received telegrams."[28]

So who, then, did send telegrams? The answer: businessmen and newspapermen. And, indeed, they sent a lot of them. According to Blondheim: "The major users of the telegraph line were members of the commercial community and of the press corps."[29] Moreover, accounting records from the 1870s show that the telegraph's most loyal customer was the Associated Press (AP), whose charges made up 10 percent of Western Union's total revenue.[30] A typical reporter sent dozens of telegrams per week. And with so much content to send, with time and money on the line, reporters compacted the intelligence sent in these numerous telegrams into a unique, coded language (i.e., cablese). Moreover, once this compressed form of linguistic intelligence arrived at press headquarters, it was deciphered, translated, and expanded into printable prose intended for widespread consumption. In other words, the information went from canned scoop to mass media article.

The linguistic upshot of this information-processing formula—i.e., from gathering, compacting, encoding, and sending, to receiving, decoding, expanding, and printing—was a new journalistic style that paved the way for modern standards in print media. In particular, this new style prioritized objectivity, unembellished prose, and accuracy of content. "Because of restrictions on the amount of text that could quickly be sent across a telegraph wire," Baron contends, "and thanks to the growth of nationwide wire services, a new 'telegraphic' form of journalism emerged. The new style gradually began replacing the sometimes rambling, typically regional, often-biased reporting of the nineteenth-century newspapers."[31] And a key player in this upsurge of telegraphically circulated news, and the concomitant linguistic effects on journalistic style, was the AP.

Our space is—alas!—too limited here to delve into it in detail. Suffice it to say, though, that the AP owes its existence to the telegraph.[32] Heavy competition among reporters, to be first to get their story transmitted, ended up hurting everyone. Often, those first to show up at the operator's desk would tie up the line for long periods (sometimes even sending fake reports) just to bar their rival stringers' access. A solution was reached in 1846, when five daily New York newspapers agreed to share the costs of telegraphing news. This quintet's financial arrangement marked the beginning of the AP.

Important for our discussion here, however, were the new conglomerate's on-site reporters. Strewn throughout the country, their single assignment was to get the scoop, and get it fast. And then send it to their agency, of course. The AP kept thousands of these "stringers," as they were called, on the payroll. And each one got explicit instructions from their boss: "Reporters for the wire service were instructed to send 'bare matter of fact.' No coloring, no personal preferences or opinions were permitted."[33] Furthermore, when these pared-down telegraphic reports arrived at the main office, editors were asked to abide by similar guidelines. "The concise, matter-of-fact language of the regional agents was hardly altered in the editing process."[34]

This amounted to a new style of journalistic writing that the great communications theorist and historian James W. Carey described as "something closer to a 'scientific' language, a language of strict denotation in which the connotative features of utterance were under rigid control."[35] Within a few decades of the AP's founding, newspapers across the country were littered with this newly objective, quasi-scientific style. "By the 1880s, more than 80% of the copy found in western American newspaper consisted of AP dispatches."[36]

There are even reports that at least one American literary giant might have absorbed some of this telegraphic style. (Though we emphasize here the modifiers *might have* and *some*.) Ernest Hemingway began his writing career as a foreign correspondent for the *Toronto Star*. A big part of his job was, in fact, sending by telegraph daily accounts of events. And these were transatlantic telegrams, which meant they were even more expensive. So Hemingway probably felt obliged to be economical with his wordage, while still upholding accuracy and expressiveness of content. In other words, Hemingway became a skilled and frequent user of cablese. Which, so the story goes, bled over into the unique style he cultivated for his fiction. In a 1985 interview with *The New York Times*, legendary journalist George Seldes recalled:

> I met him in Paris in 1922 when he was sending mailers back to his paper in Toronto. One day he came to me and several other correspondents, including Lincoln Steffens, and asked us to teach him how to file by using cablese—the shorthand that combined words to save cable charges. You had to pay by the word then, so you turned three words, like "as well as," into one, "swells." Hemingway became excited. He told us, "It's a new language—no adjectives, no adverbs; it moves!" I think by teaching Hemingway cablese we were responsible for changing his writing style.[37]

Baron maintains that Hemingway "was strongly influenced by the strictures of 'cablese,' [which] helped him to pare his prose to the bone, dispossessed of every adornment."[38]

We'd be remiss, though, if we failed to mention here that not all scholars agree on the extent to which the telegraph affected journalistic style. On one hand, for instance, Hochfelder quotes former *New York Tribune* London correspondent George Smalley: "It was the [telegraph] cable which first taught us to condense [our writing]."[39] And while Hochfelder acknowledges that "the matter-of-fact style and inverted-pyramid structure of the modern news story originated with telegraphic newsgathering,"[40] he nevertheless temporizes that "effects of telegraphy on journalism and written language are more complex than these accounts indicate."[41]

New Ideas about Language and Communication

Earlier we remarked that the telegraph represents the first-ever decoupling of communication from transportation. Put another way: in the pre-telegraph world, the only way to get information to another person was through some physical form of travel. You could whisper life-or-death details into a messenger's ear—but the courier still had to walk, ride, or sail from one place to another to deliver it. You could write your estranged sibling a poignant letter of apology—but the mailed envelope still had to find its way to the intended recipient by foot, horseback, wagon, train, or ship. You could even jot down sweet nothings to your paramour on a slip of paper and attach it to a pigeon's foot—but . . . (You get the idea.)

Even the terms "communication" and "transportation" were synonymous. "Before the telegraph," Carey writes, " 'communication' was used to describe transportation as well as message transmittal."[42] But then it became possible to send that life-or-death message (or family letter or love note) through a static wire. At the speed of light! As a result, people began to think differently of what it meant, conceptually, to *communicate information*. Speakers' perceptual paradigm shifted: *I don't need someone or something to travel a long way and take a long time to get my information from here to there*, they started thinking. *This whole idea of "to communicate" means that I can expect information to move really, really fast, regardless of how far I want my information to go . . .*

Or something to that effect.

Suffice it to say, the telegraph not only influenced language's structures (e.g., Morse Speak, Morse Jargon, and journalistic style), it also transformed people's gross notions about how "communication" worked. In Carey's words:

[The telegraph] opened up new ways of thinking about communication within the practical consciousness of everyday life. [It] altered the spatial and temporal boundaries of human interaction, brought into existence new forms of language as well as new conceptual systems, and brought about new structures of social relations.[43]

Thus it was in great part due to the telegraph that people came to expect linguistically packaged information—whether news story or personal note—to arrive quickly and irrespective of distance. People wanted information, and they wanted it now and from everywhere. It's telling that, in his groundbreaking work *Understanding Media*, McLuhan refers to the telegraph as "the social hormone."

Part 2: The Telephone

In Part 1 of this chapter we deepened our technolingual argument by examining a technology that abstracted the *written* form of language. The telegraph, we saw, ousted the letters and numbers from the page and turned them into electric pulses that defied the constraints of time, place, and physicality. In Part 2 we're going to level our sights on a technology that did the same thing to the *spoken* form of language: the telephone. And in due technolingual fashion, we'll explore both how language shaped and was shaped by this speech-abstracting technology.

Phonetic Inspirations, or How the Articulatory, Physical, and Auditory Properties of Speech Shaped the Telephone

What do we mean by "phonetic inspirations"? Recall from our earlier discussions that phonetics is the scientific study of sounds. A phonetician is interested in how we make speech sounds (articulatory phonetics), what they're made up of (acoustic phonetics), and how the human ear processes them (auditory phonetics). So when we say that the invention of the telephone was "phonetically inspired," we mean that one or more of these sound-related aspects of language played a role in how the technology came about.

Alexander Graham Bell is widely known as the guy who invented the first commercially successful telephone. What's less known, however, is that he was a passionate student of phonetics. "Long before he conceived of the telephone," Anthony Enns notes in *The Human Telephone: Physiology, Neurology, and Sound Technologies*, "Bell was already actively engaged in the technological reconstruction of the organs of human sound production."[44]

As a child Bell was already curious about how the lips, tongue, and throat worked in concert to make the sounds of English. He and his brother even constructed models of the human vocal mechanism. They once built an automaton that, when air was bellowed through it and the operator worked a series of levers, could "speak" a range of vowels and consonants. The articulatory working of speech fascinated Aleck most; consequently, he made it his mission to understand the physiology and movements in detail. Ultimately—and in classic technolingual fashion—the phonetic discoveries he made through observation and experimentation steered his inventive mind, inspiring his prototype's unique feature: the magneto-diaphragm, which was modeled after the human ear's own medial membrane, aka the eardrum.

Now, the precocious young Bell didn't stumble upon linguistics on his own; it was, literally, a family affair. His Scottish grandfather, David Charles Bell, had been a celebrated authority on articulation; his book *The Standard Elocutionist* went through more than 200 editions.[45] As was the custom in those days, David drafted his son Alexander Melville into the same vocation. And by his early 20s, A. Melville was lecturing at the University of Edinburgh on elocution and the sounds of speech. And by the time *his* sons were tinkering with their speaking automaton, the noted "professor of elocution and vocal physiology" had already published a handful of respected books on speech.

This was the intellectual milieu in which Aleck came of age. Language, for the Bell family, was a spellbinding puzzle to be "solved." How does the air move up and out of the lungs? How and why does the voice box make this air vibrate? Where do the tongue, palate, and teeth go when we speak? What would vowels and consonants "look like" if we could see them? And how does our ear "hear" all these fluctuations in air pressure as "speech sounds"? On cold winter evenings and rainy summer days, the family would work on this puzzle together. They played language-inspired parlor games. They discussed these and other questions at length. And all the Bell children received formal training in elocution.

And perhaps most importantly of all, the Bell patriarch would issue his sons phonetic challenges, intended to encourage them to consider the Family Puzzle from new angles. The "speaking" automaton we mentioned above, for instance, came about because A. Melville offered his sons a prize if they could build a "talking" machine. "The most important years of his education," Snyder writes about Aleck, "were not those spent in the classroom, but those spent being trained by his mother, grandfather, and father at home in subjects relating to sound and the mechanism of speech."[46] Thus it was within the walls of hearth and home that Aleck caught the phonetics bug that, years later, would guide him in his telephonic ventures.

His father's *Visible Speech: The Science of Universal Alphabetics* fostered Aleck's early enthusiasm for language. First published in 1867, the elder Bell stood by it all his life. Indeed, it was in many ways a brilliant precursor to today's International Phonetic Alphabet (itself formulated two decades after Bell's work). Snyder explains visible speech as "a series of symbols that represented the anatomical positions the speech organs take in uttering sounds."[47] Among other things, A. Melville envisioned it as a tool to help the Deaf[48] learn to speak. At its core, though, visible speech was a system that required its user to have a thorough command of articulatory phonetics—a key point that brings our discussion back to the younger Bell, Aleck.

Vital to our argument here—namely, that the phonetics of speech informed the invention of the telephone—is how A. Melville's system was passed on to Aleck, the eventual inventor of said technology. Though "passed on" is too light a term to describe it. According to most accounts, Aleck submerged himself in his father's universal phonetic alphabet. He internalized the symbols, and their corresponding articulatory positions, so thoroughly that his father recruited him to help out with public demonstrations.

One anecdote in particular illustrates Aleck's mastery of his father's system. It was the summer of 1864. The Bells were demonstrating visible speech, when a professor of Hindustani stood up and issued a challenge. While Aleck waited outside of the room, the professor dictated to A. Melville a sound in Sanskrit that, according to the professor, was nearly impossible for an English-speaking person to pronounce accurately. A. Melville listened, transcribed the sound into visible speech, and then sent for his son. The audience watched with bated breath as Aleck reentered the room. In a 1922 autobiographical article in *National Geographic*, A. Graham recounted the episode:

> My father handed me a piece of paper with a very simple-looking symbol upon it, and I was requested to utter the sound represented.
>
> At first I thought it was simply the direction to pronounce the letter T, but soon noted a little diacritical mark attached to the symbol that had the technical meaning of "soft palate."
>
> This I translated to mean that the point of the tongue, instead of being applied to the upper gum, as in the ordinary method of forming T, was to be coiled back in the mouth and placed against the soft palate—a thing I had never heard of or dreamed about before.
>
> I followed the direction, coiled my tongue backward, and tried to make a T-sound, with the point of the tongue against the soft palate. This resulted in a sound resembling both K and T, and the gentleman who had given the text expressed great satisfaction. He informed the audience that ... the

sound he had given was the "Sanskrit cerebral T." He expressed surprise that Mr. Bell's son should have given it correctly at the very first trial, *without ever having heard the sound at all.*[49]

Suffice it to say, Aleck knew the articulatory intricacies of speech like the back of his hand. And this would serve him well in his subsequent experiments on the acoustic properties of speech.

Which now brings us full circle: to that momentous summer of 1874, depicted in this chapter's creative (though historically accurate!) opening narrative.

Visible speech was indeed a clever way of giving graphic form to the intangible sounds of speech (to make them "readable," in other words). But for Aleck, his father's system didn't go far enough. Aleck wanted to "see" what human speech actually "looked like," and not just through symbols that represented these sounds.

He got his wish in 1874, while living in Boston. There he attended lectures on acoustics at MIT and began familiarizing himself with state-of-the-art tools for studying sound. He learned, for instance, that over in the Old World a Parisian by the name of Leon Scott had built a contraption that rendered recordings of speech on paper. It was called a "phonautograph" (literally, "self-propelled writer of sound") and was modeled after the physiology of the human ear. An open-ended barrel focused the sound (like the cartilage folds of the outer ear), a strip of parchment served as an elastic membrane to absorb the vibrations (like the eardrum), and a bristle of animal hair acted as a stylus (like the middle-ear bones) to conduct the vibrations from the quivering membrane onto another medium. When you spoke into the barrel and simultaneously moved a smoked piece of glass across the stylus, it traced out a squiggly line that, in effect, "captured" and concretized the vocal patterns of speech. Figure 3.6 shows Leon Scott's phonautograph, constructed in 1857.

Aleck was captivated. Within this technology, he thought, lay the next generation of his father's work. It would revolutionize the field of phonetics (known, at that time, as the *physiology of speech*). Moreover, he believed that the technology might be adapted to another project that he and his father had been collaborating on for years: innovative tools for teaching the Deaf to speak.

Through connections he'd made at MIT, Bell was permitted to use the university's cutting-edge acoustics laboratory. He immediately began experimenting with the phonautograph. He spent months making recordings of individual vowels and consonants, but remained largely unsatisfied with the results. His experiments exposed the limitations of what Scott's instrument allowed one to "observe" of speech sounds. Snyder writes:

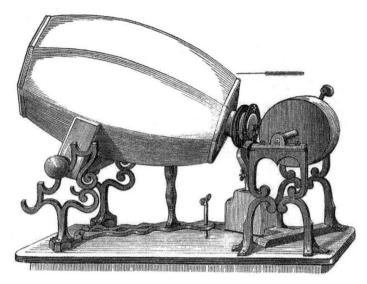

FIGURE 3.6 *Leon Scott's phonautograph. (https://commons.wikimedia.org/wiki/File:Phonautograph_1859.jpg (accessed February 5, 2017).)*

Bell constructed a number of different forms of phonautographs, using membranes of different diameters and thickness and different materials, and changing the shape of the attached lever and bristle. The results did not please him. He reasoned that the apparatus he employed must be imperfect, was not sensitive enough.[50]

The only way, Bell realized, he could get the quality of sound recordings he was after was to construct something that resembled the human ear as closely as possible. And though he himself was no slouch when it came to the anatomy of the ear, it still wasn't his field of expertise; he needed to consult a specialist.

Enter Dr. Clarence John Blake, a lecturer in otology at Harvard Medical School and a fellow phonetics enthusiast.

Bell told Dr. Blake of his frustrations with Scott's phonautograph. And Blake's response would prove monumental for the history of the telephone. Why not, Blake suggested, replace the parchment with an actual eardrum, and the bristle with the bones of the middle ear—essentially, build a human ear phonautograph?

Bell took to the idea at once; here was a chance to observe the acoustics of speech from the perspective of the actual human ear. Yes, he told Blake. He would collaborate with the otologist and the two would share their findings. Project Human Ear Phonautograph was officially green-lighted. Blake paid a visit to Harvard's cadaver lab, fetched the temporal bones from two subjects, and set about preparing them:

> The temporal bone was cleaned. The auricle and other soft parts were removed, and the lining of the external auditory canal cut away to a line close to the membrana tympani [eardrum]. Step by step, bone and tissues were cut away to expose the middle ear. The petrous portion and the stapes [middle-ear stirrup-shaped bone] were removed, leaving the inner surface of the membrana tympani freely exposed with malleus [middle-ear hammer-shaped bone] and incus [middle-ear anvil-shaped bone] in position. The specimens were kept moist with a mixture of equal parts glycerin and water. A style, made of fine wheat straw, was glued to the incus, extending downward with the free tip lightly touching a palate of smoked glass. The whole affair was mounted on a telescope stand.[51]

Blake made two of these contraptions in the spring of 1874, one for himself and one for Aleck. Over the next few months, the men made various recordings of their speech and compared the wavy lines on their glass plates.[52]

As we expressed in the opening narrative, this human ear phonautograph was a catalyst for Alexander Graham Bell's inventive approach to the telephone. Through his experimentations with the device, and after careful consideration of the physiology of the human ear, Bell came up with the idea for a "membrane diaphragm" telephone.

The design worked like this: just as our ear uses a stretched yet flexible patch of skin to catch the air vibrations of speech, so Bell's telephone incorporated a circular piece of metal for the same purpose. "Like the phonautograph," Enns concludes in *The Human Telephone*, "the telephone also represented a technological reconstruction of the human ear, so it similarly reflected a mechanistic understanding of auditory perception."[53] Some years later, while reflecting back on his days spent tinkering with the phonautograph, Bell would make special note of how he derived from his acoustic trials the inspiration for the eardrum-esque design of his telephone:

> I was carrying on experiments with the phonautograph constructed from the human ear which Dr. Blake had prepared for me. It occurred to me that if such a thin and delicate membrane could move bones that were, relatively to it, very massive indeed, why should not a larger and stouter membrane be able to move a piece of steel in the manner I desired? At once the conception of a membrane speaking telephone became complete in my mind.[54]

Our point: it was the actual physiology of the human ear—specifically the tympanic membrane, or eardrum, and the ossicles, or middle-ear bones—that steered Aleck's inventive process. In 1879, Dr. Blake delivered a paper titled "Sound in Relation to the Telephone" before the Society of Telegraph Engineers. In it, he emphasized the connection between Bell's telephone and the human ear:

> The mouth-piece of the hand telephone may be compared to the external ear, the metal disc to the drum membrane, the air-chamber to the middle-ear cavity, the damping effect of the magnet to the traction of the tensor tympani muscle, and the induced current in the coil to the sentient apparatus.[55]

Figures 3.7 and 3.8 depict one of Bell's earliest telephone designs that incorporated the membrane diaphragm. He displayed it in 1876 at the Centennial International Exhibition in Philadelphia.

Let's home in on the cross-sectional image to get a better sense of how Bell's invention was patterned after the human ear.

M is the mouthpiece; think of it like the cartilage that forms your outer ear. D is the diaphragm membrane (with a piece of iron glued to it) stretched across the cone's other end; it serves as your eardrum. C and H make up the electromagnetic relay; these act like your middle-ear bones. Speak into the mouthpiece, and your sound waves cause the membrane and iron armature to vibrate. In turn, the quivering motion of the iron armature generates a fluctuating electric current in the relay coil. This undulating current is then sent by wire to a similarly constructed receiver that reverses the process: a fluctuating electric current makes a diaphragm vibrate, thereby reproducing the original sound waves.

FIGURE 3.7 *Bell's 1876 Centennial International Exhibition telephone. (http:// commons.wikimedia.org/wiki/File:PSM_V69_D434_Bell_centennial_single_pole_ telephone.png (accessed March 8, 2015).)*

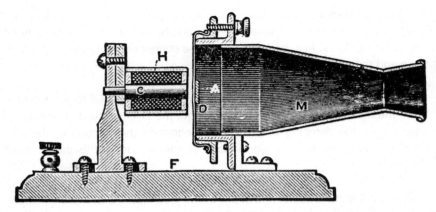

FIGURE 3.8 *Cross-sectional view of Bell's 1876 Centennial International Exhibition telephone. (http://commons.wikimedia.org/wiki/File:PSM_V69_D434_ Bell_centennial_single_ pole_telephone_sectional_view.png (accessed March 8, 2015).)*

Just so we're clear: our argument is that it was precisely Alexander Graham Bell's background in phonetics—in particular, the acoustic and physiological mechanics underlying both the production and perception of speech—that uniquely positioned him to construct the first practical telephone. According to Robert Hopper, former linguist at the University of Texas at Austin: "Bell defeated superior electricians in the race to his invention because of his knowledge about the facts of human speech."[56] Indeed, both prior to and during the time that Bell labored over his invention, there were a number of bright minds working on devices for transmitting the human voice through wire.[57] But ultimately it was Alexander Graham Bell—professor of vocal physiology and elocution, master of articulatory phonetics, and tireless investigator of the acoustic ins and outs of speech—who came out on top.

Science writer Todd Timmons concludes that Bell "was uniquely situated to invent the telephone," because "[his] background and training in the teaching of the deaf gave him insight into the physical characteristics of speech."[58] The phonetics of language—from the articulation and acoustic properties of speech, to the aural physiology involved in its perception—inspired and guided the first successful design of the telephone.

Of "Faceless" Conversation and Telephonic Etiquette: The Telephone's Effects on Language

In line with our technolingual framework, we now turn the discussion around and consider how the telephone affected language.

First, we look at the linguistic repercussions of "faceless" discourse; in other words, how language adjusted to the novel context of neither speaker being physically present for the linguistic exchange. We see that this novel, "faceless" context for conversation led to new linguistic structures, and new strategies for negotiating discourse.

Then we turn our attention to language ideologies. Like most of the technologies we've considered so far (and consider in later chapters), the telephone inspired speakers to formulate new ideas and attitudes about how language ought to be used with the new technology. Language authorities waxed pedantically on the linguistic no-nos and yes-yesses of telephonic interaction. They published usage manuals for the office, self-help guides for aspiring social climbers, and of course children books (because every language authority knows that you've got to get to them while they're still impressionable!). Parents drilled into their offspring proper telephone etiquette, which, for many, was as important as table manners or personal hygiene. Even the telephone service providers got in on the ideological dervish, with pamphlets and advertisements meant to edify their customers.

Ultimately, all of this linguistic novelty—the forms, patterns of discourse, ideas, attitudes, and prescribed usages—resulted in an expansion of speakers' linguistic repertoires. This expansion, as we've seen and will continue to see, is a compelling corollary of technolingualism. It testifies to the boundless adaptability and creativity of human language.

When Conversation Goes Faceless: New Linguistic Structures and Discourse Strategies

Before we wade into the details of our discussion here, some food for thought: spoken human language probably arose between 50,000 and a 100,000 years ago, and for about 49,850 or 99,850 years of this timespan (that's 99.7% and 99.85%, respectively, for all you numerophiles), the *only* way you could talk to another person—aside from yelling or using some version of a rally girl megaphone—was if you were both *there*. Oral conversation required both parties to be visible to each other.

Not only could you hear your interlocutor's words, you could also *see* their expressions and body language. And for thousands of years, your ancestors had learned to interpret these nonverbal forms of communication together with the actual speech sounds. So when you saw a raised hand, you'd expect to hear words expressing a greeting or farewell. When you saw a nodding head (or if you were in South Asia, a bobbling head), you'd expect words of encouragement or approval. Or when you saw a middle finger extended at you (or if you were India, someone flicking a thumb off their teeth in your direction—a gesture known as the "cutis" which, roughly translated, means "screw you and your family"[59]), you wouldn't be surprised to hear the unsavory remarks that follow. You get the drift. Humans learned to understand verbal and non-verbal communication in tandem.

Then the telephone comes along and does away with this age-old sociolinguistic arrangement. "The telephone," Henry Boettinger puts it, "was the first device to allow the spirit of a person expressed in his own voice to carry its message directly without transporting the body."[60] And so there you are, left to interpret *only* someone's words. The gesture-deciphering skills that your forbearers developed over eons and passed down to you—they're as useful as a candle in a bright room. Dilemma? No. Because you're fortunate enough to have language, an incredible system of communication that can adjust to novel circumstances just like this.

And that's what happened, over a century ago, when it suddenly became possible to hold a spoken conversation without actually seeing the other person. Our language adapted. Our linguistic repertoires expanded. And "all was good" in the Land of Technolingualism.

To get a better idea of how language, in its structures and discourse strategies, adjusted to the telephone, let's review some basic components of "a conversation." What goes on, linguistically and pragmatically, when we converse with another speaker?[61] Well, we know that every discourse (a fancy term for "conversation") has a beginning and an end. So, all speakers must have agreed-upon structures and tactics for initiating and concluding discourse. Next, we know that, while we chat with other people, we manage the flow of information: we bring up various topics, change these topics, wait for our interlocutor to answer, request or decline more information, correct ourselves, allow for pauses, and even interpret. In other words, we operate within a pragmatic framework that tells us how to negotiate turn taking; govern informational exchange; and construct, maintain, and test social relationships.

When you and a friend meet for chitchat over coffee (or chinwag over a pint, if that's your fancy) you're participating in a more elaborate choreography of language and pragmatics than you realize. "A conversation by telephone," Mark Twain penned in his 1880 parodic sketch *A Telephonic Conversation,* "is one of the solemnest curiosities of this modern world." Part of what Twain was getting at is that telephone conversations eliminate all visual factors, leaving only the auditory cues for speakers to rely on. And for this very reason, telephonic exchanges have offered linguists a valuable source for studying the systematic goings-on when two speakers converse. It isn't for nothing that noted discourse analyst Robert Hopper extols the telephone as "our century's speech teacher."[62] He furthermore sizes up the potential that this teacher bears for its pupils, in their quest to understand language:

Telephony undergirds our theories about communication. Telephone speech splits sound from the rest of the senses, splits the dyad [speaker pair] from the rest of society, and splits communication from other activity. Telephone conversation is pure dialogic speech communication. Hence, descriptions of telephone conversation are central to theories of language, conversation, and interaction.[63]

The telephone, in other words, was (and still is) a linguistically potent technology. It has affected the structural and pragmatic patterns of our language; more specifically, the parts that make up a "conversation."

Take the way that you open a conversation. Recall from our thought experiment above that, before the telephone, you generally saw the other person before you initiated dialogue. Maybe the other person smiled and waved emphatically. Maybe they gave you an expressionless nod. Or maybe they looked at the ground and sighed. Each of these visual stimuli would help you choose a fitting linguistic path to go down. (Perhaps: "Great to see you!" for the first; a simple stating of the other person's name, for the second; and "How are you holding up?" for the last.)

When you pick up the receiver, though, none of these visual cues is at your disposal. Thus one of the more pressing matters, in the early days of the telephone, was: what should one say into the receiver immediately after picking it up? "The telephone," Baron notes, "engendered a need for working out appropriate linguistic conventions, beginning with the simplest challenge of a conversational opener."[64]

Certainly, a lot hinges on the context in which the entire phone conversation takes place. A business, for instance, might opt for a bland-yet-professional announcement of its name (e.g., "Mighty Mouse Tires" or "Herbert Hobbies"). But what about, say, the average household? How should you answer the phone there? Conceivably, there are oodles of options. You might pick up and prompt the caller with a curt *speak*. Or you might announce your name, as they typically do today in Germany and Holland.[65] Perhaps you err on the side of politeness and answer with an anodyne *good morning/afternoon/ evening*. Or maybe you look for guidance from an outside party; in 1880, for instance, the first US public telephone exchange in New Haven issued a manual instructing customers to answer with, "What is wanted?"[66] Indeed, there are a lot of possibilities.

Bell himself appears to have had a fondness for the all-too-nautical-sounding *ahoy!*—though, to be accurate, he suggested this in the early days of the telephone, when the line connecting the devices was always live. The *ahoy!* actually served to alert the recipient that they were being called (like you would use it to hail a ship).[67] The salutation *hello!*, which has become the familiar greeting for most speakers of English—though many language communities have also adopted their own native version *hello!* for answering the phone; notably in Greece,[68] Korea, and Japan[69]—is widely credited to Thomas Edison.

As early as 1877, in a letter to the president of the Central District and Printing Telegraph Company, Edison suggested using the snappy, monosyllabic term in place of a call bell, because "Hello! can be heard 10 to 20 feet away."[70] Edison's proposal evidently struck a louder cord with the telephonic crowd than did Bell's. By 1880, for example, the attendees at the first National Convention of Telephone Companies, in Niagara Falls, were brandishing badges with a big *HELLO* preceding their name. The organization's president himself called attention to the little word's telephonic prowess, noting in his welcoming address: "The shortest speech that I could make to you and that would express a great deal to you, probably would be the one that is on all your badges—'Hello!'"[71]

Just so we're clear, though: The word itself (i.e., *hello*) wasn't an Edisonian brainchild, like the incandescent bulb or the kinetoscope. Edison didn't suddenly coin the term one fine whimsical afternoon at Menlo Park. *Hello*, in fact, had been kicking around in colloquial speech long before Edison scribbled it down in that dispatch from 1877. The *OED* lists the word as first attested in 1827 in the *United States Telegraph*:[72] "Hello, sez Joe Laughton, wher's Bil Perry un Olla Parsons?"[73] Its next documented appearance was 1853, in the weekly entertainment tabloid *New York Clipper*. "Hello ole feller, how are yer?"[74] We cite both attestations, in full, in order to make the following point: *Hello*'s sociolinguistic realm was idiomatic. It wasn't a word you spoke among high society. And you definitely wouldn't deign to use it in writing. But it was alive in everyday parlance long before Edison and his consultations with the Central District and Printing Telegraph Company.

So it wasn't that the telephone birthed a lexical singularity. What it did do for *hello*, though, is similar to what modern social media (think YouTube) has done to otherwise lesser-known personages and phenomena: it catapulted the word into widespread public consciousness. But unlike the oft short-lived fame á la YouTube, *hello*'s spot in the vernacular big time hasn't fizzled. Once marginalized to the domain of spoken language, and deemed too vulgar for sitting room guests, modern-day speakers don't bat an eye when they come across *hello* in print or hear it used in mixed company. Figure 3.9 shows an n-gram of *hello!*'s occurrence in millions of English-language books, published between 1800 and 1900, that Google has scanned into its immense database.

Note, in particular, the jump between 1870 and 1900. Bearing in mind that there was an orchestra of sociolinguistic motivations at work, it's nevertheless conceivable that the telephone contributed to *hello*'s rapid ascent—in the United States and internationally. *Hello* has become a staple salutation in

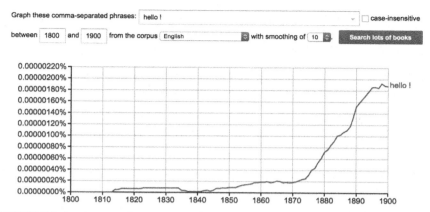

FIGURE 3.9 *N-gram of occurrences of* "hello!" *in English-language books printed 1800–1900.*

tongues across the globe. Wikipedia lists nearly fifty languages that use the word for answering the telephone or as an informal greeting.[75] As for *ahoy!*— if you'll pardon the pun—its ship never did come in.

But let's move on. Because, not surprisingly, telephonic chat is much more complex than the single word or phrase you say upon picking up the receiver. In fact, linguists have authored lengthy studies on how people handle the sequence of tos and fros that form the opening of a phone conversation— depending, especially, on whether the caller and answerer recognize each other's voices. In his paper, "Identification and Recognition in Interactional Openings," Schegloff declares:

> The openings of telephone conversations generally do have a distinct- ive shape. We regularly find a sequence not found in "face-to-face" conversation—a sequence where the parties identify and/or recognize one another. Even where no such sequence occurs, the issue (recognition/rec- ognition) is worked through.[76]

Using hundreds of recorded phone conversations as the empirical basis of his work, Schegloff identifies nine distinct linguistic constructs that condition the opening sequence of a telephonic exchange, after the party being called has picked up and spoken *hello* into the receiver:

1. Simply greeting the caller in return; e.g. *Hello/Hi/Howdy/Good morning*

2. With a rising tone, offering the name of the person who answered, or the person whom the caller intended to call; e.g. *Jane? / Miz Doe? / Dr. Doe? / Mom?*

3. With an even or assertive tone, stating the name of the person who answered, or the person whom the caller intended to call; e.g. *Jane. / Miz Doe. / Dr. Doe. / Mom!*

4. Inquiring or commenting on the answerer's state; e.g. *Oh! You're home. / Were you sleeping? / Can you talk?*

5. Stating the reason, actual or assumed, for the call; e.g. *I said I'd be there in 5 minutes! / Yeah I'm on my way. / I got a message to call this number back.*

6. Requesting to speak to another party; e.g. *Is Jane there? / Can I talk to Mom?*

7. Identifying oneself; e.g. *It's Jane. / Yes, this is Dr. Jane Doe calling. / Jane here.*

8. Inquiring about the identity of the answerer; e.g. *Good morning, is this Dr. Doe? / Hello, am I speaking with Miss Doe?*

9. Starting a joke, or making a joke out of the telephonic context of the linguistic exchange (through mimicked intonation, giving false information on purpose, using a comical accent, etc.).[77] A few examples, where C = caller and A = answerer:

e.g. 1:
> A: *Hello?*
> C: *Hello?*
> A: *Hello . . .?*
> C: *Hello??*
> A: *Hello? Can you hear me?*
> C: *Haha. Gotchya.*

e.g. 2:
> A: *H'llo.*
> C: *H'llo* [spoken as if an echo]
> A: *H'llo?*
> C: *H'llo?* [spoken as if an echo]
> A: *Who is this?*
> C: *It's Jane. Sorry, just playing around.*

e.g. 3:
> A: *Hello?*
> C: *Yes, is this the Hells Angels' HQ?*

e.g. 4:
> A: *Hello?*
> C: *Yeah this is Chuck Norris calling about the acting gig.*[78]

Each of these linguistic constructs gives way to a unique subsequent exchange, and both speakers negotiate this exchange with adaptive structures and pragmatics.

But, you might be thinking, these constructs are also possible in a face-to-face conversation (some, naturally, more than others; for instance, it might prove difficult to pull off a convincing Chuck Norris lookalike). Keep in mind, however, that the telephone posed for speakers a hitherto unknown linguistic challenge: faceless oral dialogue. You the caller can't *see* if you have, in fact, just woken up the other person. And you can't *see* if you do, indeed, have the person whom you intended to reach on the other end of the line. Neither problem existed back in the days when both you and your converser were present for the linguistic deed.

The telephone brought with it a new sociolinguistic ball game. And language, in its structures and pragmatics, had to adapt to the new rules. "The beginning of telephony," Hopper concludes, "wrought changes in the ecology of speech communication by emphasizing the oral and by promoting the importance of the dyad steered by a purpose-centered caller."[79] How speakers negotiate the start of a faceless telephone conversation are the sort of "ecological" changes Hopper is getting at.

Let's now step away from structures and pragmatics and consider how the telephone interfaced with language ideologies.

Of Ad Campaigns and Etiquette Guides: Telephonically Inspired Language Ideologies

In previous chapters we've seen that technology can affect more than just the structures of language; to wit, writing, the printing press, and the typewriter also spawned new modes of *thinking about* language and language users—a sociolinguistic phenomenon we're calling *language ideologies*.

As you can guess, telephonic technology was no exception. As Bell's invention become more commonplace in the office and household, it too gave rise to new ideas, attitudes, and judgments on how speakers should or shouldn't use language in association with it. "Among the first generation of Americans to use the telephone," NYU sociologist Sidney Aronson insists, "were those who were concerned about the ways in which people behaved while talking on the phone and the rules evolving to govern that behavior."[80]

In this final section of our chapter on the abstraction of language, we'll consider some historical material that was instrumental in shaping language ideologies related to the telephone. For the most part, our discussion will concentrate on telephone companies' early efforts to regulate linguistic behavior, and on etiquette guides aimed at instructing the public—especially women and children—in the linguistic and social proprieties of using the telephone. Although, for reasons of space, our discussion will largely be limited to language ideologies among speakers of English in the US, we will nevertheless work in a few remarks on telephonically inspired language ideologies in present-day Japan.

We can thank Mark Twain and his literary prolificacy for giving us one of the earliest attested examples of a telephonically inspired language ideology. In his droll *A Telephonic Conversation*, he notes that the words of the woman he was observing on the phone were "all shouted—for you can't ever persuade the sex to speak gently into a telephone." Moreover, at the end of the sketch, Twain has the woman say "good-by" five times in turn before she finally brings the conversation to a close. His explanation for this iterative and drawn-out leave-taking: "A man delivers a single brutal 'Good-by,' and that is the end of it. Not so with the gentle sex."

Thus it would seem that in 1880—only four years after Bell's demonstration of the telephone at the Centennial International Exhibition in Philadelphia—at least one speaker (i.e., Mr. Twain) had already begun mentally associating the separate sexes with specific language patterns and habits while on the phone. Twain expressed—even if cloaked in the convenient mantle of parody—the notion that women, when on the phone, use a louder-than-normal voice and different pragmatics. Accurate or not, his comments represent an abstract belief or judgment about women's linguistic conduct on the telephone; it is, in other words, a clear example of a language ideology—one inspired by the technology.

But there were other printed media that contributed to the formation and spread of speakers' ideas about language and the telephone, such as advertisements put out by the telephone industry itself. "In the first few decades of telephony, companies faced not only the task of finding uses but also that of managing customers' use of the telephone, showing them how to work it and how to use proper etiquette."[81] Strategically placed in popular magazines and on billboards, or circulated as standalone flyers, these ads functioned as didactic primers on how speakers should act on the telephone. AT&T issued one particularly vivid ad in 1910 with the ominous caption, "Dr. Jekyll and Mr. Hyde at the Telephone." The ad is shown in Figure 3.10.

The ad didn't explicitly prescribe or caution against any language or conduct in particular. It did, however, offer the gentle reminder that "courteous and considerate co-operation is as essential at the telephone as in the office."

First and foremost, this meant no swearing. "Many industry people complained of profanity, yelling, and abuse on the telephone," writes Claude Fischer, professor of sociology at the University of California, Berkeley. "Through notices, direct chastisement of customers, and occasional legal action, the

Dr. Jekyll *and* Mr. Hyde
At the Telephone

Courteous and considerate co-operation is as essential at the telephone as in the office or home.

In every use of the telephone system, three human factors are brought into action—one at each end, one or both anxious and probably impatient, another at the central office, an expert, at least as intelligent and reliable as the best stenographers or bookkeepers.

For the time being, this central office factor is the personal servant of the other two and is entitled to the same consideration that is naturally given to their regular employees.

Perfect service depends upon the perfec. co-ordinate action of all three factors—any one failing, the service suffers. This should never be forgotten.

All attempts to entirely eliminate the personal factor at the central office, to make it a machine, have been unsuccessful. There are times when no mechanism, however ingenious, can take the place of human intelligence.

The marvelous growth of the Bell System has made the use of the telephone universal and the misuse a matter of public concern. Discourtesy on the part of telephone users is only possible when they fail to realize the efficiency of the service. It will cease when they talk over the telephone as they would talk face to face.

AMERICAN TELEPHONE AND TELEGRAPH COMPANY
AND ASSOCIATED COMPANIES

One Policy, *One System,* *Universal Service.*

FIGURE 3.10 *AT&T ad from 1910. (http://arstechnica.com/tech-policy/2010/08/ what-would-emily-post-say-about-droids-in-cafes (accessed March 19, 2015).)*

companies sought to improve telephone courtesy."[82] AT&T took the matter even further and sent each of its subscribers a "Telephone Pledge" card with the declaration: "I believe in the Golden Rule and will try to be as Courteous and Considerate over the Telephone as if Face to Face."[83] Customers were asked to sign and return the pledge. And those who violated their oath ran the risk of having their service disconnected. A few companies even lobbied for laws to penalize the most egregious offenders.

The telephone industry also recruited from its own customer base to help spread its ideology of phone etiquette. In the same year as the Dr. Jekyll and Mr. Hyde ad, *Telephone Engineer* magazine issued a competition for an essay that best described correct telephone decorum. And guess where AT&T promised to have the winning entry included? In each of their hundreds of thousands of telephone directories. This was yet another venue for spreading new language ideologies tied to the phone, and for inculcating speakers.

One of Bell System's more entertaining efforts to educate their customers was its illustrated booklet—rolled out sometime between 1921 and 1939—with the quaint title *How to Make Friends by Telephone*.[84] The cover is shown in Figure 3.11.

To modern-day users of the telephone, its campy images and stuffy language seem almost comical. "How often you meet folks whose voices delight

FIGURE 3.11 *Bell System's booklet "How to Make Friends by Telephone." (http://www.amusingplanet.com/2009/10/how-to-make-friends-by-telephone-guide.html (accessed March 20, 2015).)*

you!" the pamphlet implores the reader in its introductory passage. It continues: "There's something in the way they say almost anything—the inflection, the emphasis, the tone, the timing—that lets you know at once that here is a person who is gracious, sympathetic, understanding, and charming." The reader is then supposed to think: *Yes, I know exactly what you mean! I enjoy speaking with such people! And I want to be* that person *on the phone!*

Figure 3.12 shows one of the booklet's lessons, urging telephone users to "visualize the person you call" because "you're more apt to be pleasant and understanding."

Elsewhere, as illustrated in Figure 3.13, the booklet advises callers: "Be attentive: The person to whom you are talking will appreciate your listening attentively."

FIGURE 3.12 *"Visualize the person you call." (http://www.amusingplanet.com/ 2009/10/how-to-make-friends-by-telephone-guide.html (accessed March 20, 2015).)*

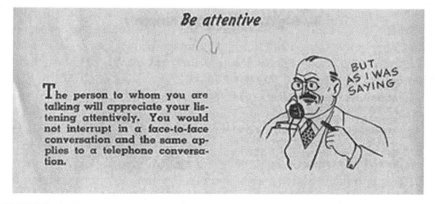

FIGURE 3.13 *"Be attentive." (http://www.amusingplanet.com/2009/10/how-to-make-friends-by-telephone-guide.html (accessed March 20, 2015).)*

Though it strikes us today as corny—in spots even downright patronizing—in the early twentieth century this booklet was earnestly intended to educate speakers in "correct" linguistic behaviors for personal and business dealings over the phone. In the (unknown) author's introductory remarks, the reader gets the following rationale for the booklet's ensuing pages of dos and don'ts: "Over the telephone, your voice and your voice alone—is you. It's not just what you say but how you say it that results in making friends and that smooths the way for the quick, pleasant transaction of the business at hand." Note that the author couches their rationale in the same unique sociolinguistic context we began this section with, namely, "faceless" conversation. Even five decades after Bell upended the world of communications with his telephonic device, people still marveled at the technology's language-abstracting effect (i.e., its divorcing of spoken language from the immediate and physically present speaker). *How to Make Friends by Telephone* suggests that, as late as the 1930s, there was still a need to instruct fellow speakers on the "correct" ways to conduct themselves in this new and curious setting of linguistic estrangement.

The industry weren't the only ones who formulated and spread language ideologies about the telephone. Private individuals also chimed in. By the late nineteenth century, the drumbeaters for social decorum had added telephone etiquette to their lists of priorities. And they were particularly keen on instructing the gentler sex.

In his impressively researched *America Calling: A Social History of the Telephone*, Claude Fischer looked at twenty-one etiquette guides published between 1891 and 1955.[85] He observed that, among other subjects, these guides counseled female readers on: issuing social invitations via phone; answering the phone; the proper way to instruct servants to transmit messages to others; referring to oneself and others on the phone; handling wrong number dialers; and ending a conversation.

Interestingly, it seems that the first of these—using the telephone to extend invitations for social functions—was both the most discussed and disagreed over topic. In the subsection "Inviting by Telephone" of her social etiquette guide from 1901, Anne Randall White warns that this "is never excusable, save among very intimate friends."[86] By 1922, however, there were voices challenging this societal edict. "With the exception of those of a very small minority of letter-loving hostesses," Emily Post observes in the first edition of her widely read *Etiquette*, "informal invitations are sent and answered by phone."[87] And yet, only two years later, the Washington society editor for *The New York Times* criticized that "there are persons who should know better who give invitations by telephone, and others who accept or decline in the same casual method. In both instances there is a deplorable lack of form."[88]

Although these social guides were generally written by and for women, another social group, younger and more suggestible, was also targeted: children. And what better venue to reach this group, and to propagate new language ideologies, than books? Here we'll take a look at three examples: *Telephone Time: A First Book of Telephone Do's and Don't's* (1986); *Manners on the Telephone* (2007); and *Good Manners on the Phone* (2009). Ultimately we'll see that, though charmingly narrated and illustrated, these books' teacher-y prose and relatable images are meant to instill notions of proper phone conduct, linguistic and behavioral, into impressionable tot minds.

Let's zoom in a bit on the instructive content this trio of books lays out. The star of Ellen Weiss's *Telephone Time* is "Ringalina, the Telephone Fairy." Drawn by Hilary Knight, this bell-shaped pixie flutters into the room and announces to wee Lily and Willy (whose mother, it seems, has momentarily stepped out) when the telephone rings: "I can see you need to know some things about using the phone."[89] Figure 3.14 shows Ringalina and the siblings.

FIGURE 3.14 *"Ringalina, The Telephone Fairy." (http://awfullibrarybooks.net/ telephone-time (accessed March 22, 2017).)*

FIGURE 3.15 *"The Grumple." (https://realizinggrace.wordpress.com/2016/04/25/book-review-telephone-time-a-first-book-of-telephone-dos-and-donts-reading-with-pearl/img_6707 (accessed February 12, 2017).)*

Among other things, Ringalina instructs the children not to be rude or use foul language on the phone; to hang up right away if they don't hear anyone or if they "hear words that don't sound nice"; never to tell unknown callers if they are home alone; and how to correctly and politely take messages. But perhaps the most persuasive section of the book is the "Telephone Fairy's Gallery of Phone Monsters," where Ringalina introduces the children to the six abhorrent specimens in her "very own gallery of the world's greatest telephone pests."[90] Alongside the negligent "Message Monster," irksome "Button Bopper," and aloof "Tie-Uppasaurus," there's the surly "Grumple." Clad in a white undershirt, holding a pop-top can of beer, and with a heart tattoo on his arm that reads "Mommie," the Grumple—shown in Figure 3.15—is shown barking "Yeah? Whaddya want?" into the transmitter.

The back cover of Carrie Finn's *Manners on the Telephone*, with illustrations by Chris Lench, catches readers' attention as follows: "What should you say when you answer the phone? Find out how manners make the telephone a useful tool for everyone." It takes a more sober approach than *Telephone Time*, emphasizing the "fun factor" associated with using the phone. "Using the telephone to call friends or family can be fun," it promises the young reader, continuing: "Everyone wants to talk without any problems. Good manners on the phone help make that happen. There are lots of ways you can use good telephone manners."[91]

FIGURE 3.16 *Lydia modeling good phone manners. (https://books.google.com/ books?id=o3TBBAAAQBAJ (accessed March 22, 2015).)*

What follows are twenty pages of telephone-related scenarios in which a youngster exhibits good linguistic manners. Figure 3.16 illustrates one such scenario. Elsewhere, Little Naomi is shown sitting on her bed; she "speaks in a clear voice on the phone. She does not yell or whisper."[92] In other instance, Kyle picks up the family's landline and dutifully announces, "Hello, this is the Jackson residence."[93]

Last, there's *Good Manners on the Phone*, written by Katie Marsico and illustrated by John Haslam. The back cover, shown in Figure 3.17, suggests the kind of linguistic indoctrination it has in store for children: "May I ask who is calling?" The message, therefore, is that a well-bred child would never say, "Can I ask who's calling?" (implying that *may* is more "proper" or "correct" than *can*, and that less well-mannered kids use contractions like *who's* on the phone). Not to mention something as linguistically uncouth as "Who's this?"

We shouldn't be too hard on these authors, though. They do seem to genuinely believe that they're "helping" today's youngsters and, as a result, laying the groundwork for future generations of polite phone users. Indeed: all indications point to benign, well-meaning intentions.

Nevertheless, the sharp-eyed linguist recognizes that—like the advertisements and etiquette guides discussed above—these books are vessels for spreading language ideologies; in particular, beliefs about "proper" or "correct" language for the telephone. Ultimately, these texts perpetuate opinions and attitudes about language—ideas originally borne out of technology and which therefore count as products of technolingualism.

FIGURE   3.17 *"May   I   ask   who   is   calling?"   (https://books.google.com/books?id=cCDofBydIDsC (accessed March 22, 2015).)*

Naturally, telephonically inspired language ideologies are not unique to English. Regardless of language or culture, within *any* speech community that has the telephone, there will be attendant conceptions about what constitutes "good" or "acceptable" language for using it. Before concluding our chapter on the abstraction of language, we'd like to broaden our cultural perspective to include one example of phone-related language ideologies in a non-English-speaking community: professional telephone etiquette in contemporary Japan.

"Formal phone answering is serious business in Japan, with many rules intended to head off offensive or awkward moments," *New York Times* correspondent Hiroko Tabuchi explains in an article from December 2013.[94] And in fact, the Japanese—businesspeople especially—value phone etiquette so much, that each November they hold a nationwide contest to find Japan's "Best Phone Answerer." Begun in 1962, the competition's purpose, according to its official website, is to "preserve correct, eloquent Japanese, as well as measuring the improvement in the service-level and words of each firm's response to telephone calls."[95]

Now, the evaluative terms "correct" and "eloquent" to describe the type of Japanese language that the competition promotes will strike most linguists as a clarion call for prescriptivism. (Prescriptivism involves telling people how they should or should not speak; as opposed to descriptivist perspectives, which favor straightforward, judgment-free descriptions of language.) Despite the in-your-face judgment, thousands of Japanese (mostly female) take part in the competition every year. In November 2014, for example, 13,362 aspirants from all parts of the island nation flocked to the western Japanese coastal city of Kanazawa to showcase their skills.[96]

Even outside of the office setting, concern for correct language usage on the telephone is rampant among the Japanese. Tabuchi reports that "a search on Amazon's Japanese website found more than 60 books specifically on phone manners."[97] In other words, the legions of annual hopefuls have a lot of formal resources at their disposal as they prepare for the competition. And the basis for every one of these how-to guidebooks? Abstract, pervasive ideas about how the Japanese *ought* to linguistically comport themselves when they use the telephone.

These mental constructs then map onto concrete linguistic structures, that is, the words, phrases, and grammatical forms that authors prescribe as the "best" or "most correct" language to use while telephoning. "The [Japanese phone] conversation itself," Tabuchi writes, "is carried out in a formal, honorific spoken form of language—peppered with exclamations like 'I'm horrified to ask this request, but . . .' "[98] In addition, these manuals advise Japanese phone users to pay close mind to good tone, volume, speed, and pronunciation, and the use or avoidance of certain words.

Keep in mind, however, that this prescribed style of language doesn't come naturally to the Japanese speaker. They have to practice. They have to work hard to mimic the linguistic hows and whats that someone else—someone with fervent opinions and attitudes about language—is dictating to them. Take Mika Otani, for instance, a promising contender at the 2013 All-Japan Phone-Answering Competition. According to Tabuchi, Ms. Otani "trained six months for the competition by writing out sample answers and practicing in front of a mirror to make sure she was properly opening up her larynx and articulating."[99] As it did in the United States, Bell's invention led to new ideas, attitudes, and regulatory trends for language in Japan as well. And every year, these byproducts of Japanese language ideologies are brandished, ratified, and showcased by a panel of judges at the All-Japan Phone-Answering Competition.

The Abstraction of Language and Technolingualism

In this chapter we looked at two technologies that abstracted language—in time, location, and physicality. We showed that the telegraph and telephone were the first technologies to decouple communication from transportation: the former for written language, the latter for spoken language. Both inventions abstracted language away from the immediate speaker, converting concrete manifestations of language—scribbled letters or uttered sounds—into invisible and instantaneous packets of electricity.

More importantly, however, the abstraction of language grants us more compelling insights into the overarching argument we've labeled technolingualism—that is, language and technology are engaged in a mutually shaping arrangement.

Writing systems and letter frequencies influenced the codes developed for sending information over the telegraph: the Chinese logographic system, based on characters signifying entire words, lent itself best as a numeric code, whereas the English alphabetic system, comprised of symbols representing (mostly) discrete sounds, proved more suitable as a dot-dash code for transmitting letters. In this vein, we also saw that, in a manner echoing the construction of the typewriter keyboard, letter frequencies in English affected the design of Morse code; letters that tend to be used more often were assigned a shorter dot-dash combination, and vice versa for letters used less often.

We then made the case that the telephone was phonetically and anatomically inspired; to wit, Alexander Graham Bell's unique background in the science of language—specifically, in elocution, articulation, acoustics, and the physiology of sound perception—informed his inventive process. We argued that this was most evident in Bell's early experiments with the human ear phonautograph. This apparatus simulated the anatomy of sound perception and inspired the breakthrough idea for building the first practical and commercially successful telephone: the diaphragm membrane.

On the other hand, we also considered how this duo of language-abstracting devices shaped language, both structurally and ideologically, and resulted in an expansion of speakers' linguistic repertoires. The telegraph, we argued, gave people trained in Morse code a new "language" to communicate in; yielded a new jargon (aka cablese) for news correspondents; contributed to the development of a new journalistic writing style; and inspired new understandings of what it means to "communicate." As for the telephone, we saw that the novel context of "faceless conversation" gave rise to new linguistic structures and pragmatic strategies (e.g., how to answer the phone, navigate the opening sequence of a telephone conversation, etc.) as well as language ideologies (e.g., telephone etiquette).

In Chapter 4, our exploration of technolingualism will bring us into more contemporary times: to the computer. As we'll see, this game-changing technology took the abstraction of language phenomenon, begun with the telegraph and telephone, another step further—into the realm of digitization.

4

Digitization of Language: The Computer

The Many Faces of Email, or Professor Ferraro's Inbox Irritants

Professor Ferraro unloads an armful of books and term papers onto her desk. She glowers at the slipshod stack of exams on the floor. They've been loafing there for a week, refusing to go away on their own. She groans. Courtesy of this fresh batch of term papers, and coupled with the seven-day-old recalcitrant exams, her weekend is now set: ten hours of grading. (And that's a conservative estimate, i.e., one that assumes no more than two glasses of red wine per grading session.)

She jiggles the computer mouse to wake up her screen. Only five new emails—two of which, she now sees, are mass mailings from publishing companies. *New and exciting textbooks to jumpstart your fall semester.* Delete. *See what's new from your number one publisher of academic texts!* Junk.

The next email's subject line isn't much better (*Excellent opportunities at the Center for Faculty Excellence*) but she recognizes the sender's name, a junior—and irritatingly upbeat—colleague in the Department of Economics.

Dear Colleagues,

Allow me to take a moment out of your busy day to make you aware of three excellent opportunities for professional development through the CFE this fall semester.

Not interested—no matter how "excellent" the opportunities. She clicks delete.

The third message's subject line reads *Registration Question*. The sender's name looks familiar, though she can't visualize a matching face. Probably one of her newly assigned advisees. She selects "open message" and reads:

Dr. Ferraro,

We haven't met but my name is Ryan Crowley. I got an email that you're my adviser so I'm writing you with a question. I'm trying to register for classes for the spring and it keeps telling me that I need a registration code. Is this something I should have gotten from the college or do you have it? If so could you please send it to me ASAP? There are some classes I'd like to get into before they fill up. Okay thanks!

Without realizing it, she rolls her eyes. (An involuntary habit she developed not long after earning tenure.) Two weeks prior she'd sent all her new advisees an email explaining that they would need to schedule a meeting with her to discuss their spring course schedules. And that during this meeting she would give them their spring course registration code. But apparently this important email had gone unheeded by one Ryan Crowley, who now requires this information "ASAP"—and who, it occurs to her now, has neither the time nor awareness to end his email with a salutation.

She highlights the message and selects "Follow-up Tomorrow." If he wants the code so badly before then, he can stop by her office.

The last of the new messages has a single lackluster word in its subject field: *Course*. The sender isn't familiar. She double clicks to open it.

Sup prof,

Hey I was wondering if its still cool that I sit in on your 10 am class. Remember I talked to you about it last spring. Thanks!

Sent from my Verizon Android

For a long moment she just stares at the screen, too stunned even to roll her eyes. In her time as an instructor at an institution of higher learning she's gotten plenty of bizarre emails, from students and colleagues alike. But this message blows them all out of the water. *Sup prof*!? *Wondering if its still cool* . . . !? Had this student really sent this email? To a professor?

Unbelievable.

She finally comes to, and banishes the offensive specimen to the trash.

Maybe, she thinks to herself, it's time to augment her course syllabi with a lecture and some exercises on the proper etiquette for writing emails . . .

❖

Our opening narrative flashes several points about the technolingual relationship between email and language—points that we return to and flesh out later in this chapter. We'll see that writing, like speech, isn't a monochromatic and uniform medium of linguistic communication; rather, it displays colorful variation in its structures and practices. Thus we can speak of multiple varieties of written language. Second, with respect to *how* it conveys linguistic information (i.e., as a medium) email differs from traditional writing in that it's *computer mediated*. It is, then, an example of *computer-mediated communication*— what we henceforth refer to as CMC. Third, we'll see that, similar to other CMC-based technologies (e.g., instant messaging, text messaging), email exhibits a wide stylistic range: at times its structures and practices approximate informal speech, while at others it approaches a more formal or standard written idiom. And finally, like all varieties of language, we'll see that email is fraught with ideologies. To wit, speakers who use email—indeed, even people who don't use it but simply know *about* it—collectively and individually create, harbor, and pass on perceptions, opinions, and judgments about the structures and practices of the language of email. Moreover, these language ideologies of email aren't static; on the contrary, they vary from person to person and often change over time.

∞

In Chapter 3 we looked at how language, in its structures and ideologies, both shaped and was shaped by the telegraph and the telephone. The upshot of this technolingual development, we argued, was a tripartite abstraction of language: in location, time, and substance. The telegraph allowed us to send written language across vast distances, in an instant, as pulses of electricity. The telephone did the same thing for spoken language (but as fluctuations in current instead of electrical pulses).

In this chapter we focus on a technology that propelled the abstraction of language still further—into the digital realm. In what follows we see how the computer[1] amounted to a sweeping digitization of language, converting it into abstract data that a machine can understand. Speech was rendered into electronic diagrams. Writing was transformed into strings of ones and zeros.

Maintaining our hallmark theoretical scaffolding—a framework we call technolingualism—we consider how language-digitizing technology, exemplified by the computer, both affected and was affected by language. And don't forget, too, that under "language" we understand structures (i.e., sounds, words, sentences) as well as ideologies (i.e., opinions, attitudes, and beliefs about language and speakers).

We begin with language's influence on the computer, fleshing out two trains of thought. First, we consider the impact of writing systems on the development of digital word processing. Next, we go back to the pioneering days of computer programming and consider the role—albeit indirect, as we'll see—that theoretical linguistics (in particular, formal language theory) played for advancements in programming languages.

The latter part of our chapter addresses the alternate side of our techno-lingual case, namely, the computer's effect on language. To this end we concentrate on two digital technologies: email and the internet. Regarding the first, we explore the extent of email's influence on written language. We follow this with a look at how the internet—inasmuch as it affords a panoramic and quantitatively unprecedented vantage point from which to study linguistic events—has led to fresh insights and questions about language. As before, we won't limit our discussion to only structures and practices; instead, where appropriate, we also bring language ideologies into the mix.

Of Writing Systems and Formal Grammar Theory: How Language Shaped Computer Technology

Let's consider two ways that language has informed the technical evolution of the computer. We start with writing systems. Recall from previous chapters that a language's writing system shaped, to various degrees, the mental models and mechanical decisions that underlay the printing press, typewriter, and telegraphic code. Well, the same applied to the computer. Engineers began working on computer word-processing technology in the 1960s.[2] And they quickly realized that a language's particular writing system required them to adjust their inventive schema, especially in terms of the digital encoding of linguistic symbols.

We then step back into the 1950s and consider the role that an obscure branch of linguistics, known as *formal grammar theory*, played for the evolving field of computer science. We see that one linguist's work in particular, through subtle (yet important) ways, contributed to the theoretical and methodological groundwork for developing programming languages.

The Symbol Is King, or How Writing Systems Informed Software and Hardware

We're often told that computers are intrinsically dumb. That it takes a human to "make" them smart. For many of us, this truism conjures an image of a computer geek pecking away at a terminal and filling the machine's empty "brain" (or CPU) with information—that is, programming it.

Less widely known, however, is what this programmed information looks like when it's stripped down to the basics. Not the odd-looking strings of punctuation marks and bracketed terms that make up a programming language like C+ or Java, rather, the "language" behind these strings—the form of communication the machine understands: ones and zeros. People understand sequences of spoken sounds or written letters. Computers are digital dolts; they comprehend only ones and zeros.

Say I invite you to a party at my house. And since you've never been to my place before, I jot down:

- go north on country rd. 281 for 2 miles
- turn right onto Amerman Rd.
- in 1/4 mile turn left onto Sprocket St.
- mine is second house on your right

As you read these directions, your brain recognizes each word as a collection of distinct and abstract sounds (or phonemes). In other words, your brain processes linguistically encoded data.

To a computer, though, these letters mean nothing. Its "brain" processes digitally encoded data. It understands only *on* or *off*, that is, the presence or absence of voltage flowing through a circuit. This two-state condition can be encoded as one ("current flowing") or zero ("no current flowing"), and its informational value is known as a "bit," a portmanteau of "binary digit." "Digital computer memory stores only bits," Charles Petzold explains in his wonderful *Code: The Hidden Language of Computer Hardware and Software*, "so anything we want to work with on a computer, must be stored in the form of bits."[3]

Therefore, if we wanted to invite our computer to the party too, we'd have to tell it something like:

on-off-on-off-off-off-on-on-off-off-on (or 10100011001, for "go north");
   off-off-on-on-off-off-on (or 0011001, for "country road");
   "on-on-on" (or 111, for "2")

And so on. Suffice it to say, it would be a colossal concatenation of ones and zeros.

Granted, this is a pitiably oversimplified description of what goes on in your brain[4] versus a computer's "brain." Yet the takeaway point is relevant for our ensuing discussion: humans had to come up with unique and clever ways to translate their multifaceted linguistic code into the binary lingo that computers need.

Digital word-processing technology is a prime example. In order to get a computer to render a symbol that humans can read—whether alphabetic letter, syllabogram, or logogram—a programmer must instruct the machine through lines of binary code (which, remember, indicate either the absence or presence of voltage flowing through a circuit). The letter *A*, for instance, could be captured as the binary sequence 01. And every time the computer receives this off-on voltage input, it "knows" to produce an *A* as output. *B* could be programmed as 10, *C* as 11, *D* as 001, and so on. This procedure, called binary encoding, allows for linguistic text to be represented in a computer's memory.

We should point out, however, that this idea of enciphering letters along a binary scheme wasn't an original contribution of the computer age. As we saw in Chapter 3, already in the nineteenth century letters were being encoded as combinations of dots and dashes. Telegraphic code was essentially binary: a dot served as a zero, a dash as a one (or vice versa). You also recall that this dot-and-dash code worked swimmingly for idioms written with an alphabet. Their symbol sets are relatively small, and each symbol in these sets can be combined to form words. Alphabetic languages thus required a less complex dot-and-dash code system. Logographic writing systems, however, were less conducive to this coded form of telegraphic transmission. Symbols in these systems usually stand for entire words. And they don't break down easily into a manageable number of discrete components. So the symbol sets for Japanese kanji and Chinese hànzí run into the tens of thousands. It simply wasn't feasible to assign each character its own dot-and-dash encryption.

When we extend this train of thought to word-processing technology, it becomes clear that the number of symbols your writing system contains determines how long your digital coding sequence must be; that is, how many bits (or units having either a one or zero value) you need in order to accommodate the full set of written symbols.

Let's take a quick look at the math behind this. If one bit represents two potential values, then two bits give us four. Three bits expand the options to eight. And if we choose to go with a four-bit coding scheme, we'd arrive at sixteen binary combinations. Table 4.1 gives a mathematic description for a two-, three-, and four-bit system.

As you can see, even a four-bit system allows us to encode only sixteen symbols. This is clearly not enough for writing in any language—except, maybe, in Rotokas, a language spoken in Papua New Guinea that has only twelve letters.[5] But even then we'd still be left with only four more binary encoding slots. There'd be no room to represent uppercase letters. And what about the ciphers 0–9, punctuation marks, or operation keys like the space bar or backspace? Forget it. We'd need to extend our encoding system to five or even six bits. This would then give us thirty-two and sixty-four slots, respectively.

TABLE 4.1 Mathematic description of two-, three-, and four-bit encoding systems.

Bits	Math Formula	Potential Value	Binary Options
2	2^2 (or 2 x 2)	4	00, 01, 11, 10
3	2^3 (or 2 x 2 x 2)	8	000, 001, 010, 011 111, 100, 110, 101
4	2^4 (or 2 x 2 x 2 x 2)	16	0000, 0001, 0010, 0100, 1000 1100, 1110, 1111, 1010, 1001, 1011, 0101, 0111, 1110, 1101, 0011.

For adequate word processing in English, early programmers determined that they needed seven bits, or 128 encoding options. To understand why, let's again do some math. The Latin alphabet for English includes twenty-six letters, which we double to fifty-four to include uppercase. We add the numerals 0–9 and arrive at sixty-four. Now, this would suffice for English, if alphanumeric symbols were the *only* things programmers needed to encode. But take a closer look at your computer keyboard. There's a collection of keys for punctuation, a few mathematical symbols, and a bunch of control keys (e.g., return, arrows) and modifier keys (e.g., shift, alternate). All told:

> You still have less than 100 distinct things that need to be encoded. That means that in fact to encode English you really only need (less than) $2^7 = 128$ positions, which means in turn that English can be encoded using only seven bits ... And this is exactly what was done in the first encoding systems.[6]

English's writing system thus motivated a seven-bit encoding platform. Developed in 1963, developers of this system named it the American Standard Code for Information Interchange (ASCII). Figure 4.1 illustrates this seven-bit scheme for encoding the symbols needed for word processing in English.

At first glance it looks downright byzantine. But here's how it worked. Binary integers 1–4 are headed, in descending order, in the first four columns on the left. You notice that sixteen rows extend below these first four bit columns; recall from Table 4.1 how a four-bit coding scheme translates into sixteen binary configuration possibilities. The remaining three bits, 5–7, are headed in a single field above the columns for bits 1–4. The nine possible binary configurations for this three-bit coding scheme run to the right in a row. Thus, to determine the binary representation of lowercase *c*, we find the

USASCII code chart

b4 b3 b2 b1	Row	0	1	2	3	4	5	6	7
0 0 0 0	0	NUL	DLE	SP	0	@	P	`	p
0 0 0 1	1	SOH	DC1	!	1	A	Q	a	q
0 0 1 0	2	STX	DC2	"	2	B	R	b	r
0 0 1 1	3	ETX	DC3	#	3	C	S	c	s
0 1 0 0	4	EOT	DC4	$	4	D	T	d	t
0 1 0 1	5	ENQ	NAK	%	5	E	U	e	u
0 1 1 0	6	ACK	SYN	&	6	F	V	f	v
0 1 1 1	7	BEL	ETB	'	7	G	W	g	w
1 0 0 0	8	BS	CAN	(	8	H	X	h	x
1 0 0 1	9	HT	EM	)	9	I	Y	i	y
1 0 1 0	10	LF	SUB	*	:	J	Z	j	z
1 0 1 1	11	VT	ESC	+	;	K	[	k	{
1 1 0 0	12	FF	FS	,	<	L	\	l	|
1 1 0 1	13	CR	GS	-	=	M	]	m	}
1 1 1 0	14	SO	RS	.	>	N	^	n	~
1 1 1 1	15	SI	US	/	?	O	_	o	DEL

FIGURE 4.1 *ASCII character-coding chart. (https://commons.wikimedia.org/wiki/ File:ASCII_Code_Chart-Quick_ref_card.png (accessed June 22, 2015).)*

corresponding four bits on the left (1100) and then the three bits above (011), and put them together. So each time you push the button marked *c*, the computer comprehends "1100011" and renders a "c" on the screen as output.

Now, this seven-bit coding scheme worked fine for languages written with an alphabet. A check on *ethnologue.com* shows that about half of the world's known languages are written,[7] most with some form of alphabet. Moreover, among the various alphabets in use around the world, the Latin and Cyrillic systems are the most widely used.[8] And because alphabets generally include 20–35 letters, programmers could rely on a seven-bit platform.

But keep in mind: this seven-bit scheme only sufficed to encode the symbols of any *individual* alphabet. Say, for instance, you were a Russian-English bilingual and wanted to use the same computer to work with documents in separate languages/alphabets or with one document containing both languages/alphabets. Your computer would only have enough binary space to handle one or the other. In other words, you'd need two computers (and a lot of spare cash to buy that extra machine!). You also notice from the ASCII chart that there are no encodings for various letters common to other Western European alphabets, like Spanish *ñ* or Danish *å*. People wanting to word process in these alphabets were out of luck.

So beginning in 1985 the International Organization for Standardization (IOS) expanded the coding scheme to eight bits (or one *byte*). Now able to handle

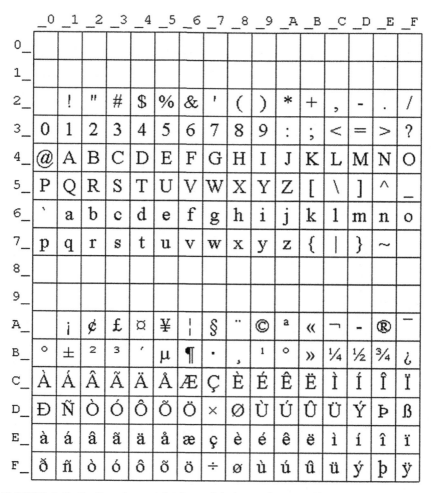

FIGURE 4.2 *Coding chart with ASCII alphabet and non-English Western European symbols.*

a character set of 256, the first IOS coding scheme, shown in Figure 4.2, contained both the ASCII characters *and* those characters needed for most non-English Western European alphabets. In 1988 the IOS released another one-byte scheme that incorporated the Cyrillic alphabet. Figure 4.3 shows this coding chart.

By now you've probably sensed where this discussion is headed: what if you wanted to word process in Japanese or Chinese? As you recall, these languages are traditionally written with logograms, that is, symbols that (generally) stand for an entire word. In fact, with Japanese the situation is even *more* complicated, because it's written with both logograms (kanji) and syllabograms

	-0	-1	-2	-3	-4	-5	-6	-7	-8	-9	-A	-B	-C	-D	-E	-F
0-																
1-																
2-		!	"	#	$	%	&	'	(	)	*	+	,	-	.	/
3-	0	1	2	3	4	5	6	7	8	9	:	;	<	=	>	?
4-	@	A	B	C	D	E	F	G	H	I	J	K	L	M	N	O
5-	P	Q	R	S	T	U	V	W	X	Y	Z	[	\	]	^	_
6-	`	a	b	c	d	e	f	g	h	i	j	k	l	m	n	o
7-	p	q	r	s	t	u	v	w	x	y	z	{	|	}	~	
8-																
9-																
A-		Ё	Ђ	Ѓ	Є	Ѕ	І	Ї	Ј	Љ	Њ	Ћ	Ќ	-	Ў	Џ
B-	А	Б	В	Г	Д	Е	Ж	З	И	Й	К	Л	М	Н	О	П
C-	Р	С	Т	У	Ф	Х	Ц	Ч	Ш	Щ	Ъ	Ы	Ь	Э	Ю	Я
D-	а	б	в	г	д	е	ж	з	и	й	к	л	м	н	о	п
E-	р	с	т	у	ф	х	ц	ч	ш	щ	ъ	ы	ь	э	ю	я
F-	№	ё	ђ	ѓ	є	ѕ	і	ї	ј	љ	њ	ћ	ќ	§	ў	џ

FIGURE 4.3 *Coding chart with ASCII and Cyrillic alphabets.*

(kana).[9] In order to accommodate the tens of thousands of characters, engineers had to broaden the coding schemes to two bytes (i.e., sixteen bits), giving them 65,536 slots. Unfortunately this demanded a lot of memory space on a computer's hard drive and often slowed down processing.

Coding issues aside, word processing in Chinese and Japanese posed challenges on the hardware front too. William Hannas describes what it was like, as late as 2003, to digitally create text in Chinese: "Unlike alphabetic writing whose units consist of a few elements, Chinese characters must be input on large keyboards with several thousand key choices, or by pressing keys that correspond to character components."[10] In fact, Hannas is critical of both approaches. Of the first, he writes:

> [It] typically puts several characters on each of a few hundred keys. One finds the right key, and then selects the proper character by pressing another key, like the function keying done on alphanumeric boards. If you

have trouble remembering which functions are associated with the "Ctrl" and "Alt" keys on an alphanumeric keyboard, or lack the dexterity to execute these commands, multiply the confusion by a hundred to get an idea of the task users of large character keyboards face.[11]

The second approach breaks down characters into root shapes or strokes. By selecting a root and then additional components, special software analyzes the sequence of input, assembles a range of characters, and displays these options. While this system sounds ideal and efficient, Hannas argues:

> Unfortunately, the elements that make up the Chinese character set are neither few nor well defined. [A] lot of memorization and guesswork is involved simply to produce this *range* of options.[12]

Software engineers have also developed a third solution that allows users, on a standard-sized keyboard, to word process in Chinese or Japanese: phonetic conversion. Using pinyin for Chinese, and kana (a syllabic character script) and *Romaji* (the Latin alphabet) for Japanese, the user spells the word as it's pronounced. The computer matches up this input with one or more possible characters and shows it on the screen. Newer phonetic conversion software uses canny algorithms to analyze preceding words, determine the syntactic and semantic context, and then offer the likeliest or most fitting character. The user chooses the character they were after and then goes on to the next word.

Say you wanted to write "I like dogs" in Japanese. Using the Romaji (or "Roman letter") keys on your board, you would type *watashi wa inu ga suki*. As you enter each syllable, the software immediately replaces it with a kana syllabogram and underlines it. A window pops up on the screen and displays kanji options. You can either keep the kana syllabogram (which are often used to indicate grammatical inflections or particles) or choose the kanji you were after.

To see how this works, let's consider the word *watashi*, which is the Romaji spelling of "I" in Japanese. When you enter *wa* on the keyboard, the syllabogram わ appears and is underlined. Typing *ta* brings up the underlined た. And punching in *shi* gives you し. You then hit the spacebar twice. A separate little box appears and displays the kanji character 私 as an option. Figures 4.4 to 4.7 demonstrate how this phonetic conversion process unfolds.

Continuing in this vein, you eventually get the entire sentence 私は犬が好き, which includes both kanji ideograms (私 for *watashi* ["I"], 犬 for *inu* ("dog"), and 好 for *su* ("like")) and kana syllabograms (は and が for *wa* and *ga*, grammatical particles that mark the immediately preceding word as a subject and object, respectively, and き for *ki*, a first-person verb conjugation).

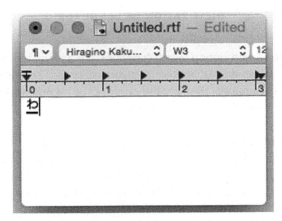

FIGURE 4.4 *Typing Romaji syllable* wa *to get kana* わ *using phonetic conversion software.*

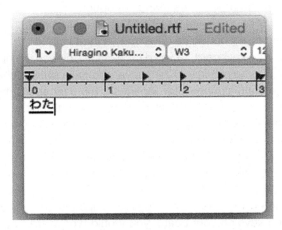

FIGURE 4.5 *Typing Romaji syllable* ta *to get kana* た *using phonetic conversion software.*

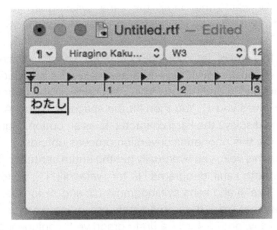

FIGURE 4.6 *Typing Romaji syllable* shi *to get kana* し *using phonetic conversion software.*

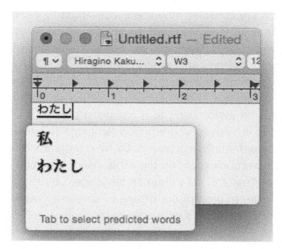

FIGURE 4.7 *Pop-up window displaying kanji 私 ("I").*

Seem complicated? To those accustomed to typing their language with an alphabet, it is. But for millions of Japanese and Chinese it's the most practical way of word processing. "As far as Asian input systems go," Hannas concedes, "this is the best of the lot."[13] Hannas nevertheless maintains the critical tone characteristic of his book. "No matter how adept software becomes at divining a user's intent," he concludes, "there will always be an intermediate stage where one must confirm or revise the suggested text."[14] Hence, for Hannas, even state-of-the-art word-processing software for handling the character-based orthography of Japanese and Chinese "requires that an inordinate amount of time be spent on processes that contribute nothing to content, and tend to act as a substitute for it."[15]

Of Formal Language Theory and Computer Programming, or How Computer Science Benefitted from an Obscure Subfield of Linguistics

Most people today—even those who (gasp!) care little or nothing about linguistics—will sense that the engineering masterminds behind their computer or handheld smart device had to know something about language. Typed or spoken, we can now interact linguistically with our gadgets with relative ease. This technology wouldn't be possible without the science of language. Someone had to instruct that piece of technology how to make sense of our distinctly human system of communication. And in order to do this (i.e., to linguistically endow that machine), this hypothetical someone had to figure out a few things about how language works.

In this section we consider how linguistics—broadly defined here as the scientific pursuit to understand and explain language—has contributed to the world of computing, specifically, our ability to interact linguistically, as a means of "communication," with digital machines.

First off, we distinguish between two levels of this human-to-computer communication: machine and phonetics. Machine-level communication is the way we pass on instructions to a computer's CPU. The most common way of doing this is with a programming language (which is further translated into computer-friendly machine code by a program called a compiler). Phonetics-level communication, on the other hand, is using typed or spoken natural language ("natural" as in human language, i.e., the opposite of programming language) to prompt our device to do something it's programmed to do. For instance, computers with speech recognition software can "understand" our sounds, words, and sentences. How this speech-recognition technology works, and the key linguistic insights that drove it, will be our focus in Chapter 5.

In this chapter, though, we focus on machine-level communication. We see that early developers of programming languages (and compilers) drew trailblazing insights, in particular, from one linguist's work in formal language theory, an abstruse subfield of linguistics. "Noam Chomsky developed the Chomsky hierarchy in the field of linguistics, a discovery which has directly impacted programming language theory and other branches of computer science."[16] We show how Chomsky's mathematical and formal approach to studying language, in particular grammar (note that by "grammar" we mean here the abstract device in a speaker's mind that governs how words can be strung together into sentences), buoyed computer scientists in their efforts to formalize and develop "languages" for telling computers what to do, that is, programming them.

But first we need to acquaint ourselves—briefly!—with what programming languages are and why computers need them.

Programming languages are formally constructed systems of communication that allow us to "talk" with a computer. These languages provide the basis for what has come to be called software, the "set of machine-readable instructions that directs a computer's processor to perform specific operations."[17] Before software was invented, engineers had to arrange a computer's hardware a certain way to instruct it to do something. In other words, every computer had to be individually hardwired to perform a task or solve a problem.

Say, for instance, you wanted a machine to do your taxes. So you go into your garage and solder a bunch of circuits, attach a keyboard and monitor, run a current through it all, and presto—it spits out your prepared tax forms. And then your next-door neighbor drops by. He's so impressed, in fact, that he offers you a hundred bucks if you can rig up his own computer to do the same thing. Now, today, we might just respond with something like, "You should just go out and buy TurboTax." But this hypothetical incident is taking place before software, as we know it today, was invented. So you explain to him that either you need to take apart his machine and refunctionalize its hardware entirely, or you have to build a new machine from the ground up.

This was one of the motivations for inventing software: it made the computer more malleable in terms of functionality. Instead of reconfiguring their digital pet's hardware each time they wanted it to turn a new trick, computer scientists used a special code to write programs, and these programs "communicated" the new information to the computer's CPU.

Now, remember that a computer understands only groups of binary values, or bits. Thus the earliest software, from the 1940s, was actually written in binary code—to wit, massive concatenations of ones and zeros. Imagine how tedious that must have been: just one misplaced digit and the program wouldn't work! In short, the introduction of programming languages went a long way toward easing a coder's cognitive woes. Programming languages replaced digits with something that humans can work with much better: words.

The first programming language that did this was assembly language, in which mnemonic tokens stood for digits. Once entered, a device called an assembler would translate tokens into the binary code that the computer understands. An example of assembly language might be:

LOAD BASEPAY
ADD BASEPAY
STORE BASEPAY

The first word establishes an operation (i.e., instructions for what the computer should do) and the second word establishes a location (i.e., where the information is stored or should be stored in a computer's memory). Thus, the word LOAD might exit the assembler as, say, "00111" (which, again, signified some specified operation), and the word BASEPAY might be translated into the numeric code "0111 0001 0011" (again, a certain memory address).

Though a step up from binary coding, assembly language was still an awkward way to tell a computer's mainframe what to do. First, the programmer had to learn hundreds of "English-like" terms, each associated with a specific machine-language instruction. Second, because there was a one-to-one relationship between assembly code and machine instruction, programs written in assembly language tended to be pretty long. Finally, assembly language wasn't portable across machine hardware: "Each assembly language is specific to a particular computer architecture."[18] This is why assembly language is called a "low-level" programming language.[19]

The solution was to develop a type of programming language that abstracted the programming instructions further away from the computer's instruction set architecture. And the best way to do this? Well, since the computer speaks digital, and humans speak language, computer scientists decided to integrate more features of natural language into programming. And this is just what so-called "high-level" programming languages do: they use English words and familiar symbols to specify operations.

Developed in the 1950s, COBOL, FORTRAN, and ALGOL are examples of early high-level programming languages. Instructions written in high-level languages pass through a compiler program that translates them into machine code. But unlike assembly language, high-level languages are portable between architectures: as long as they're equipped with their own compiler, both Macs and PCs can read programs written in the same high-level language.

Now that we've covered the basics of how humans communicate with computers on the machine level, let's bring our discussion back to the technolingual argument: language's influence on computer programming.

In the spirit of full disclosure, we should note that language's influence on computer programming took an indirect route. Programming languages weren't inspired by the anatomy of sound perception, as we saw with the telephone. Nor did computer scientists derive conceptual cues by observing phonetic frequencies and orthographic patterns, as we saw with the typewriter. Rather, the influence that language exerted on computer programming is rooted more in theory than practice.

In the 1950s a promising young theoretical linguist at MIT became interested in grammar. Not the grammar that comes to mind when you think about your seventh-grade English teacher or college professor of German. The grammar that Noam Chomsky took on was more abstract: "A grammar can be regarded as a device [in a speaker's mind] that enumerates the sentences of a language."[20] The emphasis of his research was on syntax, the rules that allow a speaker to generate and understand sentences.

Chomsky's approach was revolutionary. For one, he used mathematical theory to explore the nature of grammar. For another, he described syntax through rewrite rules,[21] a formal technique common in logic and computability theory. And finally, he argued that language could be studied with the same scientific formalism that physicists and other natural scientists used to interrogate their theories. In 1956 he wrote:

The grammar of a language can be viewed as a theory of the structure of this language. Any scientific theory is based on a certain finite set of observations and, by establishing general laws stated in terms of certain hypothetical constructs, it attempts to account for these observations ...

A mathematical theory has the additional property that predictions follow rigorously from the body of theory. Similarly, a grammar is based on a finite number of observed sentences (a linguist's corpus) and it "projects" this set to an infinite set of grammatical sentences by establishing general "laws" (grammatical rules) framed in terms of such hypothetical constructs as the particular phonemes, words, phrases, and so on, of the language under analysis.[22]

Put in our own words: Chomsky regarded the grammar of any given language as a theory of the structure of that language. And in order to test the theory of, say, English, he chose to use mathematical proofs. For example, he used mathematical variables to define any given grammar, or G:

The basic system of description that we shall consider is a system G of the following form: G is a semi-group under concatenation with strings in a finite set V of symbols as its elements, and I as the identity element. V is called the "vocabulary" of G. $V = V_T \cup V_n$ (V_T, V_n disjoint), where V_T is the "terminal vocabulary" and V_n the "nonterminal vocabulary." V_T contains I and a "boundary" element #. V_n contains an element S (sentence).[23]

We won't go into depth on what, exactly, this all means. Our purpose is simply to establish Chomsky as the first linguist to describe grammar with mathematical models, and to investigate theories of grammar. He described his *Syntactic Structures* from 1956, for instance, as "an attempt to construct a formalized general theory of linguistic structure and to explore the foundations of such a theory."[24]

Perhaps you're asking at this point: what does this have to do with computer programming? Well, although it seems never to have been Chomsky's stated intention,[25] his work in formal language theory got the attention of computer scientists. Hard at work on developing more efficient, human-friendly programming languages, early programmers were drawn to two aspects of Chomsky's work.

First, they liked his mathematical angle for exploring the syntax of human language. However, for them it was less about *language* per se than about understanding how rule-based systems work in producing and understanding strings of variables. Computer scientists, you see, were starting to realize that the high-level languages they were envisioning for writing programs that the computer would read—these "languages," like any natural language—would need a "grammar" with a defined "syntax."[26] Jiang and company explain:

Every programming language from Fortran to Java can be precisely described by a grammar. Moreover, the grammar allows us to write a computer program (called the *syntax analyzer* in a compiler) to determine whether a string of statements is syntactically correct in the programming language.[27]

And similar to how the human brain understands sentences by running the strings of words through a mental grammar, a computer's compiler program would translate the strings of programming language (or source code) into machine code.

To the programming pioneers trying to sort all this out, Chomsky's linguistic formalism was a welcome resource. Take the renowned computer scientist Donald Knuth, whose seminal multivolume oeuvre *The Art of Computer Programming* shaped the modern field. He writes:

> Of course [in those early days of computer programming] we had only a vague notion of what we were doing; our work was almost totally disorganized, with very few principles to guide us. But researchers in linguistics were beginning to formulate rules of grammar that were considerably more mathematical than before. And people began to realize that such methods are highly relevant to the artificial languages that were becoming popular for computer programming, even though natural languages like English remained intractable.[28]

Knuth also recounts his first, and rather inspirational, encounter with Chomsky's work in formal theoretical linguistics:

> I found the mathematical approach to grammar immediately appealing—so much so, in fact, that I must admit to taking a copy of Noam Chomsky's *Syntactic Structures* along with me on my honeymoon in 1961. During odd moments, while crossing the Atlantic in an ocean liner and while camping in Europe, I read that book rather thoroughly and tried to answer some basic theoretical questions. Here was a marvelous thing: a mathematical theory of language in which I could use a computer programmer's intuition! The mathematical, linguistic, and algorithmic parts of my life had previously been totally separate. During the ensuing years those three aspects became steadily more intertwined.[29]

Second—and even more importantly—computer scientists took note of Chomsky's "Three Models for the Description of Language." In this paper he proposed a four-part hierarchical classification of grammars: recursively enumerable, context sensitive, context free, and regular. Again, for considerations of space, we won't go into detail on each grammar and how, exactly, the hierarchy was (and still is) applied to programming languages.[30]

Suffice it to say, the Chomsky hierarchy proved especially useful to the minds hard at work on developing programming languages and compilers. In particular, it turned out that the context-free grammar that Chomsky mathematically laid out as $A \rightarrow \gamma$ (where A, a single nonterminal symbol is replaced by γ, a string of terminal and/or nonterminal symbols) was ideal for capturing the syntax of programming languages. In her insightful *Mind as Machine: A History of Cognitive Science*, Margaret Boden writes:

> Computer scientists were interested [in Chomsky's hierarchy] immediately. Similar research was already being done by some of them, but Chomsky's was a highly valued contribution. His distinction between context-free and regular grammars helped them to codify, respectively, the syntactic structure of artificial languages and the high-level structure of programs.[31]

Simply put, computer-language specialists benefitted, theoretically and—to some extent—practically, from novel ideas on language proposed in the 1950s in an obscure subfield of linguistics. Gerhard Jäger and James Rogers, the former a linguist and the latter a computer scientist, write of "the immense success of [Chomsky's hierarchical] framework, influencing not only linguistics to this day but also theoretical computer science."[32]

To sum up, we've argued that formal language theory's influence on computer technology, though ultimately trailblazing for the development of high-level programming languages, took a more indirect path. Chomsky never gave a captivating keynote address at some International Conference for Programming Geeks. He didn't personally collaborate with computer scientists to create a brilliant, new, high-level programming language. Instead, his early papers on language were published in tech journals (with tantalizing titles like *IRE Transactions on Information Theory*) that computer scientists read. And they took notice. So much so, in fact, that in their hefty manual *Programming Languages and Compilers*, authors Cocke and Schwartz conclude: "The systematic syntactic definition of ALGOL given in the two famous ALGOL reports, together with the work of Chomsky, aided greatly in popularizing the systematic view of syntax, in particular, the syntax of programming languages."[33]

Computer Technology's Effects on Language

Let's now relocate our analytical lens to the other side of our technolingual argument. In this latter part of our chapter we explore the fascinating and often under-recognized ways that the computer has shaped and continues to shape language. As always, we consider structures, practices, and ideologies of language, both written and spoken. And while much of our discussion and examples revolve around English, we nevertheless take pains to bring in research on computer-mediated communication (CMC) in other languages as well.

We open with a general overview of CMC. In this regard our discussion centers on the terminological and theoretical background for describing and categorizing its novel linguistic character, forms, and practices. Ultimately we see how linguists have wrestled with the question of whether and to what extent CMC is more like written or spoken language.

We follow this with a closer survey of two examples of CMC: email and the internet. For the former, we once again make the case that this technology has triggered an expansion of speakers' linguistic repertoires. To wit, computers have given speakers a virtual and seemingly boundless linguistic playground for experimenting with, challenging, and outright flouting established forms and practices—and for creating new ones. We also connect our discussion of this point back to our chapter's opening vignette. Moreover, as Danet and Herring show in their fantastic collection *The Multilingual Internet*, this phenomenon (i.e., the expanding linguistic repertoire) is also observable outside the English-speaking world. To this end we touch on the findings from studies of CMC in Egypt, Hong Kong, and Germany.

Thereafter we turn to the internet, where we make the case that, inasmuch as it's become a cavernous collecting basin for linguistic instantiations, the internet has revolutionized our knowledge base of language. Essentially, so our argument goes, this unprecedented repository of digitized data—linguistic and otherwise—has given researchers fresh insights, and led to new questions, about language. And in fact an entire new field of linguistic study has emerged.[34]

One quick note on the scope of our discussion, before we plunge in: As much as it pains us to admit, this chapter isn't the place to comprehensively tackle CMC and its multifarious effects on language. Keen minds have written prolifically and (mostly) superbly on this voluminous topic in the last three decades, and the pile of data that we'd want to consider now towers high—in short, we'd need a lot more time and space than afforded here to do an admissible job of covering the subject. But fret not, ye readers thirsty for more: in this sentence's endnote we've included some recommendations for further reading.[35]

Linguistic Encounters of a "Third Kind"? The Classification Quandary of CMC

In the summer of 2003 linguists descended on Toronto for the Eighth International Pragmatics Conference. In one particular workshop, "Interactive

Language in the Internet: Written, Spoken, or a Third Kind?" attendees explored whether internet users' words, grammatical structures, and pragmatics were closer to the way they would write or speak, or whether this computer-mediated linguistic communication presented a "new kind" of language altogether.[36] The investigative lead-up to this workshop, however, was more than two decades in the making.

In the early 1980s linguists took an interest in what they termed computer-mediated communication. At the time, examples of CMC included emails, list servers, and the "old-school" terminal program-based bulletin board systems. The study of CMC quickly blossomed into a linguistically and sociologically capacious field, with linguists leveling their sights on the structures (e.g., words, sentences, discourses, spelling, and punctuation), behavioral habits, and ideas that followed from people exchanging information through computational venues. And in fact, early on the same question that would occupy linguists twenty years later in Toronto—let's call it the "Classification Quandary"—came up: are the linguistic corollaries of CMC more like writing or speaking? "A central issue in the linguistic CMC-related discussion," Beißwenger and Storrer explain, "is the status of computer-mediated discourse relative to the distinction of orality and literacy, especially its status within the dichotomy of writing and speaking."[37]

In 1984, for instance, a young professor of linguistics at Brown University, Naomi Baron, argued that the "linguistic concept of 'register' [should be] extended to computer-based communications."[38] Speakers, she maintained, adopt a particular computer-mediated register or style of language, in effect "[using] computers as a replacement for writing and as a replacement for speech."[39] Ultimately, though, along her communication continuum she places computers next to "Traditional Writing."[40] It would seem, then, that Baron à la 1984 considered writing and CMC kissing cousins; speech, on the other hand, was a cousin thrice removed.

In a 1996 study of linguistic structures and practices of bulletin board systems, Collot and Belmore call CMC a "new variety of language," ultimately dubbing it "Electronic Language."[41] As for their part in the Classification Quandary, they conclude that Electronic Language is "clearly a 'hybrid' variety of English."[42] And by 2010, Baron's own terminological preferences have shifted. In her award-winning *Always On: Language in an Online and Mobile World* she refers to CMC as "electronic language" and "Internet language," designating platforms like instant messaging, blogs, and text messaging "new forms of language [that] are having profound impacts upon both the linguistic and social dimensions of human interaction."[43]

Elsewhere, popular linguist David Crystal adds his own bit to the Classification Quandary, calling the internet a "fourth dimension of linguistic communication."[44] His view holds that CMC "cannot be compared with either spoken or written language, even though it shares some features with both."[45] (This sounds a lot like Collot and Belmore's "hybrid variety.") Nevertheless, when push comes to shove it appears that Crystal leans toward Baron à la 1984: "On the whole, Internet language is better seen as written language which has been pulled some way in the direction of speech rather than as speech which has been written down."[46]

More recently, Jan Blommaert proposed the term "supervernacular" to capture CMC's novel forms and practices. "Supervernaculars," she explains, "are a particular and new type of sociolinguistic object: patterned semiotic forms that circulate in networks driven, largely, by relatively new technologies such as the Internet and mobile communication devices."[47] As such, she continues, speakers of supervernacular forms "share none of the traditional attributes of speech communities—territorial fixedness, physical proximity, socio-cultural sharedness and common backgrounds."[48] Blommaert offers mobile texting codes as an example. Referring to text messaging as both a "small vernacular" and "mini-language," she presents a series of symbols, linguistic and sociolinguistic rules that govern speakers' use.

Here we suggest that in order to resolve the Classification Quandary, you have to accept that there is no definite answer. The solution instead lies in a perspectivistic[49] approach to the problem. If you come at, say, instant messaging looking for attributes of written language, you'll find them. Just as you're sure to find traits of spoken language, if that's your aim. Whichever of the two perspectives you adopt, it will fit.

It would seem, then, that digital technologies (read, especially: the computer) have given us a slippery yet compelling instantiation of language—one that's redolent of both speaking and writing.

Behold: The Speech-Writing Continuum

Because of its dualistic qualities, most linguists prefer to describe CMC in terms of a multipoint cline instead of an either-or paradigm.[50] Crystal explains it thusly:

> It is more realistic to think of speech and writing as being the endpoints of a multidimensional continuum, within which varieties [of language] can be located as being "more or less like speech" or "more or less like writing." The varieties that form the Internet can be approached in this same way.[51]

Figure 4.8 is a vertical illustration of this kind of Speech-Writing Continuum. Descriptive characteristics of the medium are given on the left. Examples of the resulting linguistic communication are on the right.

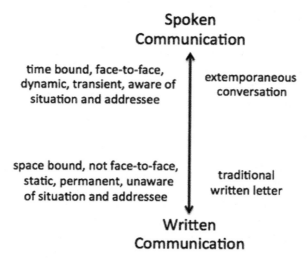

Spoken Communication

time bound, face-to-face, dynamic, transient, aware of situation and addressee — extemporaneous conversation

space bound, not face-to-face, static, permanent, unaware of situation and addressee — traditional written letter

Written Communication

FIGURE 4.8 *Speech-Writing Continuum. (Table based on Crystal,* Internet Linguistics; *Baron,* Always On; *and Christa Dürscheid's* Einführung in die Schriftlinguistik *(Göttingen: Vandenhoeck & Ruprecht, 2006), 32–62.)*

First, keep in mind that this continuum is conceptual; it stands for the notional constructs, residing in a speaker's mind, about how written and spoken language is "supposed" to look and sound. The descriptions on the left describe the characteristics of each form. Spoken language, you note, is restricted in time, place, and situation, yet fleetingly free and unruly in its delivered form. You also know at whom you're directing your language; thus you can accurately gauge the sociolinguistic situation. Take the following hypothetical exchange between you and a coworker at the water cooler (because, naturally, that's where all insipid office conversation occurs):

YOU: I really like your new hairstyle.
COWORKER: Thanks. I had it done yesterday and—okay, at first, you know, when I looked in the mirror, I wasn't—I guess you could say—entirely, a fan. But yeah . . . Thanks.

Your exchange passes only in that moment and within each other's presence, leaves no physical traces, and its linguistic structures are dynamic and variable. This *extemporaneous conversation* is what speakers notionally associate with "spoken communication."

At the other end of the continuum are the characteristics that speakers conceptually equate with "written communication." Think: a letter to your grandma. (Yes, an old-fashioned handwritten dispatch, crafted with that antique doohickey called a pen.) On the one hand, your language is freed from the clutches of time, transience, and variability. On the other hand, it's now in permanent form, spatially bound (i.e., as to the length and width of the paper), and largely fixed (i.e., you follow letter-writing conventions you were probably taught in school). And with written communication—unless you deliver it by hand, demand that the recipient read it in your presence, and then burn it on the spot—you can never be entirely certain about your addressee and the circumstances in which they read it. This isn't the case with spoken communication. Apart from being spied or eavesdropped on, you generally know the who/when/where/how your language is being received.

So where does CMC fall along this perceptual cline? The answer (which has a patent quantum-mechanical ring to it) is: everywhere in between and at many spots at once. Take instant messaging (IM). The linguistic forms and practices that you find among IM users don't occur face to face, but they are more time, situation, and addressee sensitive than a traditional written letter. You type in a comment, press send, and instantly it appears on your addressee's screen. As for the addressee and the situation, you're more aware of these than with a traditional letter, but not to the extent of an extemporaneous face-to-face conversation. Moreover, the IMs you send are clearly more permanent than the ephemeral sounds of speech. These features of IM would suggest a placement along the continuum closer to written communication. But the linguistic structures of IM tend to be dynamic and fluid (i.e., less orthographically and grammatically conventional), which suggests a placement more toward the opposite pole.

The takeaway here is that the forms and practices that have sprung up within this new computer-mediated linguistic landscape—to wit, the language we use for communicating through email, text messaging, IM, the internet, etc.—is something foreign, confounding, and fascinating. It's a linguistic encounter of a third kind.

The Incredible Expanding Linguistic Repertoire: The Language of Email

This section covers some of the linguistic forms and practices traceable to email technology. We consider, in turn: the variation in how users open and close messages; the spoken-dialogic character of email; and the text-manipulation capabilities of email that have spawned novel rhetorical practices—all features that, according to Crystal, "are central to the identification of email as a linguistic variety."[52] We round out this section with a look at language ideologies; we compare two style guides and the linguistic advice they offer email users. Similar to what we've seen with other communication technologies, all of these things (i.e., the structures, practices, and ideologies of email) amount to an expansion of speakers' linguistic repertoires.

Hard as it may be for the younger generation to believe, until roughly forty years ago the commonest way of exchanging written information across distances involved a tool that left marks on a material surface, which then had to be physically transferred between points of origin. And then, in the early 1970s, the traditional industry of letter correspondence was turned inside out when contractors working on the military's ARPANET—a computer-networking scheme generally recognized as the precursor to today's internet[53]—figured out a way for users to send "mail" to each other on their computers. One of these contractors, a programmer by the name of Ray Tomlinson, made perhaps the greatest linguistic mark on CMC posterity: it was his idea to include the @ symbol in every email address.[54]

Another important thing to keep in mind about email: because the technology was originally developed in a professional context, for communication among corporate and military personnel, Tomlinson and others modeled email on relevant forms and styles of written communication—in particular, the office memorandum. This is where email got its header formatting—the "To," "From," "Subject" or "Re," and "Date" fields, followed by a field for the actual message. Figure 4.9 compares the common layout of each communication type.

This new electronic option of sending messages took like wildfire to dry kindling: "Within a couple of years, 75% of all ARPANET traffic was email."[55]

It took another couple of decades before the service, by then commonly known as e-mail (with a hyphen), moved out of strictly academic and military domains and became available to the greater public. As you know, this group embraced the technology even more fervently. Such that by the time of this writing, the technology market research firm Radicati Group Inc. calculates that "the number of emails sent and received per day total[s] over 205 billion."[56] For Joe Schmo or Plain Jane down at the office, this translates into an average of more than 120 emails per day, whether sent or received.[57]

As you can imagine, when millions upon millions of people use language to communicate this often over a new medium, there's bound to be a lot of variation and novelty in both forms and practices. (In fact it would be downright weird and nonhuman-like if there weren't!) Linguists have been quick to note the variant character of the forms, practices, and ideologies associated with email communication. By the end of her *Alphabet to Email*, Baron concludes: "Email is clearly a language in flux."[58] Crystal, after sifting through piles of emails (among other electronic data), declares that "there is an enormous amount of idiosyncrasy and variation seen in e-encounters."[59] As for Crystal's eventual summation: "Email, in the final analysis ... is formally and functionally, unique."[60]

BUILDING + CODES DEPARTMENT
LES CROCKER, DIRECTOR

MEMORANDUM

TO: **Building Contractors & Electrical Contractors**

FROM: **Mike Baker**
             Building Official

RE: **Electric Permits**

DATE: **September 19, 2011**

Effective October 3, 2011: The City of Clarksville Building & Codes Department will issue electrical permits for projects inside the jurisdiction of the city.

This does not apply to Federal and State projects or projects located in the jurisdiction of Montgomery County government.

Should you have any questions with regard to this matter please do not hesitate to contact the office, 931-645-7426

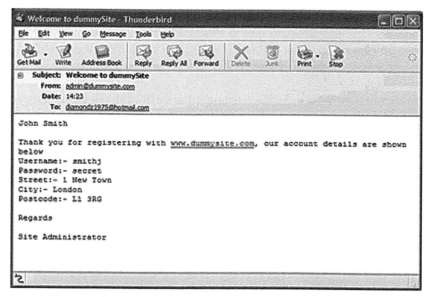

FIGURE 4.9 *Comparison of office memo and email common layouts. (http:// www.clarksvillehba.org/codes.htmlandhttp://www.bitethebullet.co.uk/ EmailTemplateFramework.aspx (accessed December 1, 2015).)*

Do you remember, back in elementary school, learning the proper way to write a letter? If so, you'll probably remember that the *first thing* you learned was how to start the correspondence: "Dear (name or appropriate title and name)" followed by a comma, space, and indentation for your impending paragraph. Well, this sociolinguistic convention was fine and good for correspondence by pen, typewriter, or digital word processor—which you still had to place in an envelope and trust would get to the intended recipient. There was something "formal" about the entire process. You *felt* that it demanded those standards you learned in school.

But then suddenly that physicality, of both medium and message itself, is taken away. Replaced by an altogether new medium—one that's immaterial and instant. What, then, of those learned standards? Do they still apply? If so, how do you know? If not, which new forms and practices should you substitute for the old ones? And with that, linguistic dithering ensues . . .

It's likely that something like this—call it, an emerging sense that linguistic norms previously learned and thought of as steadfast are beginning to wobble—these inklings of linguistic instability started to crop up in speakers' minds. This most likely would have unfolded in the 1990s, when email invaded offices and households en masse. Users started to question the sociolinguistic conventions they'd been indoctrinated with and that they'd been using for as long as they could remember.

Which brings us back to your schooling. (We're going to assume that you always paid perfect attention during class.) At some point during your education, you learned to start and end a letter with a "correct" word or phrase. A list of the salutation and valediction options you might have learned are given in Table 4.2.

Moreover, you're likely to have learned that each of these salutations corresponds to how you view your relationship with the recipient(s): whether you're on a first-name basis; how much you know about their job role; if it's the first time you're contacting them; etc.

In the early days of email, this two-part sociolinguistic paradigm (i.e., formal/informal) didn't apply as much. Inspired by the office memo form and style, email was used predominately for professional communication. But years later, as email took off within the general populace and people began using email for all kinds of communicative purposes, users fell back on the sociolinguistic paradigm they were taught in school.

But here comes the twist: some of email's technical features align it with written, and some with spoken, aspects of communication. First, email is mostly read and not heard. Second, an email's text can be edited before it's transmitted. On the other hand, email is like speech in that it often tends toward relaxedness in style and a more fluid organization of ideas. "With regard to such parameters as language style, assumptions about recipient responses, identity of audience, and presuppositions about durability of message, email seems to be Janus-faced—at once resembling and not resembling face-to-face speech."[61] What's more, as Baron argues in *From Alphabet to Email*, in the timespan that email was being developed and widely adopted, the enterprise of writing in general was undergoing a drift toward speech-like informality, begun in the mid-twentieth century.[62]

This broader textual trend, coupled with speech-redolent features of email, has resulted in some blurring of the sociolinguistic model once learned in school. In a 2001 opinion piece in *The New York Times*, Baron described—with an undertone of irritation—an email she got from a graduate student (whom she didn't know) that opened with "Hello Naomi" and closed with "OK NAOMI ... I really need your information as soon as possible."[63] Clearly, the flippant writing style doesn't reflect the student's real-world acquaintanceship with the recipient. Over the years we have ourselves experienced the occasional email whose greeting or closing prompted a raised brow. Table 4.3 shows a few of our all-time "favorites".

It would seem, then, that the openings and closings in Table 4.3 reflect what Baron calls the "three attributes that characterize a significant proportion of the messages sent today: informality of language style, psychological assumption that the medium is ephemeral, [and a] high level of candour."[64] However, in the students' defense we must clarify that student-to-instructor

TABLE 4.2 Salutations and valedictions for formal and informal traditional letters.

Formal Letter		Informal Letter	
Salutations	Valedictions	Salutations	Valedictions
[Title] + [last name]:	Best,	[First name],	Thanks,
Dear + [last name]:	Sincerely (yours),	Dear + [first name],	Ø +
Dear Sir or Madam:	Yours truly,	Dear + [familial title; e.g., Grandpa/	[first name],
To Whom It May Concern:	Very truly yours,	Mom].	Warmly,
[Professional Title] + [last name]	Cordially (yours),		Yours,
	Respectfully (yours),		Love,
	(Personal/Kindest) regards,		Fondly,

TABLE 4.3 List of author's favorite salutations and valedictions in student-sent emails.

Salutation	Valediction
Hi (Professor/Prof)	Let me know,
Hey (Professor/Prof)	
Hello (Professor/Prof)	∅
∅	Please respond,
Prof,	Confused,
Sup Prof,	:-)
Hola,	(or other smiley variant)
Question:	

emails with these kinds of questionable salutations and valedictions are still in the minority; most emails we get from students indicate that they're aware of traditional conventions for formal writing—conventions that they're carrying over into the new digital medium.

As for the office setting, it seems of late that workers' emails reveal just as much variety in their openings and closings. In a 2013 piece for *Forbes*, for instance, staff writer Susan Adams polled colleagues and four "people she'd consider experts" on how to conclude emails for the workplace, and the connotations the various sign-offs might have. Alone the title of Adams's piece should suffice to make our point: "57 Ways to Sign Off on an Email."[65]

But let's look at some empirical data. Table 4.4 gives the findings from our survey of thirty messages, chosen randomly, in the Enron email corpus.[66] All emails were sent between 2000 and 2002, either from former Enron CEO Jeff Skilling or his assistant Sherri Sera. The survey reveals a similar mix of salutations and valedictions, ranging from colloquial to formal.

These data suggest that, even in a decidedly professional setting, email as of 2001 was being adapted for multiple sociolinguistic conditions, from formal to personal, and with shifting openings and closings to accommodate this range of contexts. In fact, these observations dovetail with Waldvogel's 2007 study "Greetings and Closings in Workplace Email." Waldvogel looked at greetings and closings in more than 500 emails sent among the employees of two professional institutions—an educational organization and a manufacturing plant—in New Zealand. "The results of this study," the author concludes,

TABLE 4.4 Selection of salutations and valedictions in Enron emails.

Salutation	Valediction
Ø	Ø
Greetings + [first name],	[First name]
Dear + [title] + [last name],	Thank you, + [first name]
Dear + [first name]	Regards, + [first name]
[First name],	Best regards, [first name]
Gentlemen,	[Initials]
Ladies and Gentlemen,	Thanks + [initials]
Hi + [first name]	Regards, + [initials]
	Thank you + [first & last name]
	Yours faithfully + [first name] + [smiley]
	[First name] + [smiley]
	Sincerely + [first & last name]

"show considerable variation in the use made of greetings and closings in the two organizations."[67]

Apart from openings and closings, linguists have pointed out the dialogic character of email communiqués. This is especially apparent when an asynchronous email exchange (i.e., there's lag time between sent email and response) turns into a semi-synchronous back-and-forth volley of missives (i.e., I shoot you an email while you're at your computer, and you immediately read it and reply). Here's what we mean:

Original Message

FROM: JohnRoe@example.com
TO: JaneDoe@example.com
DATE: Tuesday, Dec 1, 2015, 1:20 pm
SUBJECT: Email Transcriptions
Hi Jane,
I'm doing some research on emails. Would you be willing to help out with the transcriptions?
-John
____

Reply #1

FROM: JaneDoe@example.com
TO: JohnRoe@example.com
DATE: Tuesday, Dec 1, 2015, 1:32 pm
SUBJECT: Re: Email Transcriptions
Hi John,
Thanks for your message. Yes, I'm willing to help out. Approx. how many emails are we talking about?
-Jane
____

Reply #2

FROM: JohnRoeexample.com
TO: JaneDoe@example.com
DATE: Tuesday, Dec 1, 2015, 1:33 pm
SUBJECT: Re: Email Transcriptions
Great, thanks! There are fifty emails in the data set. Is that doable?
-JR
____

Reply #3

FROM: JaneDoe@example.com
TO: JohnRoe@example.com
DATE: Tuesday, Dec 1, 2015, 1:34 pm
SUBJECT: Re: Email Transcriptions
When would you need this by?
-Jane
____

Reply #4

FROM: JohnRoe@example.com
TO: JaneDoe@example.com
DATE: Tuesday, Dec 1, 2015, 1:35 pm
SUBJECT: Re: Email Transcriptions
By the end of next week at the latest. Thoughts?
-JR
____

Reply #5

FROM: JaneDoe@example.com
TO: JohnRoe@example.com
DATE: Tuesday, Dec 1, 2015, 1:37 pm
SUBJECT: Re: Email Transcriptions
That works. Send them over.

Reply #6

FROM: JohnRoe@example.com
TO: JaneDoe@example.com
DATE: Tuesday, Dec 1, 2015, 1:38 pm
SUBJECT: Re: Email Transcriptions
Great! Folder with emails attached.

Most users of email have experienced this kind of semi-synchronous exchange. The result is often a staccato, dialogic structure of communication more redolent of speaking than writing. Crystal also associates with this dialogic character "a greater intensity of questioning than in traditional letters."[68]

In addition, the technical features that let users manipulate emailed text have spawned new linguistic practices. Text intercalation is a case in point. To "intercalate" basically means to insert something between existing layers of something else. Imagine a five-layered cake. (Feel free to make said imaginary cake your favorite flavor.) After baking the layers and letting them cool, you stack them. But then you decide you want icing between each of the four layers. So you fill a pouch with icing, stick the tip between each layer, and squeeze in the saccharine gooeyness. Ergo, you've intercalated the cake with icing. Figure 4.10 gives a basic illustration of the intercalation process.

Now replace the cake layers with the text of a sent email, and the layers of icing with the text of the response to this email. For instance, John Roe gets the following message from Jane Doe:

FROM: JaneDoe@example.com
TO: JohnRoe@example.com
DATE: Thursday, Dec 3, 2015, 8:06 am
SUBJECT: Reports
Hi John,

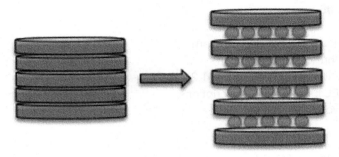

FIGURE 4.10 *Basic illustration of intercalation process. The flat cylinders are the cake layers. The round blobs represent the intercalations of icing.*

I finally heard back from the higher-ups about the reports we sent last week. They have a few questions regarding both the formatting and content. So it looks like we'll need to get the group together again and go over some things. Can you and I meet tomorrow first thing and get this started? Apologies in advance if I'm late in getting your response. (I'm leaving the office now for a doctor's appointment.)
    Thanks,
    Jane

John then intercalates the text of his reply with segments from Jane's original message:

FROM: JohnRoe@example.com
TO: JaneDoe@example.com
DATE: Thursday, Dec 3, 2015, 9:01 am
SUBJECT: Re: Reports
Jane,
Got your email. Below my comments:
I finally heard back from the higher-ups about the reports we sent last week.
Finally! I was starting to wonder if all that work was going to go unnoticed . . .
They have a few questions regarding both the formatting and content.
I suspected they might . . . If you get this message in time, can you pass on their questions so I can start thinking about solutions?
Can you and I meet tomorrow first thing and get this started?
Yes. I'll be in the office at 8. Does that work?
(I'm leaving the office now for a doctor's appointment.)
Everything ok?
-John

As this example shows, email technology enables users to manipulate text in ways that, though physically possible (e.g., reprinting the sender's comments in your own paper reply), were not practiced in traditional letter writing. Email's text-editing functionalities—especially intercalation—give it a unique stylistic profile. When email users adopt new forms and practices like this, they're effectively expanding their existing linguistic repertoire.

Beyond English: CMC's Effects on Other Languages

Outside of the English-speaking landscape, we find evidence that email has influenced, and continues to influence, language in similar ways. In a 2007 study, Carmen K. M. Lee, a professor of linguistics at the Chinese University of Hong Kong, examined forms and practices involving emails sent by Cantonese speakers in Hong Kong. Using nearly 200 messages, collected from seventy-two subjects, ages 15–24, she looked at Cantonese-English code mixing, and the variation in how speakers represent Cantonese graphically. Her study ultimately "identified five forms of 'code' created and used in different combinations by Hong Kong CMC users: standard English, standard Chinese, Cantonese represented in characters, romanized Cantonese, and morpheme-by-morpheme literal translations."[69] Prior to email (and other CMC technologies) this much variation in, and experimentation with, written communication was uncommon in Hong Kong.

A similarly new and exciting linguistic phenomenon has been observed by Warschauer and company in their study "Language Choice Online: Globalization and Identity in Egypt."[70] In the early 2000s, the research team administered questionnaires among, and collected emails from, forty-three young professionals in Cairo. The questionnaire targeted linguistic forms and practices common among the participants' interactions through email. Analyses of their actual digital correspondences then looked for empirical evidence supporting or contesting the questionnaire's results. The linguists were shocked to find that participants largely used a mixture of English and Egyptian Arabic—which, by the way, the participants wrote with Roman letters and not in the traditional Arabic *abjad*—in their e-communications. In the researchers' words:

> Classical Arabic in Arabic script, the most common form of writing in Egypt, was seldom used by any of the 43 participants. Rather, online communications featured a new and unusual diglossia—involving a foreign language, English, and a romanized, predominantly colloquial form of Arabic that had very limited use for these informants prior to the development of the Internet.[71]

Thus, beyond the microcosmic English-speaking world there is evidence that email affects linguistic repertoires in like fashion by enlarging the palette of linguistic forms and practices at a speaker's disposal.

The How-tos of Email: Language Ideologies and Prescriptive Guides

We now come to the ideologies that have emerged out of this language-digitizing technology. And instead of just presenting an arbitrary rundown of do-this-and-avoid-that excerpts from style guides, we're going to argue that these prescriptive texts themselves reflect the fluid and hybrid character of email. We anchor this argument with a survey of style guides published between 1992 and 2013, with a particular eye to how these manuals advise readers on spelling and punctuation.

A basic search on Amazon (at the time of this writing) for "how to write emails" renders dozens of results. Here is a sample of fifteen titles, published between 1992 and 2013:

The Guy Kawasaki Computer Curmudgeon (1992)
Netiquette (1994)
Elements of E-Mail Style (1994)
Wired Style: Principles of English Usage in the Digital Age (1999)
Business E-Mail: How to Make It Professional and Effective (2002)
Writing Effective E-Mail: Improving Your Electronic Communication (2003)
E-Mail: A Write It Well Guide. How to Write and Manage E-Mail in the Workplace (2005)
The Executive Guide to E-Mail Correspondence (2006)
The Art of E-Mail Writing (2007)
E-Email Etiquette Made Easy (2007)
SEND: Why People Email So Badly and How to Do It Better (2008)
E-Etiquette: The Definitive Guide to Proper Manners in Today's Digital World (2010)
Email Etiquette for Business Success: Use Emotional Intelligence to Communicate Effectively in the Business World (2011)
Email Mistakes: How to Avoid Looking Like an Idiot (2012)
Write Better Emails: How to Stand Out by Being Short, Civil, and Savvy (2013)

First, notice how the accepted standard of spelling "email" has shifted. The manuals published from 1994 to 2007 give it a hyphen and sometimes capitalize it.[72] This was probably in analogy to constructions like "A-bomb" and

"C-section." Later titles—and indeed many that we did not list here—largely jettison the hyphen, with "email" writ miniscule.

Second, notice that most of these handbooks address the how-tos of email communication for professional contexts. "Whether you're writing a thank-you to a client," the author exhorts the reader of *Business E-Mail*, "an invitation to a lunch honoring a co-worker, a reminder about a department meeting, an announcement about your company's participation in a volunteer project, a proposal, a request for a quote, or a direct sales pitch, your e-mail message represents your business."[73] The book's ensuing 100+ pages offer conservative guidance for both practices (e.g., when to send, respond, forward, cc, etc.) and forms (e.g., grammar, spelling, punctuation, and word usage) associated with emailing at the office. Fraser's self-published booklet *Email Etiquette for Business Success* offers an "emotionally intelligent" angle for professional communication via email. Largely forgoing linguistic structures, it focuses instead on how professionals can harness the "ability to recognize and be aware of [their] emotions and those of others" in order to communicate more effectively at work and, therefore, "help YOU be successful."[74]

A few of these fifteen sample titles also offer advice on using email in your personal life. In their introduction to *SEND: Why People Email So Badly and How to Do It Better*, authorial duo Shipley and Schwalbe explain:

> We are bosses and employees, mothers and daughters, and sisters, scolders and comforters, encouragers and discouragers—and we constantly blend and change roles.... Email demands that we figure out who we are in relation to the person we're writing and that we get our tone right from the outset.[75]

Complete with cautionary tales of individuals getting misunderstood, offended, lambasted, fired, and/or sued due to unwary email activity, *SEND* covers a lot of ground, on both forms and practices. Among others, it extends advice on when and when not to send emails; how to compose emails; what to do about emotional emails that you receive; and even how to avoid "emails that can land you in jail."[76]

Author and self-proclaimed "Email Etiquette Expert"—as taken verbatim from the volume's back cover—Judith Kallos casts her prescriptivist net just as wide in *E-Mail Etiquette Made Easy*. In an early chapter titled, "Who Needs E-Mail Etiquette?" she asserts:

> Everyone who is online should want to use technology with knowledge, understanding, and courtesy.... This is not an issue that only applies to certain people, countries, or locations online. E-Mail Etiquette applies to every one of us who chooses to participate.[77]

Except for the occasional reference to spelling, punctuation, word choice, acronyms, and emoticons, Kallos's guide mainly targets everyday email practices—with an unabashed emphasis on the "right" or "proper" ways of using email. She instructs on how long to wait before replying to an email or for a reply to your own email; handling rude messages; setting up auto-replies; and email privacy. The author has a starkly vested interest in e-etiquette: it turns out that she's also the founder and promoter of netmanners.com, a site dedicated to "discussing the challenges and dilemmas we all face at one point or another [as to our email habits and skills]."[78]

This, then, is a sampling of what you'll encounter if you're ever in the market for a *vade mecum* on "Achieving Professional and Personal Success with Email."

But let's get down to our central argument, namely, that a comparison of email style guides showcases the technology's stylistic and ideological shapeshifter-ness. As evidence for this argument, we've shown how the content of fifteen manuals, penned between 1991 and 2014, reflects the "linguistic elasticity" associated with the use and perceptions of email.

Take spelling and grammar. Already in the early 1990s there was wrangling over orthography. Virginia Shea reports:

> Actually, there's a controversy on the net—not exactly raging, but ongoing—over how important these issues [of spelling and grammar] are. Some people believe that electronic communication should be spontaneous and from-the-hip. They don't think anyone should worry about spelling and grammar. Others feel it's worthwhile to think before you post, and that bad spelling and grammar make a bad impression.[79]

Thus, the question was whether or to what extent the traditional norms for "writing well" should be foisted on the new medium. The fifteen manuals we canvassed illustrate differing viewpoints, furthermore echoing email's sociolinguistically dynamic character. Let's look more closely, then, at a few of these manuals.

In his cheeky, Ambrose Bierce–inspired[80] *The Guy Kawasaki Computer Curmudgeon* from 1992, the author recommends "[ignoring] stylistic and grammatical considerations," because "e-mail is supposed to be fast, tit-for-tat communication."[81] The authors of *Wired Style* are even more unabashed in their casting off of traditional orthographic rules. Email, they insist, is "a cross between a conversation and a letter," in which "spelling and punctuation are loose and playful."[82] Overall they make a vehement plea for the colloquialization of email style:

> Write the way people talk. Don't insist on "standard" English. Use the vernacular, especially that of the world you're writing about. And avoid lowest-denominator editing: don't sanitize and don't homogenize.[83]

As we've seen, the observation that email trends in the direction of informal, speech-like writing was far from new. And it wasn't just linguists. Style guides also took note of this. In *The Elements of E-Mail Style*—Angell and Heslop's digital twist on Strunk and White's classic—the authors concede that email "makes different demands on writing style and has its own unique conventions."[84] Moreover, they note that the technology "encourages an informal, conversational style of writing because it's an instantaneous and one-on-one medium of communication."[85]

Nevertheless, Angell and Heslop are still advocates of pre–digital age standards. For instance, they include a fifteen-page chapter on "Minding Your Mechanics," in which they emphasize the importance of checking spelling and capitalizing correctly.[86] Indeed, there's a palpable, old-school grammarian tang to many of the subchapters listed in the book's table of contents. A small sample: "Use Commas for Clearer Prose," "Use the Active Voice Most of the Time," "Control Your Dangling and Misplaced Modifiers," and "Avoid Sentence Fragments and Run-on Sentences." Thus, while Angell and Heslop acknowledge email's budding vernacularism—"it has its own needs and conventions," they note[87]—they nevertheless fall back on established forms and practices.

As for the authorial coterie of *E-Etiquette: The Definitive Guide to Proper Manners in Today's Digital World*, published in 2010—when it comes to advice on spelling, grammar, and style in electronic communication, these authors come across as dye-in-the-wool traditionalists. "Pay close attention to your usage and grammar," they advise.[88] They furthermore remind the reader that "an e-mail is not a telegram," and instruct them to "write in complete sentences; not write in all lowercase letters; avoid the overuse of punctuation; and not have more than one or two topics in your email."[89]

These four style guides, taken as a representative sample for the dozens of handbooks on the market between 1991 and 2014, offer differing advice on the linguistic forms that one may or may not, or ought or ought not, use for communicating via email. As such, they reflect the linguistically pliable character of the technology itself.

Where No Linguist Has Gone Before, or How the Internet has Revolutionized Our Knowledge Base of Language

So far, we've considered how the computer has affected linguistic structures and ideologies in direct ways, that is, the words, forms of discourse, and language-focal beliefs that have emerged out of speakers' digitally mediated communication. In this last section, however, we pull our analytical lens back from the structural and ideological specifics of how CMC technology has shaped language. Our argument here is more general: we propose that one computer-based technology in particular has transformed the potentiality of language exploration. The internet, we contend, has given linguists a never-before-seen vantage point for studying, and ultimately understanding more about, language. Moreover, this technolingual development has hatched a new field of language study altogether: internet linguistics.

We start by looking at what makes the internet particularly exciting and useful for linguistics—namely, linguistic corpora. We then turn our attention to internet linguistics and describe its main topics, approaches, and goals. We wrap up by presenting a case study—more specifically, a web-based research project—that illustrates the potentiality of language exploration when language corpora and internet linguistics meet.

Piles and Piles of Language: Linguistic Corpora

Peer into every nook and cranny of the World Wide Web and you find some form of language—written, spoken, or signed. This ethereal, globally entwined network of digitized information has become, in Crystal's words, "the largest database of language the world has ever seen."[90]

Most of this language is heterogeneous. The internet does not demand this or that standardized form of language (as opposed to other media venues like radio, TV, or newspapers); instead, the language of cyberspace flaunts a kaleidoscope of variation—whether socially, geographically, or ideolectally motivated.

Just as you can find a vlog (i.e., video blog) from a woman in Madrid articulating a well-honed variety of standard Castilian Spanish, you can just as sure find another vlog from a woman in Mexico City who speaks in a colloquial, slang-riddled variety of Latin American Spanish. In fact, "[the] web is stylistically so diverse that it makes little sense to talk about 'the language of the web' at all."[91]

Thus, what we find on the web, albeit expressed through various outputs (e.g., tweets, blogs, email, gaming, IM), is a mirroring of the linguistic diversity in the real world—except that this diversity, scattered and ephemeral in the physical world, exists within a contained and timeless cyberspatial arena.

Never before in the history of our species has so much language, and so many different manifestations of this language, been pooled together and housed in a single place. And here's the cherry atop the linguistic sundae: a good chunk of it is free for the taking, covered by neither copyright nor intellectual property laws. All you need is a digital device, an internet connection, and a lot of time on your hands to cruise the vast expanses of the cyber-linguistic steppes. "With little effort," Beißwenger and Storrer argue, "linguistic data can be retrieved from public access CMC platforms or from the archives of client programs of e-mail, news and instant messaging services."[92]

Say, for instance, that your research interest is artistic performativity and variation in African American Vernacular English (AAVE). And your targeted data set is the lyrics of underground hip-hop: its words, sounds, syntax, and language ideologies. No problem—the internet has what you need. Rap Genius, for example, is a crowdsourced online repository of thousands of hip-hop songs. It contains both the audio and textual transcriptions of song lyrics, so you can read along as you listen.

But Rap Genius is more than just listening and reading along. The site also "breaks down text with line-by-line annotations, added and edited by anyone in the world."[93] In other words, this online software gives linguists more than just structural linguistic data. When other speakers contribute comments on and annotations of the songs, they are providing sociolinguistic and perceptual data as well. "While lyrics databases have been around since the days of Usenet," Charlie Lock writes in *Wired*, "crowdsourced tools like Rap Genius have been a boon to linguists."[94] Darrin Flynn, an associate professor at the University of Calgary whose research focuses on rap linguistics, is one such linguist who's benefited from Rap Genius.[95] "For any huge-scale study of language," he notes, "there's now this database with thousands upon thousands of songs."[96]

From personal emails and open chat rooms to crowdsourced knowledge-base sites like wikis and social media—the internet is a bottomless yet centralized receptacle for linguistic forms and practices that occur around the clock and on an enormous international scale. Baldly put: it's a linguist's dream come true.

Believe it or not, though, there's almost *too* much content on the internet for linguists to handle. "There has never been a language corpus as large as this one," Crystal writes, adding that "this constitutes a challenge to linguists wanting to explore this medium."[97] But linguists are a crafty, relentless bunch. And early on they began organizing material into smaller, more workable corpora.

The idea of assembling corpora was first formally addressed in 1989 at the annual conference for the Association of Computational Linguistics.[98] Three years later a thirty-three-page article appeared in Oxford University's journal *Literary and Linguistic Computing*, in which the authors aimed "to identify the principal aspects of corpus creation and the major decisions to be made when creating an electronic text corpus."[99] A few years after that (1997, to be exact) a trio of linguists gave a paper at the Eighteenth International Conference on English Language Research on Computerised Corpora (ICAME), focusing specifically on "Language Corpora and the Internet." Their main argument: corpora and the internet are "a joint linguistic resource."[100]

By the turn of the millennium the internet was no longer some bashful ingénue at the linguists ball; it was a respectable grande dame. In 2001, for instance, Australian linguist David Lee launched a website dedicated to corpus-based linguistics. In addition to general information on software, conferences, and journals, Lee started a list of language corpora available on the web. At the time of this writing, his list includes dozens of corpora for several languages[101] and in various modalities (i.e., written, spoken, contemporary, and even historical collections of language).

Another popular online locale for web-based language corpora is Brigham Young University's site, created by Professor of Linguistics Mark Davies. As of January 2016 it reports that "more than 130,000 distinct researchers, teachers, and students each month" use it to explore language in the digital age.[102] Finally, 2008 saw the first book-length publication on the topic of internet-based corpus linguistics: *Corpus Linguistics and the Web*.[103] "This publication constitutes another important step in the establishment of web linguistics as the currently most rewarding approach in corpus linguistics," one reviewer praised.[104] The volume includes fifteen articles, reviews, and case studies informed by linguistic data taken from web-based corpora.

And just what are these "corpora" we speak of, you ask? For starters, the word itself is the plural form of Latin *corpus*, meaning "body"—in the figurative sense of "a body" or "collection" of something. Thus corpora are "bodies" or "collections" of language, whether spoken, written, or signed. Second, these collections of language aren't just randomly thrown together; on the contrary, creators often assemble specific modalities and varieties of language, for targeted research. Which means that, third, many corpora include transcriptions of linguistic data. And all this makes many a linguist—whose professional lifeblood often depends on the availability of empirical data—very, very happy. Table 4.5 gives five examples, and short descriptions, of notable corpora available on the web (at the time of this writing).

A Newcomer to the Field: Internet Linguistics

As mentioned above, this revolutionary state of linguistic affairs (i.e., the presence and accessibility of an unprecedented amount of linguistic data on the web) has given rise to a new field of study. Internet linguistics investigates all manners and forms of linguistic expression facilitated by, cataloged in, and emerging within, the global digital network. Linguist David Crystal gets credit for delivering the first official guidebook, aptly titled *Internet Linguistics*. "What I, as a linguist, see on the Internet," Crystal asserts, "is a remarkable expansion of the expressive options available in a language."[105] This point should sound familiar to you, Dear Reader; it's

TABLE 4.5 Examples of notable corpora on the web.

Corpus	Description
sms4science	Large-scale collection of multilingual Swiss text messages[106]
British National Corpus (BNC)	100 million–word collection of samples of written and spoken language from a wide range of sources, designed to represent a wide cross-section of British English, both spoken and written, from the late twentieth century[107]
Corpus of Contemporary American English (COCA)	Contains more than 520 million words of text; is equally divided among spoken, fiction, popular magazines, newspapers, and academic texts; includes 20 million words each year from 1990–2015; and is updated regularly[108]
National Center for Sign Language and Gesture Research (NCSLGR) Corpus	Substantial corpus of American Sign Language (ASL) video data from native signers. Multiple synchronized high-quality video files (available in a variety of formats) showing signing from different angles as well as a close-up view of the face[109]
Bulgarian National Reference Corpus	Collection of 400 million tokens of written Bulgarian, taken from various genres[110]

cousin to our argument that technologies often prompt an expansion of their users' linguistic repertoires.

And, in fact, Crystal argues that this "expansion of expression options" should form the fulcrum of the new field. The linguistic smorgasbord on the internet "far exceeds the kinds of stylistic expansion that took place with the arrival of printing and broadcasting," he writes, stressing that "we need to understand how electronically mediated language works, how to exploit the strengths and avoid the dangers."[111] In this respect, Crystal's vision of internet linguistics—which, in 2011, he claimed was still in its infancy—departs from the sociolinguistic approach and leans toward the applied side of things. Note, here, that by "applied" we mean using theories, models, data, methods, and findings to solve real-world problems, and not just the issues that intellectuals in the academy identify and study (although these issues can and often do have real-world value, too!).

Crystal's book offers descriptive chapters on the internet as a new medium, language change and the internet, the multilingual nature of the internet, and applied internet linguistics. In one chapter he even recounts a case where internet linguistics was used forensically—specifically, to capture internet predators. In fact he concludes that it's through criminological applications such as these that "the developing branch of Internet linguistics can make a significant contribution."[112]

At the time of this writing, at least one institution of higher learning has even started a degree program in internet linguistics—with a discernible slant toward the applied track. At the Philipps-University of Marburg, located in the central German state of Hessen, you can earn a master's degree in linguistics and web technology.[113] Per the program brochure posted on the university's website: "The aim of this program is to prepare graduates for professions and/or to expand occupational fields by combining the theoretical contents of linguistics with modern technologies and methods for the application of this specialist knowledge."[114]

Wordnik: A Case Study

Finally, let's take a look at a recent (and fascinating) linguistic endeavor made possible by the internet. And keep in mind our overarching argument with regard to language and the internet, namely, that exploratory undertakings of this sort, facilitated by digital technology like the internet, deepen our meta-linguistic knowledge base (metalinguistic in the sense that we learn about language through researching language).

Our case in point is Wordnik, an online dictionary of the English language first launched in 2009 by Erin McKean, Grant Barrett, and Orion Montoya. Their linguistic credentials are solid: each worked in Oxford University Press's US dictionaries division, helping to keep current one of the largest—containing more than 300,000 lexical entries—and most prestigious dictionaries of English, the Oxford English Dictionary (OED). Wordnik, you might say, is an effort to go where the OED cannot so easily go. Wordnik endeavors to capture and catalog the overlooked words of old—in printed material from all genres and from all ages—and the newest of new words in English. It targets the words kicking around in cyberspace, whether in a random person's partially sober, late night blog entry or a journalist's stone-cold-sober piece in the Huffington Post—words that haven't yet reached, or would find resistance from, established lexical authorities. Co-creator McKean summarizes the philosophy behind Wordnik as such:

We believe that every word of English—no matter how new, old, obscure, slangy, or specialized—deserves a place in the dictionary, and that as much data as possible about every word should be easily and openly accessible by both people and computers.[115]

Indeed, McKean and her colleagues have been busy putting this idea into practice. Wikipedia reports that "Wordnik has collected a corpus of billions of words which it uses to display example sentences, allowing it to provide information on a much larger set of words than a typical dictionary."[116] But what makes Wordnik even cooler is that it invites subscribers to contribute to its lexical database. "To add a word to Wordnik," the website explains on its FAQ page, "simply look it up! If we haven't seen the word before, we'll add it to our database and start tracking it."[117] Thus Wordnik not only draws from the extant pool of analogically and digitally logged words, it's also a crowdsourced, bottom-up enterprise.

Now, any linguist worth their salt will tell you that the size of the English language lexicon (i.e., its inventory of words) is unfathomable: English is spoken, as an acquired first or second language, or as a foreign language, by around 500 million people in dozens of countries.[118] Moreover, embedded within each of these major speech communities are innumerable sub-speech communities: speakers with varying regional dialects, social registers, slang, occupational jargon, etc. And that's just present-day English. Add a *historical* element to this sociolinguistic equation and you're looking at billions upon billions of words.

But this Sisyphean undertaking doesn't seem to daunt Wordnik's founders. In September 2015 they began a month-long Kickstarter campaign to add a million missing words to the dictionary. With the rallying cry, "Let's give a million missing words their rightful places in the dictionary," the Wordnik team set a fundraising goal of $50,000.[119] And apparently there were other netizens out there who shared McKean et al.'s interest in the "lexical 'dark matter' "[120] of English: by the third week of the campaign, the monetary goal was reached. At the time of this writing, the latest blog update on the million-word effort reports that they have already begun "parsing roughly 3.5 billion words."[121] Truly a remarkable linguistic venture—made possible by the internet.

The Digitization of Language and Technolingualism

This chapter focused on technology that, we've argued, resulted in a digitization of language. The graphic markings of writing were turned into abstract sequences of ones and zeros. Language, multifaceted and uniquely human, became binary code for computer consumption. Moreover, we adhered to our technolingual platform, that is, we considered how language both shaped and was shaped by computer technology.

We began with language's influence on computers. We showed how writing systems interacted with digital word-processing technology, that the way a language is captured by written symbols—as a single phone, syllable, or word—informed the digital-coding schemes that software engineers invented for representing text in a computer's memory. Thus, while seven or eight bits were enough to digitize alphabets, logographic writing systems prompted coding schemes of (at least) sixteen bits.

Next, we described the role that linguistics played for computer programming. Although this influence unfolded along a less direct route, we nevertheless showed that Chomsky's work on formal grammars and theoretical syntax moved programmers to view their work in new ways. As a result, the budding field of programming-language theory started shifting toward the formalized, linguistic-y framework that has become today's standard.

For the second part of this chapter we fixed our investigative monocle on the other side of our technolingual argument. We considered how two language-digitizing technologies—email and the internet—have affected and continue to affect language. Our overall assertion was that these technologies have motivated an expansion of users' linguistic repertoires.

Email in particular, we saw, brandishes stylistic elements of both written and spoken language, and a broader range of variation than traditional writing. In other words, email has spawned new linguistic forms, practices, and language ideologies. We saw that speakers use a range of salutations and valedictions, often in ways that differ from traditional writing. And in Egypt, email has even breathed orthographic life into a formerly non-written variety of Arabic. Moreover, email's digital format and text manipulation functions allow users to craft written exchanges in novel ways, for example by intercalating text.

We also reviewed several prescriptive texts on email—since, we argued, such texts play a role in how speakers form their attitudes, beliefs, and judgments (i.e., language ideologies) of email. We showed that these guides differ in their proclamations of "correct" email forms and practices. We concluded that this divergence of prescribed norms reflects the linguistically hybrid state of email itself.

We finished our discussion of the digitization of language with a look at how the internet has impacted language. Our primary claim was that the internet has revolutionized the potentiality for exploring language. To wit, the web has increased our knowledge base of language by: 1) serving as a limitless repository of language, in all modalities and varieties, and 2) giving linguists (and others interested in language) access to this linguistic data. Accordingly, the internet has yielded an entire new discipline for linguistic investigation, internet linguistics.

In Chapter 5 of our technolingual exploration, we're going to consider the reciprocal influence of language and mobile phones—a technolingual phenomenon we're calling (surprise, surprise!) the *mobilization* of language.

Second Interlude

Comparing Linguists' and Nonlinguists' Takes on CMC's Effect on Language

When pressed, most linguists will acknowledge that computerized technology does shape—to varying degrees—language structures, practices, and ideologies. But as we'll see below, linguists often leaven their opinions with diplomatic delicacy, tending toward roundabout phrasing or judicious hedging. Why? Well, no linguist wants to be accused of unscholarly sensationalism.[1]

Nonlinguists, on the other hand, have traditionally been quicker to the punch, louder, and both more direct and pessimistic in their claims about how technology affects the way people write and/or speak. Moreover, while the two camps (i.e., linguists and nonlinguists) tread common ground in the general belief that devices like computers and cell phones do influence language in some way, we'll see that they clearly part ways when it comes to particulars, especially as to the extent and nature of how the one influences the other.

Linguists' Take

Let's begin with the linguists. A few examples, each from a different linguist, should suffice in making the following point: linguists largely agree with nonlinguists that digital technologies can shape language; however, scientists of language are more rhetorically diplomatic. "It can now be said with confidence," Rowe and Wyss declare in the preface of their 2009 volume *Language and New Media: Linguistic, Cultural, and Technological Evolutions*, "that the particular characteristics, features, and uses of the medium strongly affect the nature and, usually, the resultant form of the communication."[2] In that same year, Bodomo Adams's *Computer-Mediated Communication for Linguistics and Literacy* echoed Rowe and Wyss's argument:

> There is a causal relationship between the emergence of new tools and media of communication and the creation of new forms of language and communication. New tools and media of communication demand the creation of new forms and ways of communication. These new forms compete with existing forms and ways of communication, leading to changes in the way we use language in its various forms, including spoken and written forms.[3]

And what about well-known CMC scholar Naomi Baron? Well, in her award-winning *Always On: Language in an Online and Mobile World*, she at one point advances the claim that "IM, blogs, text messages and the like ... are having profound impacts upon both the linguistic and social dimensions of human interaction."[4] At other points, however, she appears to rein in her sweeping prognosis, adopting a rhetorical sobriety more typical of academics. "Our data on IM and text messaging suggest that ... electronic language is at most a very minor dialectal variation."[5] Elsewhere she sneaks palliative "mays" into her summations. For example, of digital media's role in shifting language ideologies she writes: "[The] outpouring of text fostered by informational communication technology may be redefining our standards for the written word."[6]

Finally, David Crystal approaches the subject with even more tentativeness. In his *Language and the Internet* from 2006 he stresses that "it is important to think twice before making overextended claims and wild predictions about the stability or endurability of the technolinguistic changes of the moment."[7] And five years on, in his *Internet Linguistics*, his tone is similarly guarded: "Only a very small proportion of a language's vocabulary, grammar, and orthography has been affected [by the internet]."[8] Still, he does acknowledge the internet's overall potential to affect language. "The main evidence of language change on the Internet," he concludes, "is [to be found] in the discourse patterns that characterize the various outputs."[9]

Nonlinguists' Take

So how does the popular (i.e., nonlinguist) scene view the issue? Their take boils down to two words: exaggeration and pessimism. As we'll see below, when it comes to the question of digital technology's impact on language, nonlinguists—especially in the print media—have tended toward hyperbole and general prognoses of impending linguistic doom. In an opinion piece for *The Irish Times*, for example, one exasperated reader, seemingly fed up with what they see on cell phone screens, asks: "Am I the only person in Ireland, I wonder, who considers this kind of bastardisation of English the most pernicious assault on spelling, grammar and punctuation that we've ever encountered?"[10]

Much of this linguistic angst is impressionistically conditioned, that is, it stems from this or that person's personal (and often vaguely reconstructed) "experiences" with CMC. Such impressions also tend to be anecdotally based, tying in with this or that distressing account of "What Technology Is Doing To Language." One famous case from 2003 was the Scottish schoolgirl who, the *Daily Telegraph* alleged, treated an assigned essay like a text message.[11] The article reported that the girl began her composition: "My smmr hols wr CWOT. B4, we usd 2go2 NY 2C my bro, his GF & thr 3:- kds FTF. ILNY, it's a gr8 plc."[12] (See this endnote, if you need a translation.)[13] It's worth noting that the girl, the teacher, and the school weren't identified in the report. In fact, the slew of newspaper, magazine, radio, and TV retellings of the original story *never* confirmed any reliable particulars of the anecdote.

Speaking of the media, recent decades have seen countless reports decrying the social and linguistic consequences of the computer, internet, or cell phone. Each of these technologies has at one time or another been vilified as socially and/or linguistically "ruinous," "erosive," "threatening," etc. One Canadian paper branded online language a "new communicable disease [that] has developed into a shorthand that all but obliterates the Queen's English."[14] In 2007, the *Daily Post* ran a trenchant editorial from award-decorated Welsh broadcaster John Humphrys. Its title alone leaves no doubt as to its message: "I h8 txt msgs: How Texting Is Wrecking Our Language."[15] Most tellingly, though, is a 2003 study that Crispin Thurlow conducted of print-media accounts of digitally mediated language use, structures, and general practices. The media coverage, he argues, amounts to a "popular framing" or "metadiscursive construction" of CMC.[16] In other words, the articles, op-ed pieces, and news-y reports that bombard the public's eye have ultimately shaped Joe Public's perceptions of digitally mediated language and its users. Thurlow's survey of more than 100 articles unearthed the following provocative headlines, among others:

> *Texting "Is Not Bar to Literacy"*
> *Over to You: Is Text Message Threatening Literacy?*
> *E-business: How Text Messages Destroy Language*
> *On the Internet, the Spelling Is a Disaster*
> *A Langwidge Going from Bad 2 Worse*
> *Teens' Love for Email "Ruining" Their Grammar*[17]

But it's not just Average Joes and journalists who've framed the discussion of CMC in a doomsday-esque tone. In a 1996 interview for the *Observer*, former president of France Jacques Chirac called the internet a "major risk for humanity."[18] His fears were largely linguistically motivated: Chirac intuited the technology's potential to impact language, in particular his beloved *langue française*.

Even academics have dealt jabs that smack of sociological fatalism. In a 1991 exposé for the *Boston Review*, American author and literary critic Sven Birkerts waxed dolefully on the "morbid symptoms" that have resulted from our dependence on digital tools. To his mind such technologies are essentially communication-corrupting thugs that assail traditional—read: "better"— paradigms of written and verbal interaction:

> There is no question but that the transition from the culture of the book to the culture of electronic communication will radically alter the ways in which we use language on every societal level. The complexity and distinctiveness of spoken and written expression, which are deeply bound to traditions of print literacy, will gradually be replaced by a more telegraphic sort of "plainspeak." ... Language will grow increasingly impoverished through a series of vicious cycles.[19]

In a similar malcontent vein, New Jersey Institute of Technology Professor David Rothenberg voiced concerns that the internet "destroys" the style and creativity of his students' writing. In a fiery piece that appeared in the *Chronicle of Higher Education* in the late 1990s, Rothenberg huffed:

> [This past semester] I noticed a disturbing decline in both the quality of the writing and the originality of the thoughts expressed. What had happened since last fall? Did I ask worse questions? Were my students unusually lazy? No. My class had fallen victim to the latest easy way of writing a paper: doing their research on the World-Wide Web.[20]

These are but two examples of the diatribes that academics have lobbed at digital communication technologies. It goes without saying that not *all* nonlinguists—whether in the media, academia, or elsewhere—fall into the glum characterization we've described here. Without a doubt there are just as many professors who either don't observe, or don't feel the need to publicly lament, technology's negative impact on their students' linguistic performance. Our aim here is not to traffic in general characterizations. Rather, our goal is to show that these views are out there and not hard to find.[21] "While it would be untrue to suggest that there were no positive claims made for the effects of CMC," Thurlow hedges, "for the most part the nexus of popular discourses about language, about technology, and about young people gener-ates an overwhelmingly pessimistic picture."[22]

Back to the Linguists' Take

Linguists, on the other hand, tend to be less emotional and fatalistic when it comes to evaluating the manner and extent that digital technologies shape language. In his analysis of thirty scholarly papers—nearly half of which were penned by American or British linguists—Thurlow determines that these "were shown to be more unequivocally positive in their evaluation of CMD [computer-mediated discourse] and CMC."[23] Take, for instance, the sage comments of linguist Peter Schlobinski, who's taught about and researched CMC for more than three decades. In a post-lecture interview with the South Tyrolean Cultural Institute, Schlobinski responds as follows to the question of whether native German speakers should be concerned about CMC leading to language decay (*Sprachverfall*) or a lack of linguistic competence (*mangelnde Sprachkompetenz*):

> Departures from the [linguistic] standard oughtn't be equated with language decay. Language is constantly in a state of change, and the new media must certainly bring with them new forms of writing. These, however, do not cancel out the [linguistic] standard, rather they exist in parallel—or bet-ter put—below the standard norms. It is possible that some forms estab-lish themselves from the bottom up, but we needn't be afraid of any decay in language because of this.[24]

As Schlobinski's comments suggest, linguists prefer to frame the subject in more mitigated discourse, avoiding sensationalizations and generalizations.

Indeed, linguists often cast the subject in a positive light (much as we have above, in our discussion of text messaging and the resultant expansion of speakers' linguistic repertoires). Take, for instance, Carmen Frehner's book *Email—SMS—MMS*; its subtitle touts the "linguistic creativity" of CMC.[25] Elsewhere, David Crystal extols the human capacity to react to the new—and often challenging—contexts into which digital communication technologies strong-arm language:

> I see the arrival of Netspeak as similarly enriching the range of commu-nicative options available to us.... What is truly remarkable is that so many people have learned so quickly to adapt their language to meet the demands of the new situations, and to exploit the potential of the new medium so creatively to form new areas of expression.[26]

You might be even more surprised to learn that, for some time now, linguists have been suggesting that, in fact, digital communication technologies are linguistically *beneficial* for users. In an empirical study of Finnish teenagers' text-messaging forms and behaviors, conducted by the Information Society Research Center at the University of Tampere, researchers argued that adolescent males in particular might reap linguistic benefits from certain practices associated with crafting texts:

> Our research suggests a benefit [from composing text messages]. Boys describe how they will spend 15 to 30 minutes composing a single message if they consider it significant. Boys' messages are not produced without forethought. They look for suitable words to encapsulate what they want to say, and they reflect on whether the recipient will interpret the content correctly. These concerns and activity suggest that their writing is not simply mechanical and device oriented but is purposeful and emotional.[27]

Put a different way: whenever teenagers take the time to fashion a deliberate text message, they're actually sharpening cognitive skills that carry over into their writing in general.

And because linguists realize that nonlinguists are likely to react with fervid skepticism to this texting-might-even-benefit-language argument, linguists eschew conclusions based on impressions or anecdotes. Remember that theirs is a scientific trade, ergo: evidence driven. So instead of relying on personal inklings or broad hearsay, linguists undergird their studies with empirical data, that is, they reach out to actual users of digital technology to solicit, observe, and analyze linguistic data.

Case in point: A 2009 study out of Coventry University that "presented evidence that facility with texting literacy is positively associated with standard English literacy."[28] The research team asked eighty-eight school kids, between the ages of 10 and 12, to compose text messages to a range of people in a range of situations. They analyzed this data set in terms of twelve categories of "textisms."[29] For the second data set, they administered standardized tests to measure the children's vocabulary, and reading and writing skills. After comparing the data sets, the authors arrived at the following twofold conclusion:

> First, there was little evidence that using text language was damaging to pre-teen children's standard English ability. Second, there was, in contrast, a strong positive relationship between their use of textisms and other measures of their English ability.[30]

Two other studies that, like the Coventry research, offer an empirically grounded take on the relationship between text messaging and literacy—and which are worth reading if you're interested in getting away from impression-istically and anecdotally suffused viewpoints—are Drouin and Davis's "R u txting? Is the Use of Text Speak Hurting Your Language?"[31] and Grace and Kemp's "Undergraduates' Attitudes to Text Messaging Language Use and Intrusions of Textisms into Formal Writing."[32]

On a closing note, we'd like to offer our own two cents on the matter. The way we see it, the new forms, practices, and ideologies that computer-mediated communication technologies have set in motion in languages the world over—all of this linguistic novelty is neither maleficent nor beneficent; rather, it's "par for the course."

This is a banal way of saying that just as societies and the people who make up societies change, language naturally changes along with them. The changes aren't intrinsically "bad" or "good"—they're just "different" from previously existing norms or standards. It's the speakers who super-impose onto these linguistic changes their own evaluative notions. Perhaps one speaker embraces the changes, choosing to integrate them into estab-lished models of communication, or to create new models altogether. While yet another speaker rejects the changes, opting to wage an ideological war against integration into existing paradigms or the creation of new paradigms. Fact is—as we've seen in the previous four chapters—language both changes in response to, and effects change in, technology. Crystal holds up the inter-net as a case in point; the language of cyberspace, he writes, "seems to be in a permanent state of transition, lacking precedent, struggling for standards, and searching for direction ... with users exploring its possibilities of expres-sion, introducing fresh combinations of elements, and reacting to techno-logical developments."[33]

Whether we opt for the written form *You are great, You're great, yer grt, ur gr8*, or a string of sanguine emojis—our language isn't going to intrinsic-ally suffer or prosper as a result. Linguistic dynamism of this sort, whether motivated by technical or organic sources, is and always has been par for the course.

5

Mobilization of Language: The Cell Phone

"Stupid Autocorrect," or Life, Text-Message Style

Jill tears open the box and extracts the sleek device. It's ash gray, about half the length of a standard no. 2 pencil, and no more than a couple inches wide. *NOKIA* is printed in white capital sans serif above its small, monochrome LCD screen.

It's the spring of 2000, Jill's senior year of college. And although this Nokia isn't her first cell phone (her parents bought her one in high school "for emergencies only"), it's her first one with text messaging.

She presses the power button and waits. Her excitement builds. For months she's been watching with envy as her friends texted each other. And now, with this chic Nokia 3210 that her parents have bought for her twentieth birthday, she can finally join the ranks of texters and textees.

She punches in a familiar number and crafts her first-ever SMS:

ges who gt a fone?

She presses send. A few minutes later the phone beeps: Eric, her boyfriend since the start of the academic year, has texted her back. (He's been a member of the Fellowship of Texters for several months.)

omg thts awsm <3 ttyl

She pauses, then types:

wht is ttyl?

Eric's reply:

rotfl u hv mch 2 lrn grshpr

Jill frowns. Is all texting this cryptic?

rotfl???

Her phone soon chirps Eric's reply:

ttyl = tlk 2 u l8r rotfl = rllng on th flr lfng

She smiles. It will take a some time and effort to pick up the lingo: the clipped spelling, symbols, and abbreviations. But she looks forward to it. With the punch of a few buttons she can instantly send Eric or any one of her friends a message (of 160 characters or fewer) in this artful style of language—a style, it seems to her, that she and her friends "own." And once she masters it, she'll finally be part of the in-crowd.

Later that evening, while reviewing her German vocab flashcards, her phone announces another text from Eric.

b4 i c u my <3 = —^—^—^—
whn i c u my <3 = -^-^-^-^-
w/o u my <3 = ———

She immediately texts back:

thx 4 the luv poem ur the bst

Followed by the reply:

np:>

*

It's now fifteen years later. Jill scrolls through the contacts in her Motorola Rzr phone, stops on "Katie," and selects "send new message."

hows ur day sweetie? Will b 5 min l8 pkn u up fyi

Katie's response comes moments later: *OMG mom. No one texts like that anymore unless they're ancient*

Jill and Eric bought Katie her first cell phone a month ago for her thirteenth birthday. Since sixth grade, in fact, she'd had her heart set on one of the newer so-called smartphones. And although Eric is still convinced that it's going to infect her writing with misspellings and slang, and turn her into your stereo-typical teenage monster, their daughter now has one.

Jill, on the other hand, still cherishes the familiar simplicity of her "dumb-phone" (a Motorola Rzr that Eric got her a few years ago). Sure, it takes a little longer to compose a text than it does on an iPhone or Droid, with their fancy alphanumeric keypads, but she doesn't want all the extra gadgetry that comes with these smartphones. For her, the Motorola dinosaur fulfills all her commu-nication needs—though, Jill now realizes, with one apparent drawback: her texting style ages her.

She wonders how this could've happened. It wasn't that long ago that she and Eric were exchanging flirtatious texts in college. Back then she was technologically hip. And now her daughter is calling her "ancient."

Her phone vibrates, snapping her out of her reverie.

Can we give Jen a ride home? Her practice got canceled. Thanks! We'll be at back dork

Jill can't help herself. *ok*, she taps out as quickly as she can on her prehis-toric keypad, *c u @ back DORK rotfl*

*door, her daughter texts back at once, quickly followed by *stupid autocorrect*

Jill grins. Maybe she is behind the times, technologically speaking. But at least she doesn't have to battle with her phone each time she composes a text. At least *she's* still in charge of what she writes. She is, she concludes, the proud owner of a "dumbphone."

However fictional, our opening vignette calls attention to several points about the cell phone's relationship with language. We return to and flesh out these points in the latter half of this chapter. We see, for instance, that the cell phone has given rise to a unique variety of language: a written-spoken hybrid we refer to—adopting the term from David Crystal—as *textspeak*. Consequently, as we argued for the telegraph and telephone in previous chapters, the cell phone triggered another expansion of speakers' linguistic repertoires. Second, we see how *textspeak* is stylistically versatile and creative; to wit, speakers use it for a range of communicative purposes, from informal chitchat to cre-ative writing. Third, the language used for texting is not diachronically static; rather, its structures are subject to change over time. And finally, our linguistic interaction with cell phones has become part of our ideological landscape, that is, opinions and attitudes have emerged about users' texting styles, and about how this new mode of written communication will affect users' lan-guage more broadly.

Simply put, our illustrative intro demonstrates that *textspeak* has a lot in common with all varieties of human language.

∞

In Chapter 4 we discussed language and the computer. The development of this technology, we argued, amounted to a digitization of language: speech and writing were transmuted into electrical bits of information. In the present chapter we consider the technolingualism that came about when language, spoken and written, went mobile via the cell phone.

The beginnings of what we're calling the *mobilization of language* stretch back into the early twentieth century, with radio technology. Back then communication took the form of either Morse code or speech. Symbol-based written exchange, on the other hand, was still bound to the pen, typewriter, or telegram. And although two-way telephony like ham radios and walkie-talkies made spoken communication portable for some amateur techies, it wasn't until modern cell phones, and their text-messaging features, that both modes of linguistic communication (i.e., spoken and written) overcame the bonds of immobility.

As is our custom, we start with a look at how language has influenced the very technology that mobilized it. In so doing, we argue that the acoustic properties of speech have shaped the development and refinement of speech-recognition technology, a feature that comes standard on most cellular smartphones.

The latter part of our chapter on the mobilization of language addresses the other side of our technolingual case. With a particular emphasis on text messaging, we explore to what extent the cell phone affects written language. As always, we won't restrict our discussion to just structures and practices; we also consider attitudes and perceptions of cell phone–mobilized language, drawing on prescriptivist sources (i.e., usage guides) as evidence.

Sounds, Spectrograms, and Acoustic Modeling: How Language Shaped Cell Phone Technology

It's a sultry summer evening. On the way home from work you get a craving for a frozen treat. But you're new to the area and don't know where you can stop in for a cone. So you pick up your smartphone, hold a button down until it beeps, and ask: "Where can I get ice cream to go?" Within seconds your phone announces that it has found three places nearby.

Interactions like this, between human and computer, have become commonplace in many parts of the world. Thanks to (among other things) speech-recognition software and more powerful processors, computerized devices can now make sense of spoken natural language, with accuracy rates often running into the ninetieth percentiles.[1] In this, the first half of our technolingual treatment of cell phones, we look at how the acoustic quirks of human speech informed computer scientists' efforts to develop such accurate and reliable speech-recognition software. Put another way: this section explores how the very sounds of our language have helped engineers create smartphones that can "understand" us when we speak to them.

In particular we describe how common acoustic phenomena like idiosyncratic articulation (i.e., pronouncing something different each time you say it) and coarticulation (i.e., blending the pronunciation of two or more sounds in an utterance) have compelled—and indeed continue to challenge—engineers to rethink how they program devices to "understand" (or parse) the complex acoustic realities of spoken language.

We begin with acoustic features of speech. In order to program their machines to recognize the small acoustic differences between individual speech sounds (or phones), computer scientists needed a way to observe and catalog these features. Fortunately for them, linguists were already working with instruments that allowed them to do this. As we'll see, language recognition technology depends on one resource, in particular, from the linguist's toolkit: the spectrogram. A spectrogram allows a linguist to measure the power or intensity of phones in terms of audio frequency. "Most modern systems and algorithms for speech recognition," Juang and Rabiner write, "are based on the concept of measurement of the speech power spectrum."[2]

We then consider the effect of phonetic variation on speech-recognition technology. Just as people within a shared language community differ from each other in terms of their appearance and personality, their speech also differs. Even a single speaker will routinely pronounce the same sounds differently (though not always perceptible to our own or others' ears). Ultimately, we'll see how computer scientists have had to modify technology to handle this variation.

Of Acoustic Features and Spectrograms: Speech Models for Computers

Every sound that bears meaning in our particular language has distinct acoustic features. The human brain registers these concrete features and—through neurological processes not yet completely understood—translates them into abstract phonemes (i.e., the notional units that "mean" something for our brains, kind of like the on/off sequences that "mean" something to a computer's CPU).

To get a machine to identify speech sounds (phones), computer scientists must know exactly which acoustic features, in the natural language(s) their machine will "understand," are important for distinguishing meaning. To wit, their machine needs to be programed to differentiate between, say, *pat* and *bat*, because [p] and [b] are, obviously, different meaning-bearing sounds in English. This has to do with the distinctive feature [voice]. In English, several consonants differ only in whether or not you use your vocal chords during pronunciation. In each of the following word pairs, for example, the first sound of the first word is [-voice] and the first sound of the second word is [+voice]:

pat ~ bat tot ~ dot cot ~ got sit ~ zit chip ~ jip

For comparison, in standard Mandarin Chinese there's no acoustic feature [voice]. So speakers don't differentiate between a voiceless [p] and voiced [b]. Indeed there is no *b* sound at all in their language; rather, the sound system of Mandarin Chinese distinguishes according to the acoustic feature [aspiration]. Thus, any machine designed for spoken standard Mandarin needs to be programed to "understand" the difference between aspirated *tʰa* ("pagoda") and unaspirated *ta* ("to beat"). The distinctive feature is [aspiration] and not [voice], as in English. In his compendium *Speech and Language Processing*, Martin Jurafsky explains:

> One main use of these distinctive features is in capturing natural articulatory classes of phones. In both computer speech synthesis and recognition, as we will see, we often need to build models of how a phone behaves in a certain context. But we rarely have enough data to model the interaction of every possible left and right context phone on the behavior of a phone. For this reason we can use the relevant feature ([voice], [nasal], etc) as a useful model of the context; the feature functions as a kind of backoff model of the phone.[3]

As early as the 1940s linguists specializing in the field of acoustic phonetics began using an instrument called a spectrograph to document and analyze the acoustic features of phones in American English. "Acoustic phonetics," the phonetician Allard Jongman explains, "is the study of the acoustic characteristics of speech, including an analysis and description of speech in terms of its physical properties, such as frequency, intensity, and duration."[4] And in fact today's speech-recognition technology, featured on many of today's smartphones, is the product of discoveries made more than half a century ago in this field. "Early attempts to design systems for automatic speech recognition were mostly guided by the theory of acoustic-phonetics."[5]

In 1952, for instance, three scientists at Bell Laboratories constructed the first machine that could recognize the spoken numbers "one" through "oh" (which stood for "ten").[6] Using data obtained with a sound spectrograph—at that time, a cutting-edge device for measuring acoustic energy—the inventors configured their machine to analyze the acoustic properties of the vowels, in particular each vowel's unique frequency footprint. This was a big step forward for computerized speech recognition, Jongman argues, and it couldn't have happened without the spectrograph. "The invention of the sound spectrograph in 1945 was the major technological breakthrough that made the analysis and visualization of the speech signal possible."[7]

Basically, a spectrograph is a machine that displays intensities of sound waves along a frequency spectrum. Remember that when we produce sounds in our vocal tract, we're creating waves of air pressure (similar to dropping a stone in a calm pool of water). These waves can vary in length, amplitude, and pitch or tone—all of which the human ear can register and which our brain can interpret as meaningful. A spectrograph renders a visible representation, or spectrogram, of these acoustic qualities. Figure 5.1 is a spectrogram of the phrase "ice cream to go."

The x-axis shows time in tenths of a second. The y-axis marks the sound waves' cycles per second, or hertz. The dark bands, called formants, show concentrations of acoustic energy. Vowels and nasal consonants have distinct formant structure; in other words, formant structure is one part of the acoustic features that make up these sounds. And even where there are no formants, such as with the fricative s sound in "ice," there is still dispersed, high-frequency acoustic energy (called aperiodic noise). The frequency pattern of this aperiodic noise is a telltale acoustic feature of [s].

With some practice you can read spectrograms. It turns out, however, that a (properly programmed and trained) computer is far more efficient than

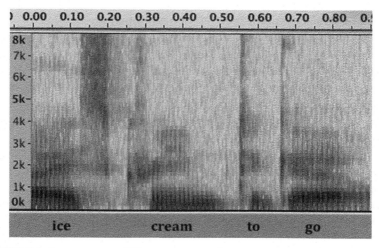

FIGURE 5.1 *Spectrogram of "ice cream to go."*

human eyes at deciphering spectrograms. Jufarsky and Martin describe the importance of spectral acoustic data for speech-recognition technology:

> It turns out that these spectral peaks that are easily visible in a spectrum are very characteristic of different phones; phones have characteristic spectral "signatures." Just as chemical elements give off different wavelengths of light when they burn, allowing us to detect elements in stars looking at the spectrum of the light, we can detect the characteristic signature of the different phones by looking at [spectrograms]. This use of spectral information is essential to both human and machine speech recognition.[8]

Another way of putting it is that spectrograms are the acoustic blueprints that a digital machine works from to pinpoint the tiny, distinctive elements of each phone. The invention of the spectrograph, therefore, was instrumental to innovation in speech-recognition technology.

The spectrograph itself was a product of classified wartime research. "Study of the auditory basis for articulatory perception," Studdert-Kennedy and Whalen explain, "became possible with the development of the sound spectrograph at Bell Laboratories during World War II."[9] From 1943 through 1946, Drs. Ralph Potter and George Kopp, together with their research assistant Harriet Green, constructed the first spectrograph and studied the visual patterns it made of speech. Initially their work remained under wraps, as the US government had a vested interest in the spectrograph as a decryption tool. After the war, however, the researchers were given permission to share their findings. Thus, in 1947 *Visible Speech*[10] was published. It was "the first comprehensive overview of the acoustic properties of (English) vowels and consonants."[11] But Potter and company didn't set their sights on the recognition of speech by machines; rather—much like the Bell family a century before—their goal was "the development of a greatly simplified and cheaper machine for the aid and relief of the totally deaf."[12]

The first linguist in an academic context to use the spectrograph to analyze the phones of speech was Professor Martin Joos at the University of Wisconsin-Madison. In so doing, Joos contributed key knowledge to the development of computer speech-recognition technology—namely, the identification and enumeration of the acoustic features that make up sound segments. During World War II he worked as a cryptologist for the US Signal Security Agency. His duties there allowed him to experiment with Potter, Kopp, and Green's spectrograph. And with the 1948 release of his book *Acoustic Phonetics*, he both coined the name for the new field and gave it its first de facto handbook. In meticulous, data-driven fashion Joos's work "discussed acoustic parameters of segments with their proper frequencies, amplitudes, phases and time dimensions, [providing] the techniques, for example, for classifying vowels ... using the first two formant frequencies."[13] Mattingly writes that *Acoustic Phonetics* "was very influential and is still worth reading today for its discussions of segmentation and coarticulation."[14]

Joos's work was a game changer not only for the field of linguistics, but also for the development of speech-recognition technology. It paved the way for the next generation of acoustic research, which focused on *acoustic feature theory*.

Above we explained that phones are made up of patterned disturbances of air pressure—patterns that our ears pick up on and which machines must be trained to recognize. Before spectrograms, the idea that phones had distinctive acoustic features was still a theory.[15] Linguists didn't yet have the tools to prove—or disprove—their hypotheses. But the spectrograph changed all that. Finally, here was a device that could give detailed, visual evidence of the physical differences among sound segments. *Visible Speech* and *Acoustic Phonetics* were the first publications to demonstrate this, laying the groundwork for future studies that yielded more comprehensive insights into the acoustic intricacies of speech sounds.

No Sounds on This Runway, or Acoustic Modeling

So how does computerized speech recognition—in particular the software built into smartphones that allows them to "understand" sounds—work?[16] Essentially, it relies on two types of modeling procedures: acoustic and language. The former distills individual phones out of the streaming, noisy mess otherwise known as speech. The latter analyzes the grammatical context of words and determines a likely sequence of these words.

Why do we need two models? Consider the example given earlier in this section: asking your smartphone, on that sultry summer evening, "Where can I get ice cream to go?" From a purely acoustic perspective, your smartphone could recognize the first word as *where, wear,* or *ware*; the third word as *I, eye,* or *aye*; the fifth and sixth words as *ice cream* or *I scream*; and the seventh word as *to, too,* or *two*. Your "smarty-pants" phone, however, posits various grammatical models, compares these with the phonetic options, and makes a decision based on probabilities of words preceding or following other words. In this case, language modeling would show it's more probable for the question word *where* to start the utterance, and for a verb to follow it, than the verb *wear* or the noun *ware*. Similar modeling procedures would establish *I* as more probable than *eye* or *aye*, and *ice scream* than *I scream*. This, in a (very simple) nutshell, is why our devices need to use language modeling, also known as the back-end process of automatic speech recognition.

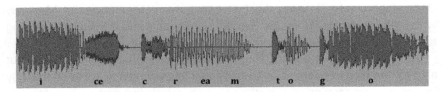

FIGURE 5.2 *Waveform of* ice cream to *go.*

Acoustic modeling, as we've pointed out, allows a machine to tease out individual sounds from long strings of spoken segments. Take the phrase *ice cream to go.* A machine has to be "taught" how to decompose this whirl of noise into meaningful phones; that is, someone has to program it to render "acoustic models [that] convert physical waveforms into hypotheses about which speech sounds were uttered."[17] So when you speak *ice cream to go*, the smartphone's "ear" receives the sound as a waveform, shown in Figure 5.2. A waveform is just what it sounds like: the rolling impression a sound makes as it passes through the air, shoving air molecules out of the way.

A waveform is an analog package of acoustic information. Recall from Chapter 4 that computers—unlike a record or cassette-tape player—run on digital data. Therefore, the first step in acoustic modeling is to convert the analog waveform into a digital format (i.e., strings of numbers) with special software or hardware in the device. Then, with the help of a swanky algorithm (called the fast Fourier transform) the digital data is converted into a spectrogram. Next, the computer breaks up this spectrogram into a spate of short overlapping fragments, or acoustic frames. Most systems today cut up spectrograms into 10 millisecond frames (i.e., a hundred frames for every one second of spectrographic data). And it's here, within each of these frames, that the magic happens: the system identifies and extracts the acoustic features.

The process sounds straightforward enough, right? You teach a smartphone's computer brain how to recognize acoustic features using spectrographic information, give it a bunch of models with which it can compare incoming data, and voilà: it can recognize speech . . .

If only it were this simple! As we see in the next section, the phonetic reality of speech is anything but straightforward.

Variation: The Mother of Innovation

All speakers of a language, at some point, recognize differences among people in the way they talk. There are lots of reasons for these differences—geography, age, ethnicity, social milieu, to name a few. Even anatomy contributes to acoustic differences in our speech. Due to the size of his larynx, a man's voice generally has a lower pitch (and therefore lower fundamental frequency) than a woman's or child's. People with a shorter, thicker lingual frenulum (that little fold of skin under your tongue) might pronounce *d* and *t* softer than a speaker with a longer, thinner frenulum. These are just two of the many ways that anatomy can account for variation in speech.[18]

Most of us, however, don't realize that even our own speech varies. To our ears it sounds the same. But if you were to scrutinize spectrograms of your own speech, you'd find variation—sometimes slight, other times moderate—in the way you pronounce individual phones within words. Maybe we're sick with a cold. Maybe we're agitated, elated, out of breath, or mopey. Or maybe we just woke up from a luxurious midday catnap. The point: changes in physical and mental states can, and often do, manifest in changes in our speech. Most of the time, though, our speech simply varies. Yet, as we just mentioned, unless the variation is extreme our own ears don't pick up on these acoustic discrepancies.

Now, to a smartphone's computer brain, even small differences in acoustic input matter. The earliest speech-recognition systems were speaker dependent, that is, they could only recognize the speech of the same speaker on whose speech they had been trained. Take the Bell Labs machine from 1952 that could recognize the spoken ciphers *one* though *oh* (for "ten"). It worked for the scientist whose speech provided the spectrographic models. But when the boss popped by to try out this incredible device for himself, things got embarrassing. Moreover, even the original scientist had to regularize his or her pronunciation as much as possible—in tone, speed, loudness, etc. The variation inherent in the scientist's own speech was liable to throw off the machine.

So while computers might be faster than humans at reading spectrograms, when it comes to coping with acoustic variability, our brains are processing goliaths. Whether due to an unfamiliar accent, articulatory or physiological impairment, decibel level, rate of speech, or background noise—the brain mitigates most of the acoustic erraticism that the ear picks up and passes on to it. That is, of course, unless the variation is too extreme, then understanding can break down. And while our brains handle this acoustic irregularity naturally, computers need to be fed lots and lots of "training data." Basically these are recordings of different speakers modeling the sorts of variation just mentioned. Sproat explains:

When speech scientists train acoustic models for ASR systems, they attempt to model [all] kinds of variation ... Typically they will train the models on a large number of speakers, include as much variation in the *ways* speakers say things as possible, balance for gender, and record in conditions that closely approximate the acoustic conditions that are anticipated when the system is deployed.[19]

As you can gather, the more examples of variation a machine gets, from its user's speech and the speech of others, the better it gets at handling variation.

But stop the presses! Something else causes variation in our speech, which—once computer scientists realized its significance for their work—revolutionized speech-recognition technology. Linguists refer to it as *coarticulation*, a decorative way of saying that when we speak we often pronounce two (or more) sounds at the same time. Sound segments, you see, don't exit our mouths in isolation from each other; instead, they tend to—ahem—"reach out and touch other ones."

Consider the words *keep* and *cope*. If you pay close attention while pronouncing each, you notice that you produce different *k* sounds. The reason is phonetic environment. The vowel in *keep* is formed in the front of the mouth, while the consonantal *k* sound originates in the back. The tongue, however, anticipates the front *e* sound while it's in position for the *k*. The result is a coarticulation of the *k* and *e* phones, and what comes out is a sound akin to the palatal fricative in German (the so-called *ich* sound). The vowel in *cope*, however, is articulated farther back in the mouth, closer to *k*'s home turf. So *cope*'s initial sound comes out more like a "standard" *k* segment.

Sounds can rub off on each other in both directions. The vowel in *lass*, for instance, is acoustically different from the vowel in *lack*. Can you guess why? The word-final sounds are generated in different places of the mouth. Granted, the difference is too subtle for human ears, but a spectrogram would reveal the discrepancy.

Coarticulation regularly occurs in every spoken language. So if you want to make a computer *really good* at recognizing natural human speech, it has to be able to handle coarticulations among these phones. Put another way: while a machine needs to know about the individual sounds in words like *keep* and *cope*, the *transitions* between the sounds in these words are just as critical. When computer scientists figured this out, they changed their programming approaches. Sproat writes:

> Most ASR systems actually consider not phones, but phones in particular contexts, such as an /a/ between a /d/ and a /g/—noted as /$_d$a$_g$/—and they also typically break each context-dependent phone into a beginning, middle, and end part. So rather than [acoustic] models for each phone, we actually have models for each portion of a context-dependent phone.[20]

During the 1980s researchers at Bell Labs put their minds to solving the acoustic variability challenge. Their pursuit was as much commercial as scientific. AT&T wanted to be the first to offer customers automated telecommunication services. So they charged their lab coats with creating a large-scale, reliable, speaker-independent speech-recognition system. According to Juang and Rabiner:

> These automated systems were expected to work well for a vast population (literally tens of millions) of talkers without the need for individual speaker training. The focus at Bell Laboratories was in the design of a speaker-independent system that could deal with the acoustic variability intrinsic in the speech signals coming from many different talkers, often with notably different regional accents.[21]

The path to success, you might say, was lined with numbers and formulas. Acoustic differences among speakers were nothing more than observed variables, researchers realized. And observed variables, given enough of them and given the right calculations, can be used to predict unexpected variables. So even if a machine doesn't get the exact acoustic input it was trained on, it can use all the input it's ever gotten to compute a well-informed guess. This realization "led to the creation of a range of speech clustering algorithms for creating word and sound reference patterns (initially templates but ultimately statistical models) that could be used across a wide range of talkers and accents."[22] In other words, reliable and accurate computerized speech recognition became all about calculating probabilities.

It's beyond the scope of our discussion here to cover the many mathematic models incorporated into speech-recognition technology for managing acoustic variability. However, one statistical formula in particular has contributed significantly to solving the variability challenge: the hidden Markov model (HMM). Ghahramani defines an HMM as "a tool for representing probability distributions over sequences of observations."[23] Applied to automatic speech recognition, an HMM "models the intrinsic variability of the speech signal (and the resulting spectral features) as well as the structure of spoken language in an integrated and consistent statistical modeling framework."[24]

Think of it this way. A computer makes hundreds of observations of incoming speech—or to be more precise, it observes the acoustic features of each uttered segment (by chopping up the spectrogram into frames). Remember, too, that the computer observes individual segments *and* the transitions between them. An HMM's purpose, therefore, is to "model the probabilities of these transitions between the phones."[25] And it's on the basis of these probability models that a machine can accurately predict the sounds it observes.

The acoustic variability of speech prompted researchers to explore creative solutions through mathematics. In particular, they discovered that statistics-based algorithms—among others, HMMs—were valuable tools for turning random content (i.e., speech) into predictable digital data. "The HMM methodology," Jiang and Rabiner conclude, "represented a major step forward from the simple pattern recognition and acoustic-phonetic methods used earlier in automatic speech recognition systems."[26] Ultimately, the variability nuisance was conquered by the last of the proverbial three Rs.

The Cell Phone's Influence on (Written) Language

Let's now turn our analysis around and consider how the cell phone has shaped, and continues to shape, language. For the sake of succinctness and space, we limit our discussion to written language.[27] In particular, we focus on the structures, practices, and ideologies associated with text messaging.

But first, let's go back to where we started this chapter. You recall that several key points about the relationship between texting and language emerged from the opening vignette " 'Stupid Autocorrect,' or, Life, Text-Message Style"; namely:

1) The technology that allows users to send messages over cell phone (aka SMS, text messaging, or texting) has given rise to a new variety of language: textspeak, a chimeric style of written communication that outpaces even email's colloquial drift.

2) Cell phones therefore added another linguistic tool to users' quiver of styles and registers. In other words, like the telegraph, telephone, and email, texting expanded speakers' linguistic repertoires.

3) Like *all* linguistic systems of communication, textspeak is stylistically versatile and creative. It's not just the haphazard backwash of "real" language; rather, speakers adopt it for, and adapt it to, many communicative ends.

4) Like *all* varieties of language, textspeak isn't immune to change; its linguistic structures, in other words, drift and shift over time—whether due to changes in technology, users, ideologies, or other external forces.

5) As with the other technologies we've looked at it in our exploration of technolingualism, language ideologies have accompanied the rise of texting. Speech communities construct ideas and attitudes about which linguistic forms and practices should or should not occur in association with text messaging.

In this section we delve into each of these points in turn—with the exception of the first two, which we address as one (the diligent reader will have noticed that point two is more a corollary of point one than a standalone idea). And as we did with email, we'll bring in examples from beyond the English-speaking world.

A "Coded Language in Its Own Right": Linguistic Structures of Textspeak

In her contribution to *The Cell Phone Reader: Essays in Social Transformation*, Janey Gordon concludes the following about the social and linguistic upshots of text-messaging technology:

> The short message service or text in particular has empowered the user in ways that were not foreseen. The text message has become a coded language in its own right. A complex subculture of codes and subtle meanings has developed.[28]

As depicted in the chapter's opening vignette—which, remember, is set in the year 2000—text messages sent with cell phones of that time did indeed often resemble a "coded language in its own right." Granted, our vignette is fictional. But as with every chapter opener in this treatise on technolingualism, this narrative draws on actually observed data.

In his 2004 *Glossary of Netspeak and Textspeak*, for instance, Crystal lists 500 abbreviations (also called initialisms) common in SMS at that time; among them: *ttyl, rotfl,* and *omg*.[29] As for Jill and her boyfriend's penchant for shunning word-internal vowels, this too was typical of SMS composed on the small, numeric international standard keypads of the time (the letters were mapped to number keys).[30] Mny txt msgs wr smply wrtn lk ths. In his superb *Txtng: The Gr8 Db8*, in which he meticulously describes, analyzes, and explains the linguistic forms and practices of text messaging, Crystal writes:

> More common [than initialisms] are the cases where texters shorten words by omitting letters from the middle (often called *contractions*) or dropping a letter at the end (often called *clippings*). Usually these are vowels ... but final consonants are often dropped too, as are "silent" consonants, and double medial consonants are reduced to singletons.[31]

Texts can sometimes grow so heavy with initialisms, contractions, and clippings—and to complicate matters further, there can be lot of variation within and between messages—that translation websites have popped up.

The site trnsl8tit.com, for instance, invites visitors to "type in SMS, text message, emoticon, smiley, slang, chat room net lingo or abbreviations and let transL8it! convert it to plain english to understand—OR—type in your phrase in english and convert it to SMS TEXT lingo slang!"[32]

Then there's the matter of orthography (i.e., the way our fictional texting lovebirds spell and punctuate their messages). Forms like *ges* for "guess," *luv* for "love," and *fone* for "phone" suggest a preference for phonetic spellings of words, especially if these forms are shorter and therefore more efficient to communicate via numeric keypad. Indeed, the *Pragmatics of Computer-Mediated Communication* lists "phonological approximation"—that is, writing words closer to how they actually sound—as one of the three " 'maxims' of text-message style."[33]

Punctuation in SMS also tends to diverge from traditional norms. Notice that Jill and Eric almost exclusively forgo capitalization, periods, commas, apostrophes, and question marks. (Note that Jill reserves *?* for conveying emotional emphasis.) In 2005, Baron and Lang collected nearly 200 text messages sent by twenty-two university students over a twenty-four-hour period. In sum, 336 sentences were analyzed for punctuation. They found that 61 percent of the students' texted passages contained *no punctuation* at all.[34] Question marks appeared in just 13 percent of the collected sentences, while periods and commas were even scarcer, occurring in only 9.1 percent and 2.1 percent, respectively, of all sentences. The authors fittingly titled their article, "Necessary Smileys[35] and Useless Periods."

A final quirk of text messaging, similarly demonstrated in Jill and Eric's fictionalized interactions, is the use of letters and numbers to stand for sounds (single phones, clusters of phones, or syllables) and words. Examples include: *4* for "for" or "-fore"; *b* for "be"; *u* for "you"; and *8* for "-ate". Though less frequent than initialisms or contractions, linguists were quick to single out this logographic practice in texting. Crystal calls it the "chief feature" of textspeak.[36] And at least one author of two separate how-to guides on texting (released in 2000 and 2001, respectively) appropriated the trend for her titles: *Wan2tlk?: Ltl Bk of Txt Msgs*[37] and *IH8U: Ltl Bk of Txt Abuse*.[38]

This logographic phenomenon is based on the rebus principle, that is, using a string of nonlinguistic images to convey linguistic, sentential information. You recall from Chapter 1, on the technology of writing, that this is an age-old technique. Among other ancient peoples, the Egyptians and Sumerians incorporated rebuses into their writing systems (which were also the world's first). Mind you, this was around 5,000 years ago. In a twist that smacks of linguistic irony, the rebus-happy texters of the twenty-first century have, in a sense, brought the technology of writing back full circle. Moreover, as

Stephan Elspaß points out in his study of personal letters between Germans in the early 1900s, speakers back then were already using numbers, letters, and other ideographs in similar, linguistically creative ways.[39]

Taken together, these structural features of textspeak (i.e., initialisms, clippings, phonetic spellings, logographs, rebuses, and lack of punctuation) give it a distinctly informal and speech-like nuance—even more pronounced (no pun intended) than the language of email.

Similar texting phenomena appear in languages around the world. Take French. Despite a robust and centuries-old tradition of linguistic prescriptivism, the French casually besprinkle their *textos* with textspeak. Between the spring of 2002 and March 2004, French linguist Jacques Anis collected and analyzed 750 text messages sent from dozens of French speakers ranging in age and sex. His unsurprising observation: "The language used in SMS messages deviates in many ways from the prescriptive norms of standard French."[40] To these deviatory structures and practices of French text messaging Anis assigns the blanket term "neography," examples of which he categorizes into "three broad types: phonetic spelling, syllabograms (rebus writing), and logograms (symbols, uniliteral abbreviations, acronyms)."[41] Table 5.1 gives examples, from Anis's corpus, of each neographic type:

In the case of ludic logography—that is, the playful use of letters and symbols to write a text—Crystal gives examples from eleven languages; among others: German's word for "eight" is *acht*, so *n8* renders *nacht*, or "night"; Spanish speakers glom a *2*, or *dos*, onto the cluster *sl-* to get *sl2* for *saludos*, or "greetings"; and in Norwegian "seven" is *sy*, so a word like *syuk*, or "sick," can be communicated with *7k*.[42]

Every day, speakers around the world tap out billions of texts, each of which includes, to varying extents, this or that feature of textspeak as described above. According to statisa.com, in 2014 the Chinese sent 763 billion texts.[43] In the United States, for the same year, the number exceeded 2 trillion.[44] In fact, we'd bet dollars to donuts that most readers who are old enough to have texted on a cell phone with a numeric keypad and 160-character-limited screen, and even those younger whippersnappers who've grown up knowing only a smartphone and its luxurious alphanumeric design—most of us have used textspeak at one time or another. (Even if some of us won't admit to it . . . ;)

A Variety for All Seasons: Textspeak's Linguistic Versatility

Textspeak might abound in speech-like vernacularisms and punctuation-light nonstandardisms, but this doesn't mean its functional use is restricted to everyday, intimate social domains (e.g., checking in, making and confirming plans, flirting, etc.). Collette Snowden, professor of communication and media

TABLE 5.1 Examples of "neographic types" in French text messaging.

Neographic Type	TextMessage	Standard Written French	English Translation	Explanation
Phonetic spelling	mon nouvo forfai	mon nouveau forfait	my new plan	Reduction of eau to o, and omission of silent word-final consonant
Syllabograms	g pa 1 kdo	j'ai pas un cadeau	I don't have a present	g and j'ai, and k and ca are homophonous
Logograms	mdr @+	mort de rire à plus	dying of laughter until later	mdr is an acronym akin to English "rotfl"; @ stands for a with grave accent over it; + is homophonous with plus

Source: Jacques Anis, "Neography: Unconventional Spelling in French SMS Text Messages," in *The Multilingual Internet: Language, Culture, and Communication Online*, ed. Brenda Danet and Susan C. Herring (New York: Oxford University Press, 2007), 97–106.

at the University of South Australia, proposes that "the construction of SMS messages can be seen as a deliberate and playful manipulation of the text to serve different purposes."[45] Baldly put, texts are more functionally versatile than colloquial bromides like *whts up gf, c u l8r,* or *ur sxy.*

Sure, empirical studies of the texting habits of Norwegian teenagers[46] and American college students[47] have shown that the younger demographic regularly uses texting to coordinate social activities with peers. But other studies suggest that texting is more sociolinguistically versatile. In her paper "Non-standard Data in Swiss Text Messages with a Special Focus on Dialectal Forms," Simone Ueberwasser, a researcher at the Zurich Center for Linguistics, shows that in Switzerland texting is also used for formal linguistic interactions. Drawing from an online corpus of nearly 18,000 German-language texts collected under the auspices of the international project sms4science,[48] Ueberwasser cites an SMS from a 15-year-old participant to their coach.[49] Fascinatingly, the 15-year-old's message amounts to a mash-up of linguistic structures and styles. On the one hand, the youth employs the formal personal pronoun *Sie* to address the coach. On the other hand, the text itself is written in Swiss German dialect—a regional variety of German without a standardized orthography—and contains elements of textspeak. But then the youth also mixes in tokens that come from more traditional writing modes, such as a formal closing in Standard German.

What's more, speakers have tapped texting's linguistic wellspring to create literary works. The particularly nimble of thumb compose narrative fiction, poetry, and even emoji stories on the digital medium. The Japanese, for example, have been crafting SMS narratives—called *keitai shosetsu* (ケータイ小説) or "cell phone novels"—since the early 2000s.[50] *The New Yorker* has since proclaimed the *keitai shosetsu* "the first literary genre to emerge from the cellular age."[51] Chapters typically run between 50 and 150 words and are sent as a text to subscribers' phones or email accounts or posted to a website. According to textnovel.com, the first website to host English language cell phone novels, the *keitai shosetsu* was born when "almost fifteen years ago a young man by the name of Yoshi started writing a novel on his cell phone consisting of short chapters that fit in a multimedia email message, sent to friends and then forwarded and spread through word of mouth and other makeshift promotional strategies."[52] The new genre has become so popular in Japan, in fact, that since 2006 Tokyo has hosted several Cell Phone Novel Awards ceremonies to recognize the year's most outstanding *keitai shosetsu.*[53]

As you might imagine, the *keitai shosetsu* genre quickly drew its share of prescriptive-minded foes—among others, the press, educators, and literary critics. According to linguist Yukiko Nishimura of Toyo Gakuen University, these critics often charge that "the language [of *keitai shosetsu*] is immature, featuring only easy *kanji*" and with prose that "deviates from stylistic conventions of standard novels in a number of ways, such as insertion of black spaces even when there is no 'necessary' grammatical effect."[54] And in fact, the innovative cell phone authors intentionally injected their language with a conversational flavor.[55] They were, after all, creating a new genre. Like so many nouveaux literati before them, the "new" of their genre extended out from the language. And perhaps it was precisely this linguistic novelty—this bucking of traditional rules for writing—that attracted readers to the *keitai shosetsu.*

Whatever it was, less than a decade after Yoshi's experiment the genre had exploded in popularity. According to one source, "in 2007 five out of the ten best selling novels in Japan were originally mobile phone novels."[56] Young adults, in particular, craved their daily fix of cellularly delivered fiction. By 2008 the largest cell phone novel site Maho-i-Land featured more than a million titles and boasted more than 3.5 billion visits a month.[57]

But the multitudes of sprightly thumbs didn't offload their artistic zeal into fictional narratives alone. Turns out, the stylistic features of textspeak, and the technological limitations of early texting (especially the 160-character limit), lent themselves superbly to another creative medium: poetry. Take Eric's goodnight *luv poem* to Jill, in our chapter's opening vignette:

> *b4 i c u my <3 = —^—^—^—*
> *whn i c u my <3 = -^-^-^-^-*
> *w/o u my <3 = —*

As you can see, texting gave the poetic soul a new tool for expressing itself through a digital medium. Common features of textspeak, like initialisms and logograms, are recruited, as is another graphic trick we haven't yet mentioned (but will have more to say on below): using ASCII characters to form icons. In Eric's poem, for instance, the linguistic concept of "heart" is denoted by the less-than sign and the number *3*, and the nonlinguistic concept of a heart monitor is rendered with a series of hyphens and carets.

The poet Norman Silver appropriated similar textspeak-y wiles (save for the icons) in his 2006 collections *Laugh Out Loud: Poems from TXT Café* and *Age, Sex, Location: Poems from the TXT Café*. Below is an excerpt from the latter. The poem is titled "flirt lines."

> hey, r u searching 4 mr rite
> ide like 2 marry u just 1 nite
>
> have u worked all ur life 2 b this cute
> bet u look the business in ur birthday suit

get your coat luv – uve pulled – lets go
havnt i seen u on a webcam show?
. . .[58]

In addition to the stylistic elements mentioned above, typical of Silver's SMS poetry are phonetic spellings ("luv" and "rite"), the use of only small-case letters ("mr" and "i"), and a widespread avoidance of punctuation ("havnt" and "ide")—all common characteristics of nonartistic textspeak.

The Guardian was the first English-language media operation to take SMS poetry seriously as a new creative genre. In 2001 the newspaper ran a "pioneering text poetry competition [that] attracted nearly 7,500 entries from 4,700 mobile phones."[59] Of the seven entries chosen for the winner's circle, four were written with conventional orthography. Three of the text poems, however—including the third-place finisher and the overall winner—were replete with textspeak. Here's Hetty Hughes's winning entry:

txtin iz messin,
mi headn'me englis,
try2rite essays,
they all come out txtis.
gran not plsed w/letters shes getn,
swears i wrote better
b4 comin2uni.
&she's african[60]

Creative and adaptable in both form and style, the language of cell phone novels and SMS poetry offers a compelling account of textspeak's linguistic versatility. Textspeak is a true product of our technolingual world: drawing on norms and resources from the past while at the same time departing from these in order to blaze its own trail in the contemporary linguistic landscape. As Snowden puts it: "The technology of SMS places a new kind of literacy in the hands of individuals, in which the official rules of the classroom have been dispensed with in favor of a unique culturally created language."[61]

A final example of the linguistic creativity that texting technology has spawned has to do with emoticons and emojis. The former is a portmanteau of emotion and icon—in other words, a picture that expresses feelings. Wikipedia defines the emoticon as a "metacommunicative pictorial representation of a facial expression that, in the absence of body language and prosody, serves to draw a receiver's attention to the tenor or temper of a sender's nominal non-verbal communication, changing and improving its interpretation."[62] Got that?:D

Here's a more relatable example. Say you're in the mood for a Burger King burger, and you'd like your significant other to grab you one on their way home from work. So you text *pk me up a bk brgr pls*. A moment later you get the response: *gt ur own brger*. Devoid of the allaying inflections of your voice and your sweet accompanying smile, your texted request came across as brusque and presumptuous. How to remedy this? An *lol* or *ha*—initialisms that commonly serve as pragmatic softeners—don't fit in this situation. You need something else to stand in as a paralinguistic cue: enter the emoticon. And so the next time you're craving that burger, you tap out *pk me up a bk brgr pls:)*. And although the reply is once again negative, this time it's nicer: *sry boo jst pst bk nxt tm 4 shr xoxo*.

According to various sources,[63] the first intentional arrangement of a colon, hyphen, and parenthesis to render:-) on a digital medium can be traced back to a Carnegie Mellon faculty member. The story goes that in 1982 a prankster posted a bogus report on one of the university's digital message boards—recall that many large research institutions of the time were connected to the ARPANET, a forerunner to the internet—announcing that there'd been a mercury spill on campus. Unfortunately, the "joke" fell flat. Most users actually took the safety warning seriously. In the aftermath, "the board's users cast about for a means to distinguish humorous posts from serious content."[64] And at exactly 11:44 a.m. on September 19, 1982, Scott E. Fahlman, a professor of computer science, contributed this post: "I propose the following character sequence for joke markers::-) Read it sideways."[65] From there the emoticon took off. As users added more and more symbol-framed visages to the pile, they became more commonly known as smileys. And within a decade of :-)'s birth, David Sanderson (aka the "Noah Webster of Smileys") was boasting of having compiled more than 650 specimens for his publication *Smileys*.[66]

Texters used, and indeed continue to use, emoticons to add an attitudinal "gist" or emotional "touch" to messages barren of paralinguistic cues—that is, nonverbal markers like pitch, intonation, bodily gestures, and facial expressions. Or, as the creator of the :-) put it: "You're not going to stop and express in lovely, flowing prose what your mood is, [so] I think emoticons humanize what is otherwise a cold medium."[67]

Emojis are the next generation of emoticons: colorful, more graphically elaborate icons that add emotional or attitudinal shades to a text. "[Emojis] add context, enable wordplay, insert nuance, and let you speak your mind while taking the edge off your message."[68] The word itself is borrowed from Japanese, where it's a portmanteau of "picture" (*e*) and "letter, or character" (*moji*). Emojis also go beyond the facial realm: there are full people, body parts, buildings, machines, animals, street signs, celestial objects, and so on. As of this writing, one source reports that 845 emojis are commonly supported on

FIGURE 5.3 *Example of emoji narrative for "I (a woman) contracted a food-borne illness after eating Indian food." (http://narrativesinemoji.tumblr.com/post/14220869946/food-poisoning-after-eating-indian-food (accessed December 26, 2015).)*

FIGURE 5.4 *Example of emoji narrative for "I (a woman) went on a date with a man, drank alcohol, and it ended romantically." (http://narrativesinemoji.tumblr.com/post/11702429714/date-nite (accessed December 26, 2015).)*

most digital devices, and that Apple's iOS 9.1 software supports a whopping 1,620.[69]

Fascinatingly, emojis aren't just used as paralinguistic markers. In a development similar to what we saw with textspeak above, users have adapted emojis for new and creative means: composing graphic narratives. One blog site on Tumblr contains dozens of narratives in emoji.[70] Figures 5.3 and 5.4 are examples of two such narratives, and an approximate translation of each:

The shrewdest emoji artists have even recast movies, operas, and books into the iconic form. The aforementioned Tumblr site showcases emoji retellings of *The Shining*, *Les Misérables*, and *Independence Day*. And in 2010, after enlisting the help of more than 800 people through a crowdsourcing website, Fred Beneson edited, compiled, and published *Emoji Dick; or* 🐋 , the first-ever line-for-line translation of a major work of fiction into emoji characters. Even the US Library of Congress got in on the action: in 2013 it purchased a copy of 🐋 for its archives.

Certainly, one could argue that this clever use of emojis is less of a linguistic phenomenon than what we see with mobile phone novels and SMS poetry. At their best, emojis are polysemous ideograms (i.e., variously interpretable pictures that stand for an abstract concept). More commonly, though, they serve as straightforward, nonverbal pictograms. A technology reporter for *The New York Times*, for instance, describes emojis as "an ever-evolving cryptographic language that changes depending on who we are talking to, and when."[71] And linguist Arika Okrent, author of *The Land of Invented Languages*, calls the notion "ridiculous" that emojis function as linguistically coded symbols (e.g., letters, syllabograms, or logograms). "They're not a language," she concludes, "they're a game of charades."[72] Linguistic phenomenon or not, speakers have nevertheless adopted the symbols to transmit information in creative ways across a new digital medium. Emojis—and their older sibling, the emoticon—belong to text-speak and, as such, are further evidence of its versatility and creative potentiality.

From c u l8r:) to See You Later ☺, or How Textspeak Has Changed Even within Its Short Lifetime

Like all varieties of language, spoken or written, textspeak is subject to change over time. It's still a linguistic newborn, relatively speaking; but in the era of digitized language, change happens fast. Even within its brief twenty-some-year existence the structures of textspeak have shifted—mainly due to upgrades in the devices and technology used for texting. The investigative literature has yet to take up this diachronic perspective on textspeak. In a recent study of undergraduates' texting practices, for instance, the authors observe:

> An increasing body of research has examined the written language used in text messaging, but little or no data exist regarding how the use of non-conventional spellings, or "textisms," may change over time as people adapt their written language to fit with advances in communication technology.[73]

In fact this chapter's opening vignette plays up this observation; namely, that textspeak itself has changed in line with technological upgrades. Compare Jill's 2000 text to Eric:

ges who gt a fone

with her daughter's text, sent in 2015 on a smartphone:

OMG mom. No one texts like that anymore unless they're ancient

Or an SMS cited in Crystal's 2008 book on texting:

if u cn send me the disk by post i'll get it copied[74]

with an exchange from 2015, posted on a website that archives comical texts:[75]

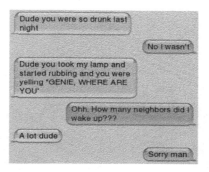

Notice that the more recently composed texts resemble traditionally written language more than early textspeak. Granted, the text from Jill's daughter bares vestiges of textspeak's original, norm-scoffing character (e.g., the acronym *OMG* and the proper noun *mom* sans capital). But in the main, her language, and the language of the "dude-you-were-so-drunk-last-night" dialogue, are closer to what you'd use for, say, a nonfiction book on the reciprocal relationship between language and technology.

So why the change from *ges who gt a fone* to *Guess who got a phone*? For starters, it's a lot easier to spell out complete words, and include punctuation, on an alphanumeric keypad. Take your basic period. On older handsets you often had to punch the same key multiple times to arrive at the symbol; on newer phones the period has its own key. Moreover, smartphones now change (prescriptivists would say "correct") your language for you. On most smartphones—unless you intentionally alter its default settings—tapping out the sequence "i luv u ur the bst" will incur the following automatic alterations: a) *i* gets capitalized; b) *luv u*, *ur*, and *bst* either get replaced with *love, you, you're*, and *best* or they get underlined in red (does this remind anyone else of their third-grade book reports?), telling you that your spelling is wrong; and c) a period gets inserted between *u* and *ur*.

In short, smartphones come preprogrammed to undo the creative variation that once trademarked textspeak. One might even say that smartphones instigate a technolingual tug-of-war. At one end of the rope stands the user, ready to communicate with textspeak's quirky code. At the other end stands the smartphone, configured to automatically adjust anything that strays from what it's been told is "acceptable" spelling and punctuation. Figure 5.5 shows this technolingual tug-of-war.

Sometimes this tug-of-war results in uncomfortable—and often humorous—mishaps. In our opening vignette, for instance, Jill's daughter means to text *door*, but something goes awry and her phone autocorrects it to *dork*. In techie circles this is known as the Cupertino effect.[76] Basically, it's autocorrect gone wrong, and the internet is becoming more and more

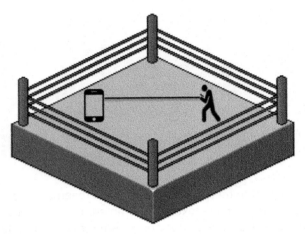

FIGURE 5.5 *Technolingual tug-of-war between smartphone and user.*

FIGURE 5.6 *Example of autocorrect gone wrong. (https://www.pinterest.com/pin/ 247557310736690444 (accessed December 29, 2015).)*

populated with (sometimes side-splitting) examples of it.[77] On Pinterest, for instance, thousands of users have posted screenshots of unfortunate text exchanges, an example of which is shown as Figure 5.6.

Incidentally, the Cupertino effect has promoted the functionality of one symbol in particular: the asterisk. When used in an SMS it conveys something like "What I meant to text was ___." Say you haven't eaten all day and want to know whether your BFF would like to join you for a bite. So you snatch your cell phone and inquire: *Hungry?* Except that your appendages don't hit their intended mark, prompting the following autocorrection:

Yikes! That's not *at all* what you meant. So you quickly add:

Asterisk to the rescue!

For the record, the use of * as a restoration device preceded autocorrection technology on cell phones. As early as 2002, Gloria E. Jacobs, a researcher in applied linguistics at Portland State University, noticed that participants in online chat rooms used the asterisk to signal repairs of typos or misspellings.[78] At one point in a live chat session, one of Jacobs's subjects wrote *i don't know whats going on her* and then quickly followed it up with *here*.[79] Jacobs explains:

According to Lisa [the participant who used the asterisk] she and her friends use an asterisk to indicate the correction of a spelling error. Lisa was unclear as to why she and her friends have adopted this convention, but preliminary analysis indicates that they use this convention only when the misspelled word could lead to a misreading of the message.[80]

In another study that looked at the textual-repair practices of five under-graduate students during live online meetings recorded in 2008, Kris Markman observed the same strategic use of *. "Although of unknown origin," she writes, "it is a commonly used convention in chat to retype the word with an asterisk either before or after the correction as a way of sig-naling repair."[81]

To recap our main point for this section: just as texting technology has changed, so has the language of texting itself. The erstwhile flagships of textspeak—the deviatory spelling and punctuation, the initialisms and contractions—are receding in the face of devices that come prewired to sup-press them. It's a showdown à la David (i.e., human linguistic creativity) vs. Goliath (i.e., the computer). And there's no way of knowing with any certainty how much longer, or to what extent, the textspeak of yore can survive the assault of digital prescriptivism. Only time, and texters' action or inaction, will tell.

The Dos and Don'ts of Textspeak: Language Ideologies of Text Messaging

By now, Dear Reader, you're well seasoned to the argument that technology's impact on language goes beyond structures and practices. As we've seen, the printing press, typewriter, telephone, telegraph, and email also spawned new *ideas* about language and the technology in question. Among other things, these ideas informed speakers on: a) how language ought or oughtn't be used with each technology; b) how and when the technology itself should or shouldn't be used to communicate with language; and c) the social, ethical, or moral standing of the person using the technology. We've used the term *language ideologies* as a catchall for these sorts of perceptions, attitudes, judgments, etc. And it should come as no surprise when we argue that simi-lar ideologies have sprung up for text messaging, too, especially as to what constitutes "proper" language and behaviors for composing and responding to texts.

Let's begin with guidebooks on text messaging. As we saw with email, these are how-to manuals written with the goal of instructing readers on the linguistic and behavioral "rights and wrongs" for communicating with the new medium. A basic search of Amazon, at the time of this writing, turned up fewer usage manuals for texting than for email.[82] Here we con-sider one manual, Izquierdo and Potter's *Textiquette: The Do's and Do Nots of Texting*.

This slim guide's mantra, posted on its final page as a kind of general con-clusion, hints at the authors' personal motivations for writing it: "Life is what happens when you're not texting."[83] It would seem, then, that they're concerned more about the social than the linguistic consequences of people's dependence on text messaging. While they admit that "with do's and do nots of texting etiquette, text messaging can be a useful tool,"[84] they nevertheless stress that they "have noticed that some people are abusing, and losing, much needed relationship skills"—all reasons why, they announce, they "are here to help."[85]

Izquierdo and Potter's "help" consists of thirty-two shibboleths, each beginning with a candid "do" or "do not." While some smack of basic common sense (e.g., "Do not make up your own abbreviations"[86]) or borderline comedy (e.g., "Do not text in the shower"[87]), others are sensible diktats that you find elsewhere online (e.g., "Do not use text to ask someone out,"[88] "Do not ever break up through a text or because of one,"[89] and of course "Do not text while driving"[90]). When it comes to language and texting, Izquierdo and Potter continue their conservative tone of prescriptivism. "Do use proper grammar and spell check," they instruct, adding that "if not maybe you shouldn't text."[91]

And to some extent Izquierdo and Potter have a point: there is evidence that speakers regularly judge—even make sweeping generalization about—a person's character based on the spelling and punctuation of that person's texts. A recent *New York Times* article, for instance, declares: "When Your Punctuation Says It All(!)" The article's author admits that she isn't immune to this kind of "you-are-how-you-text" behavior. In fact, she claims that once she even "went out with a guy based on his use of dashes [in a text message]" and "within moments of our first interaction—over text message—I was basically in love."[92] In other words, because the sender included the symbol "—" and did so correctly in the eyes of the receiver, the receiver extended this "correctness" or "goodness" to the sender's character. And thus it was love at first em dash.

What's more, when questioned on the topic of texting and grammar, the author's NYC friends showed similar attitudinal proclivities. One friend, for instance, told her that anyone who uses commas in texting runs the risk of being "viewed as straight-up 'geriatric.' "[93] And just in case you're wont to text *Boston Red Sox* instead of *boston red sox*, think again—according to Catherine Wise, a Manhattan lawyer in her early 30s, "unless you are a narc or an old person" you text in all lowercase letters.[94]

Speaking of articles … While (at the time of this writing) it's slim pickings in the book market for manuals on texting, it's a different story within print media. Since texting's arrival in the late 1990s, journalists have contributed countless articles—many to prominent newspapers and magazines—on the matter. A search for the term "texting" on *The Huffington Post*'s site returned nearly 650 pieces published between 2011 and 2015.[95] Upon closer review, a good part of these addressed behavioral practices:

> 5 Ways Texting Can Improve Your Relationship
> Sexting and Texting … the New Way to Connect?
> Why Isn't He ~~Calling~~ Texting Me?

Others inform readers of the physical dangers associated with texting:

> Walk, Text, Crash: An Orwellian Future
> This Is What Happens to Your Body When You Text
> Our Addiction to Cell Phones Is Costing Lives. Here's How We Can Stop It

Many other pieces speak to the linguistic structures of texting:

> The D*ck-tionary You Need to Decode the Crappy Texts We All Get
> The Message You Send When Your Text Reply Ends in a Period
> Textism: Is Spelling Over?

And yes, plenty of articles offer guidance on the social "rights and wrongs" of texting:

> A Much-Needed Guide to Text Etiquette
> Textiquette: Good, Bad, and Off Limits
> What Would Amy Ask? Etiquette for Young People in the Age of
>   Cell Phones

Let's take a closer look at what this last trio of "textiquette" pieces prescribes.

In "A Much-Needed Guide to Text Etiquette," author and family lifestyle expert Dana Holmes invites her readers to join her in "[learning] to manage our texting habits so that we can avoid hurt feelings and confusion among friends and loved ones."[96] Much like Izquierdo and Potter's *Textiquette*, Holmes presents a catalog of texting dos and don'ts. And in fact many of their prescriptions match; for instance, Holmes advises: "Don't use text slang unless you know what it means, either"; "Never text while another person is talking"; and "Take two seconds to proofread your text before sending it."[97]

Author and "recognized etiquette expert"[98] Lisa Mirza Grotts continues the patronizing do-this-but-avoid-that approach in "Textiquette: Good, Bad, and Off Limits." As texting has become such a "powerful tool" for communicating, she argues, it's incumbent on each of us to know that "it has ground rules and responsibilities."[99] Among others, her prescribed policies and practices include: "Don't text sad or bad news, or anything private or confidential"; "Don't freak out if you don't get a response to your text within 30 seconds"; and "Do be aware of your tone."

The third article, "What Would Amy Ask?" breaks with the tradition of simply listing dos and don'ts. Instead, it dispenses advice in paragraphed prose. "The etiquette of cell phone use is certainly an evolving one," the author, Julia Dobrow, observes.[100] Note that Dobrow is the director of communications and media studies at Tufts University (i.e., she's a linguist cloaked in another academic name). And perhaps this explains why Dobrow herself chooses not to *prescribe* any behavioral or linguistic practices in particular. Instead, she reports the responses of her university students when polled about when and what it's okay, or not okay, to text another person. They agreed, for instance, that texting is fine for run-of-the-mill communication (e.g., making plans or exchanging everyday information), but that using texting to break up with a romantic partner was a big no-no. Nevertheless, apart from these and a few other matters of texting etiquette, Dobrow found that her students "agreed that the unspoken rules about when you talk [on the cell phone], when you don't, when and what you text and snap photos of are all evolving."[101]

Not so, however, for the Emily Post Institute, whose website prescribes clear guidelines for when and how to send text messages. It's stated mission is to "evolve and maintain the standards of etiquette that Emily Post established with her seminal book *Etiquette* in 1922."[102] And this goes especially for manners in the modern digital age. "Don't text to inform someone of sad news or to end a relationship," heads up the roster of texting guidelines.[103] As to what you should do if you get a misdirected message from an unknown sender? "If you receive a text by mistake," the institute advises, "respond to the sender with 'Sorry, wrong number.'"[104] Indeed, the institute offers clear-cut instructions on the acceptable pragmatics for texting exchanges. For instance, their website advocates:

> Think of texting as a conversation: If you would respond in the conversation, then respond in the text. A short "TNX" to acknowledge that the message was received is a simple way to end the conversation.[105]

The Emily Post Institute has been preaching manners to the American masses for fourscore years. And its keepers have remained in step with the changing world around it. Texting is the latest in a long line of communication tools—going back to the telegraph and candlestick telephones of the 1930s—for which the Post prescriptivists have issued social and linguistic guiderails. Indeed, the fact that the institute recognizes texting as important or relevant enough to regulate is further testament to the technology's influence on our linguistic and behavioral practices.

The Mobilization of Language and Technolingualism

This chapter focused on a technology that, we've argued, resulted in the mobilization of language: the cell phone.

We began with language's influence on speech-recognition technology, a feature standard to most modern cellular devices. We looked at how the acoustic-phonetic realities of speech have shaped engineers' approaches to developing accurate and reliable speech-recognition technology. And we gave two examples of how, "throughout the course of development of [speech recognition] systems, knowledge of speech production and perception was used in establishing the technological foundation for the resulting speech recognizers."[106]

Beginning in the 1950s, linguists used the spectrograph to uncover the physical differences among speech sound segments, that is, the acoustic-phonetic basis for why speakers hear one sound and not the other. Speech-recognition systems, we saw, identify the acoustic features of speech by analyzing spectrograms. Moreover, the chronic variability of speech made it especially hard for machines to get it right when presented with different speakers. However, we saw that this variability motivated computer scientists to seek solutions through mathematic sleights of hand, particularly through statistical (read: probability) modeling processes (e.g., hidden Markov models).

In the second part of the chapter we considered how text messaging has impacted written language: through initialisms, contractions, clippings, phonetic spellings, logograms, punctuation, emojis, and the use of asterisks as a repairing device. And with a nod to David Crystal, we also referred to this new variety of written language as *textspeak*.

We first argued that *textspeak* is stylistically versatile, that is, it's used for formal and informal communications, to convey mundane information, and to compose creative works. Second, we made the case that *textspeak*, like all varieties of living human language, has changed over time. Last, we reviewed prescriptive sources on text messaging. These usage guides, we saw, generally agree that: 1) texting shouldn't be used to announce serious social or emotional information (e.g., tragic news, breaking up with a significant other); 2) spelling and punctuation matter, since recipients often judge the sender based on these elements; 3) users shouldn't use too many initialisms, in case the recipient isn't familiar with them; and 4) users shouldn't text while engaged in real-world conversation.

In Chapter 6—the final chapter of our exploration of technolingualism—we focus on medical matters. We see how language has both shaped and been shaped by mechanical technologies developed for the hearing impaired—an interactive process we're calling the regeneration of language.

6

Regeneration of Language: The Cochlear Implant

Between Silence and Sound, or Triumphs and Trials of Cochlear Implantation

Half giddy with excitement, half with anxiety, Emily fidgets in her chair. A plastic-coated magnet the size of a quarter sits snugly against her head, a few inches above the ear. A small cord runs from it to another device that contours around the back of her ear. A second cord, longer and only temporary, runs from this curved device to the audiologist's computer.

It's been four weeks since her surgery. Today is A-Day—activation day—for her cochlear implant. If everything goes as planned, in a few moments her life will change: for the first time in more than a decade she'll be able to "hear."

What if it doesn't work? What if my brain has forgotten what the world sounds like? No, she steels herself. *I won't expect too much . . .*

The audiologist taps on the keyboard. Emily can see her lips moving, but from this angle can't read them.

Any moment now . . .

Emily's mother stands off to the side, iPhone in hand and recording everything. In many ways today is just as important for her. Twelve years ago the 3-year-old version of the young woman sitting nervously in the chair came down with a fever that spiked to 105. Bacterial meningitis, the doctors pronounced. So severe that it robbed the child of almost all her hearing. And no matter how much the doctors assured Emily's mother that there was very little she could have done to prevent the illness, a part of her still hasn't forgiven herself.

If only I'd taken her to the hospital the night before . . . If only we hadn't gone to the mall that day, where she probably picked up the infection . . .

Yes—her mother is just as excited and anxious as Emily. Probably even more.

Just then Emily hears something. Beeps. Faint, but unmistakable.

The audiologist looks at Emily. "Okay, right now you should be hearing some tones."

Emily focuses on the series of beeps. They're still soft. Now they're getting louder. Yes, she can definitely hear them now.

"Do the beeps sound different? Some higher, some lower?"

Emily nods.

Does this mean it's going to work?

Her face warms with anticipation. Then she catches herself.

Careful, Emily. Remember what the doctors said: realistic expectations . . .

"Alright," the audiologist says. "I'm going to switch it on. Are you ready, Emily?"

She nods. Her mother gives her a thumbs-up. The audiologist moves the mouse and double clicks. The next moment, a medium-pitched whirring sound floods Emily's ear.

"Is it on?" Emily says aloud, signing at the same time, as is her habit.

At once the whirring sound is pushed aside by a loud, high-pitched robotic voice asking, "Is it on?"

Her voice—warped and Mickey Mouse sounding, but it's her own voice, a sound she hasn't heard in more than a decade.

"We're going to do a few sound tests, okay?" the audiologist says.

Again the words sound strangely tinny—and in fact she doesn't recognize them on their sound alone; she has to read the audiologist's lips. But still: she can "hear" them.

"I can hear your voice," she signs. "But it sounds weird. So does mine."

"Like a high-pitched robot?"

Emily nods.

"That's common. But it should get better after the first few mapping sessions."

"What do you mean by mapping sessions?" Emily asks.

"I'll explain shortly. Remember, too, that your brain is getting sensory input that it hasn't had to process in a long time. It usually takes a while for it to adjust."

Emily nods, wondering just how long "a while" will be.

"Now we're going to do a few things in the room." The audiologist gets up and positions herself behind Emily's chair. She takes a piece of paper and crumples it.

What is that . . .? It sounds like . . .

The audiologist crumples a second leaf. Emily's eyes light up.

"Paper!" she signs. "You're doing something with a piece of paper."

The audiologist returns to Emily's field of view and shows her the crumpled sheets. Emily takes one, smooths it out on her thigh, and balls it back up.

"It's not very loud," she signs with one hand, her face beaming. "But I can hear it."

The next sounds turn out even better: her mother's footsteps, the door slamming shut, the keys clicking on the computer keyboard—even the doctor's sneeze!

Emily's eyes start to well up. This is more emotional than she's expected. She looks at her mom. She's crying too.

"Everything looks good," the audiologist says. "Just remember to be patient with yourself. Give your brain the time it needs to adjust. Most patients go through dozens of mappings, and need months before they can understand individual words without direct lipreading."

They schedule the first of what will be several mappings over the next year. These sessions, the audiologist explains as she hands Emily a thrice-folded pamphlet titled, *MAPping Your CI: Everything You Need to Know*, will allow them to individually fine-tune the twenty-two electrodes in her inner ear. In the meantime, the audiologist assigns her "homework"—listening and concentration exercises that will encourage her brain to adjust to a range of environmental and linguistic stimuli.

As she gets up from her chair to leave, Emily glances around the room. It even *looks* different to her now.

So many sounds in just this one little room . . .

That's when it clicks: that whirring sound, the one she heard right after the audiologist turned on the implant. It was the air-conditioning unit in the window behind her, the one she notices just now. As far as she can recall, she's never heard an air conditioner.

And all at once it sinks in: outside of this room—of this building—lies an entire world of new sounds . . .

Two weeks later she's sitting with her friends at lunch. As usual, hands and fingers are flying: typical teenage gossip, complaints about schoolwork and teachers, plans for the upcoming weekend . . .

Emily's attended this school for the deaf since second grade, and most of these girls have been in her same class since then. None of them has a cochlear implant yet, although she knows that a few of them are thinking about going to the audiologist to ask about it—especially now that Emily has one. For the first few days after her activation day they'd assailed her nonstop with questions: What kinds of things can you hear? What do they sound like? Does the thing stuck to your head hurt? Does it ever shock you? Do you still have to lipread when a "hearie" talks? How long do the batteries last?

And so on . . .

By now, however, the girls' focus has shifted from Emily's new aural hardware and returned to the regular topics of teenhood.

One of her friends, Michelle, is in the middle of griping about homework when Emily sees an older girl approach their table. Emily recognizes her, but doesn't know her name. She's from a grade above. As are the three girls flanking her, taggers-along for the show.

The leader taps her foot against the table, interrupting Michelle. "People are talking about you," she signs to Emily.

For a moment Emily is finger-tied.

Who is this girl and why does she care if people are talking about me?

"Do I know you?" she finally signs.

"They're saying you think you're better than us now," the girl cuts through the air.

"Keep on walking," Michelle signs back. She's always been the more assertive one of the bunch. "We don't even know you."

The older girl scowls at Michelle then returns her attention to Emily.

"I just wanted to tell you to your face that you're not any better than any of us. In fact, you're not even one of us. You're just some half hearie who thinks she's all that."

And with that the girl and her retinue walk away. For several moments no one at the table says anything. Finally, Michelle motions to Emily and signs, "Don't even worry about that bitch. She's probably just jealous." The others quickly add their agreement, and the conversation pivots back to plans for the weekend.

Yet when the bell rings and the girls head back to class, Emily's mind is still on that girl and what she said.

Do people really think that about me?

She isn't the first kid at the school to get a cochlear implant. (Emily can think of several offhand.) Sure, she'd heard this or that scrap of scuttlebutt about those girls. But she hadn't paid it any mind. After all, she isn't one to judge others.

But now here she is, herself the target of judgment.

This change in her life, she's starting to see, is about a lot more than just being able to hear again . . .

∞

Recall that in Chapter 5 we furthered our case for technolingualism with a discussion of what we called the mobilization of language. With the cell phone as our beacon, we showed how language has both affected and been affected by this modern artifact of communication technology. We argued that the physical properties of speech informed the development and refinement of speech-recognition technology, a feature that comes standard on most cellular smartphones. Moreover, we described how the acoustic variation inherent in speech pushed engineers to come up with creative speech-processing algorithms like the hidden Markov model. Alternatively, we addressed the new variety of language that the cell phone has inspired, via text-messaging technology: a written variety that we referred to as "textspeak."

In the present chapter—which marks the final episode in our exploration of the sociolinguistic phenomenon we've termed *technolingualism*—we're going to consider technology that has aided in the regeneration of language, that is, instruments created to restore an individual's facility of speaking, hearing, or writing. Our goal, by chapter's end, is to give a convincing technolingual account of one language-regenerating technology in particular: the cochlear implant.

Loyal as ever to our technolingual framework, we come at this language-regenerating technology from opposing angles: language's influence on technology, and technology's influence on language. On the one hand we show how our body's apparatuses for processing speech steered inventers, giving them key physical and conceptual cues—information that made the cochlear implant possible. On the other hand, in the latter half of the chapter we consider the cochlear implant's sociolinguistic impact within the Deaf community. In particular, we see how language ideologies, affected by the technology, tie in with issues of group and individual identity (as alluded to in our opening narrative).

But first, let's take a short trip inside the human ear.

In the next section we offer an overview of how our amazing ear processes speech. Why? Because as Professor Philipos C. Loizou—an "internationally known leader in signal and speech processing, speech perception and cochlear implants"[1]—notes in *Mimicking the Human Ear*, "An understanding of how our auditory system works was central to the development of a successful cochlear implant."[2]

The Amazing, Pea-Sized Boney Spiral, or How Our Ear Processes Sound

In previous chapters we've described how speakers produce sounds with their lungs, larynx, nasal cavity, and various articulators in the mouth. We saw, for instance, that speakers use this posse of speech organs to utter sounds that differ in manner (e.g., voicing, aspiration, frication) and place (e.g., labial, dental, palatal) of articulation. Here, however, we're dealing with the *perception* of speech sounds. And in so doing we journey deep inside the ear to look at the physiological clockwork that allows us to do this (i.e., perceive speech, in addition to all other nonlinguistic environmental sounds).

Recall that in Chapter 3 ("The Abstraction of Language") we described how Alexander G. Bell took his inspiration, and design cues, for the telephone's receiver from a human ear that he extracted from a cadaver. And using this harvested cadaver ear, he built a phonautograph that mimicked the auditory process of *transduction* (a fancy word for "the physical conveyance of sound waves through the ear"). Specifically, Bell worked with the middle portion of the ear, as shown in Figure 6.1.

The tympanic membrane (or eardrum), and the trio of bones that conducted sound through the middle ear, were the focus of Bell's experiments. Remember too that his eureka moment, which came while Bell was musing over this anatomical arrangement, was that a series of tiny objects could carry sound waves

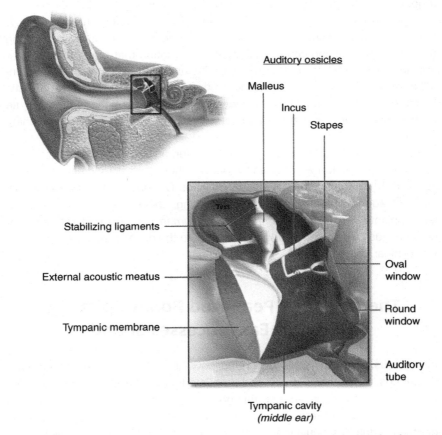

FIGURE 6.1 *The middle ear. (https://commons.wikimedia.org/wiki/File:Blausen_0330_EarAnatomy_MiddleEar.png (accessed February 21, 2017).)*

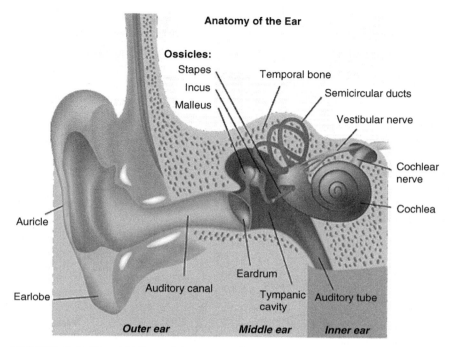

Anatomy of the Ear

Ossicles:
Stapes
Incus
Malleus

Temporal bone
Semicircular ducts
Vestibular nerve
Cochlear nerve
Cochlea

Auricle

Earlobe
Auditory canal
Eardrum
Tympanic cavity
Auditory tube

Outer ear | **Middle ear** | **Inner ear**

FIGURE 6.2 *The middle and inner ear. (https://www.earq.com/hearing-loss/ear-anatomy (accessed June 29, 2016).)*

captured by a larger, rigid membrane—even if this membrane was metallic. Bell therefore "saw his telephone as a kind of electro-mechanical ear."[3] The physical and physiological processes behind the middle ear's processing of speech, in other words, inspired the diaphragm design of Bell's telephone.

In a similar fashion, in this chapter we see how the inner ear—in particular, its physiology and its neuromechanical processes—informed the design of the modern-day cochlear implant. Figure 6.2 shows the main parts of the middle and inner ear.

Notice that the stapes bone physically links the middle ear with its inner complement. Its osseous stirrups cover one of two openings (called "windows") into the *cochlea*.

Now, as you can gather from the technology's name (i.e., *cochlear* implant), this "boney spiral" is key to regenerating the ability to hear. So from here on out we focus on the cochlea. A mere eighth of an inch long, this snail-shaped miracle of biology is the inspiration for modern implant technology. Figure 6.3 gives a cross-sectional view inside the cochlea.

As you can see, if you were to straighten out the two-and-a-half twists of its hard carapace, and then cleave it in half lengthwise, you'd essentially find

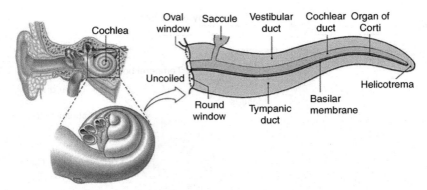

FIGURE 6.3 *Cross-sectional view of cochlea's anatomy.*[4] *(http://slideplayer.com/ slide/4280354 (accessed June 30, 2016).)*

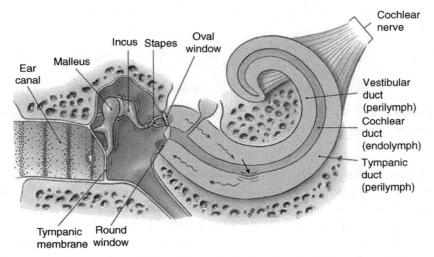

FIGURE 6.4 *How sound waves move through the cochlea. (http://slideplayer.com/ slide/4280354 (accessed June 30, 2016).)*

a "duct between two ducts." That is, in the center you'd find two cellophane-like membranes stretching from the spiral's base to its apex, in effect creating: 1) a separate intermediate passage, known as the cochlear duct (or *scala media*); 2) a passage above, called the vestibular duct (or *scala vestibuli*); and 3) a passage below, the tympanic duct (or *scala tympani*).

So, you might be asking yourself at this point, what does this mess of ducts have to do with the sounds they get from the middle ear? Figure 6.4 depicts the process.

Notice that as the middle ear bones vibrate, the stapes concentrates the energy against another membrane spanning the entrance (or oval window)

THE WATER IN THE GLASS IS VIBRATING.

FIGURE 6.5 Jurassic Park *storyboard drawing of sound ripples in water. (http://www.jurassicworlduniverse.com/jurassic-park/images/storyboards (accessed July 4, 2016).)*

to the cochlea's upper duct. All three ducts within the cochlea are filled with fluid; the vestibular and tympanic corridors contain a thin, plasma-like fluid called *perilymph*. And when the stapes pulses against the oval window membrane, it sets this fluid in motion, in effect sending ripples of sound through it.

Remember that harrowing scene in the 1992 box-office hit *Jurassic Park*, where the children are trapped in the Jeep while the tyrannosaurus approaches? There's a cup of water on the Jeep's dashboard. And each mighty stomp—gaining in intensity as the beast draws nearer—sets the liquid in motion, producing ripples, as shown in Figure 6.5.

This is basically the same mechanical-liquid process that happens in our inner ear. Tiny sound waves travel through the fluid inside the vestibular and tympanic corridors. And as they roll through, they slosh against the vestibular and basilar membranes, the sheets of tissue that form the cochlea's intermediary duct (alias "duct between two ducts," alias cochlear duct, alias scala media). Figure 6.6 shows where these membranes are located.

But wait! We're not done with membranes just yet. Figure 6.7 gives a close-up view inside the boney spiral's intermediary duct.

Notice that even within the cochlear duct there's yet another thin sheet of tissue called the tectorial membrane. (The cochlea's anatomy, you could say, is redolent of the play-within-a-play antics of a Shakespearean comedy!)

Ultimately it's here, within the membraneal funhouse of the cochlear duct, that the magic of sound perception really happens. As you can see in Figure 6.7, filling up the space between the tectorial and basilar membrane are

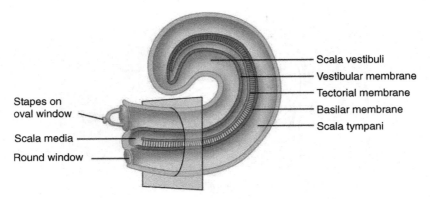

FIGURE 6.6 *Cross-section of cochlea. (http://droualb.faculty.mjc.edu (accessed July 4, 2016).)*

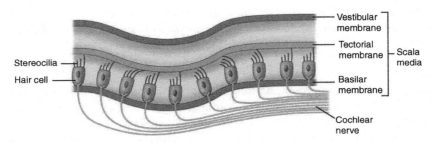

FIGURE 6.7 *Cross-sectional close-up of the cochlear duct. (http://droualb.faculty. mjc.edu (accessed July 4, 2016).)*

little bundles of microscopic "firm hairs," or *stereocilia*. There are thousands of stereosciliary bundles, each attached to a sensory cell. And each sensory cell plugs right into the cochlear nerve, which connects to the brain. So each time a sound wave displaces the inner-ear fluid in the tympanic duct, this causes the basilar membrane to bend and bulge. And guess what moves along with the basilar membrane, because they're attached to it? You got it: the stereocilia. Loizou explains it:

> The bending of the hairs releases an electrochemical substance that causes neurons to fire, signaling the presence or excitation at a particular site in the inner ear. These neurons communicate with the central nervous system and transmit information about the acoustic signal to the brain.[5]

Our cochlea essentially "functions as a transducer, converting mechanical sound waves into electrical signals carried by the auditory nerve to the brain."[6] That's one amazing, pea-sized bone.

Thus ends our explanation of how our inner ear allows us to experience, among myriad other acoustic phenomena, the sounds of human language. One tip, though, before we move on: keep the basilar membrane in mind. Below it will become clear how this microscopic, transparent stretch of tissue held the key design cue for developing auditory-regeneration technology.

Of Cochlear Mechanics, or How Language Shaped the Cochlear Implant

Now that we have our aural-physiological wits about us—that is, we have a clearer picture of how our ear processes speech—let's launch into our technolingual argument. Just to refresh our memory: by "technolingualism" we mean the reciprocally influential relationship between language and technology. And for this chapter in particular, it means we look at a technology invented to regenerate the human auditory system, through a mix of anatomical mimicry and electrical stimulation. "The cochlear implant," the editors of *Cochlear Implants: Auditory Prostheses and Electric Hearing* declare in the volume's preface, "is the most successful neural prosthesis developed to date."[7] Below we highlight one scientist in particular—the "grand-daddy of experimental cochlear mechanics"[8]—whose pioneering observations, models, and techniques contributed to the technology's present-day design and effectiveness.

Georg von Békésy: Game-Changer in Cochlear Mechanics

In yet another of the many delicious ironies one finds in the history of science and technology, the man whose "elegant and ingenious experiments"[9] paved the way for modern cochlear implant design—a Hungarian-born scientist obsessed as much with the beauty of the cochlea as he was with Oriental art[10]—it's ironic that Georg von Békésy never even studied medicine. As he describes in an autobiographical speech published after his death, his background was in chemistry, physics, and math.[11]

And yet in 1961 he was honored with the noblest of awards within the medical sciences: the Nobel Prize in Physiology or Medicine. "Von Bekesy," a colleague lauded in the official presentation speech, "has provided us with the knowledge of the physical events at all strategically important points in the transmission system of the ear."[12] Expressed in leaner terms: Békésy figured out how our ear's innards turn sounds into electrochemical fodder for our brain.

"The electrical characteristics of the cochlea are of fundamental importance in [cochlear] implant design," Daniel Geisler, emeritus professor of neuro-
physiology concludes, adding that "the modern era in this field of inquiry
begins, as it so often does in any area of cochlear research, with the work of
Georg von Békésy."[13] Accordingly, in this section we show how Békésy's discoveries, over years of observation and experimentation, contributed to the
regeneration of language. In particular we show how his insights laid the foundation for the cochlear implant's most critical design feature: the multichannel
electrode array. As we'll see, this design feature emulates the way our cochlea
actually processes sound.

Rediscovering the Cochlea, the Great Acoustic Spectrum Analyzer

The cochlear implant, Loizou explains, is science's attempt to "mimic the
human ear."[14] Engineers thus looked to the inner ear, especially the cochlea,
for their design cues. First and foremost, they needed to understand how this
little bony spiral handles complex fluctuations in air pressure with multiple
overlying frequencies, otherwise known as sound waves. And, fortunately
for them, they didn't have to start from square one. They were able to draw
on Békésy's discoveries—the most important of which was that the cochlea
functions as an *acoustic spectrum analyzer*.

The cochlea, you see, has an ingenious anatomical feature that breaks up
complex sound waves into individual strata for multilocational, frequency-
targeted processing: a "stiff structural element"[15] called the basilar membrane. And although scientists had known about the basilar membrane for
centuries before Békésy "found the inner ear so beautiful under a stereo-
scopic microscope that [he] decided to stay with that problem,"[16] no one knew
exactly how this integral part of the cochlea worked. Békésy was the first to
physiologically observe, measure, and model its functions. As such, "his discoveries serve as a basis for our conception of the cochlea as a frequency
analyzer."[17] And it turns out that modern-day implants, constructed to mimic
the cochlea's physiological gadgetry, rely precisely on this major insight.

It's worth mentioning, once again, that Békésy was far from the first scientist to take an interest in the cochlea. "Many of the general features of
the ear's structures were discovered by the pioneer anatomists of the sixteenth and seventeenth centuries," Békésy himself notes in *Experiments
in Hearing*.[18] In the centuries that followed the cochlea's initial "discovery," microscopes and preparation methods improved. And by the nineteenth century scientists could look inside the cochlea with enough clarity
to pinpoint the inner membranes as the source of its sound-processing
superpower.

Still, these avant-garde cadaver carvers remained stumped by one question: how does the cochlea actually convert sounds into neurological information that the brain can process?

To be sure, there'd been theories (i.e., science talk for "educated guess"). In the late nineteenth century, for instance, the leading educated guess came from Prussia's most respected scientist-slash-philosopher, Hermann von Helmholtz. In *Sensations of Tone*, published in 1863, he suggested that the basilar membrane works like a sound resonator, that is, it reacts to the vibrations travelling through the tympanic canal by itself vibrating at the same frequency. This idea, that cochlear processing of sound is based on a vibratory mirroring effect, was called the *resonance theory*. In Békésy's words, this theory "assumes that the transverse fibers of the basilar membrane act as tiny resonators, each one tuned to a different frequency. The tuning varies continuously along the membrane, and stimulating a particular tone sets in vibration only a small group of resonates in the region."[19]

Turns out, Helmholtz was both right and wrong. He was right that the basilar membrane handles sound in multiple places distributed along its length, depending on frequency. However, his proposal that this "frequency mapping" was based on resonance was false. (Békésy would later show that it was based on a traveling-wave model.) More importantly, though, remember that this was all still just a *hypothesis*; Helmholtz wasn't able to physically observe what was going on inside the cochlea.[20]

Fast-forward sixty years and guess who turns out to be a Helmholtz fan? Békésy, who called Helmholtz's theory "probably the most elegant theories of hearing."[21] And upon receiving the Nobel Prize in 1961 he paid special homage to the German scientist. "For me," Békésy confessed to the audience, "the most stimulating book on hearing was Helmholtz's *Sensations of Sound*."[22] He was inspired by the methodical, scientifically scrupulous approach that Helmholtz took in his studies of the human body's parts and operations. More importantly, though, through Helmholtz's work Békésy became enamored of the inner ear's aesthetics: its design, contours, and mechanisms. "It was the beauty and pleasure of the beauty that made me stick to the ear," he would later write.[23]

By the late 1920s, when he first encountered Helmholtz's book, Békésy's own career path (at this time, as a communications engineer with the Hungarian post office) had already led him to the ear. The Hungarian government, you see, wasn't satisfied with the signal quality of its telephonic technology. And so Békésy was charged with making improvements. Increasingly, however, the young engineer found himself drawn to the lingering question of how the ear processes physical sounds. This was, in fact, the start of what would become a four-decade-long research agenda. As one author says in a piece for *Physics Today*:

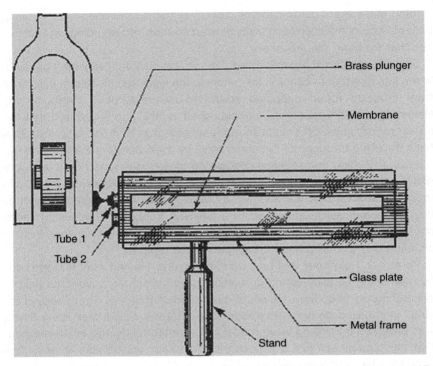

FIGURE 6.8 *Békésy's model of the cochlea. (Békésy,* Experiments in Hearing, *407.)*

> Békésy set about to discover how the ear does in fact respond to sound waves and how the cells and membranes in the tiny coiled-up cochlea vibrate in response to different frequencies.... He launched a two-pronged attack. He constructed dynamic models of the inner ear.... He also delved into the anatomy of the cochlea itself, observing stroboscopically the motions of the sensory receptors riding on the vibrating basilar membrane.[24]

Figure 6.8 shows one dynamic model of the inner ear that Békésy constructed in 1928.

As you can see, Békésy's contraption replicates the cochlea's "duct-between-two-ducts" setup. Within a larger tube (replicating the bony outer shell) there are two chambers (replicating the tympanic and vestibular ducts) filled with liquid (water, replicating the perilymph) and separated by a flexible membrane (made of rubber, mimicking the basilar membrane). Békésy describes:

> In the middle of a long brass frame was fastened a thin metal band [which] was covered with a rubber membrane that broadened gradually,

FIGURE 6.9 *Rubber "basilar membrane" of Békésy's inner ear model.*

representing the basilar membrane.... Two glass plates were cemented on the sides of the frame so as to fit tightly against the edges of the metal band, and the trough so formed was filled with fluid. The ends of two small tubes, representing the oval and round windows, were covered with rubber membranes, and on one of these was attached a brass plunger, representing the stapes. The plunger was attached to the prong of a tuning fork, which was driven electromagnetically by an oscillator.[25]

When Békésy directed vibrations of various frequencies into the model, he saw that they caused the rubber membrane to quiver most (or, as he put it, "maximally displace") at different spots along its length. Critically, he noticed that higher-frequency oscillations caused the base of the rubber membrane, where it was narrower and thicker, to vibrate more. He also noted that the top of the membrane, where the rubber was wider and thinner, moved more in response to lower-frequency waves. Figure 6.9 gives a simple illustration of this.

Next, Békésy placed his bare arm lengthwise against the brass tube. To his delight, he could actually feel the vibrations shift up and down along his arm, as the frequencies fluctuated. This, he realized, was analogous to the neural stimulation that happens with the hair cells (i.e., stereocilia) inside the cochlear duct. "From these experiments," he concludes in his Nobel lecture, "it was evident that the ear contains a neuromechanical frequency analyzer, which combines a preliminary mechanical frequency analysis with a subsequent sharpening of the sensation area."[26]

But he didn't stop there. Békésy wanted to go where Helmholtz and the other pioneers hadn't been able to go: he wanted to observe inner-cochlear activity—literally in the flesh. Put another way, Békésy wanted to watch the basilar membrane, in a still-functional cochlea, perform its frequency analysis. But in order to do this he had to use cutting-edge instruments and concoct new anatomization techniques. "I was probably one of the first," Békésy states, "who used constantly high-speed drills to drill out the cochlea and to investigate it that way."[27] Dental drills, to be specific. And—in all seriousness—he performed the dissection underwater.

Not that he himself was submerged in water, but rather, the cochlea was. In a biographical memoir, Ratcliff describes the Nobel winner's unique dissection process:

> The preparation was placed in a square bath with the fluid entering on one side and flowing out the other. Then, by using a high-speed drill, it was possible to grind off very thin layers of bone. Each time the drill was used, a cloud of bone dust was formed in the bath; but, because the fluid was continuously flowing, the cloud cleared very quickly. He was able to open nearly a full turn of the tip of the snail-shaped cochlea and thereby to expose to view a substantial portion of the intact basilar membrane.[28]

Having figured out how to access the intact insides of a functioning cochlea, Békésy then ran sound experiments with it. He set up a powerful waterproof microscope. And again using his trusty tuning fork, he sent sound waves of varying frequencies into the submerged specimen.

But there was another small hurdle: the actual basilar membrane is transparent. So even though the membrane was moving in response to the sound waves, Békésy couldn't see it. Ever the innovator, he quickly solved the problem. "He sprinkled tiny quantities of a silver powder over it," Mook explains, "and these reflected the light of the strong surgical lamp."[29] The metallic powder thus brought the membrane into bright, shiny view. And now, when the sound waves rippled through the tympanic duct, "the various patterns of vibration of the membrane produced by various pitches of sound could be observed directly."[30]

To wrap up, Békésy was a pioneer in modeling, observing, and measuring our ear's neuromechanical processes for registering sound. His work laid the basis for one of the most important anatomical principles of modern audiology: *cochlear tonotopicity*. Basically, this fancy term means that the microscopic hair cells behind the basilar membrane—the stereocilia that move when the membrane is displaced by sound waves—are arranged according to pitch or tone. And, just as Békésy observed with the basilar membrane, the hairs near the cochlea's base are most stimulated by high-frequency waves, while the hairs near the apex react most to low-frequency waves. Figure 6.10 is a barebones illustration of cochlear tonotopicity.

Tonotopicity and Cochlear Implants

At this point you might be wondering: What does all of this—the inner-ear model, observations, measurements, tonotopicity, etc.—have to do with the cochlear implant? What's the connection between Békésy and this

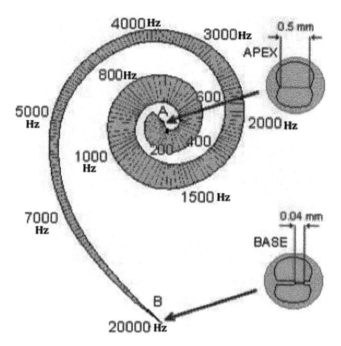

FIGURE 6.10 *Cochlear tonotopicity. (http://slideplayer.com/slide/7845732 (accessed July 14, 2016).)*

chapter's language-regenerating technology? In this section we make the connection clear.

Earlier we noted that Békésy's discoveries paved the way for a crucial "design feature" of modern-day auditory prostheses. Well, the design feature we alluded to is the cochlear implant's *multielectrode array*, an example of which is given in Figure 6.11.

Each dark notch is an electrode. (In this image there are twenty-two, but the number of electrodes varies according to the implantee's medical needs.) Moreover, each electrode is responsible for delivering a certain frequency range, or channel, of sound to the auditory nerve. Figure 6.12 shows what it looks like when a multichannel implant (here, a twelve-channel model) is inserted into the cochlea, and the approximate frequency-to-electrode relationship.

An official technical report on cochlear implants, written and made available online by the American Speech-Language-Hearing Association, notes the following about multichannel devices:

Multichannel, multi-electrode cochlear implant systems are designed to take advantage of the tonotopic organization of the cochlea. The incoming

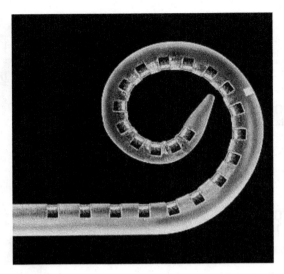

FIGURE 6.11 *Multielectrode array of modern-day cochlear implant. (https://elec-tronicsnews.com.au/new-electrode-designs-improve-cochlear-implant-performance (accessed July 14, 2016).)*

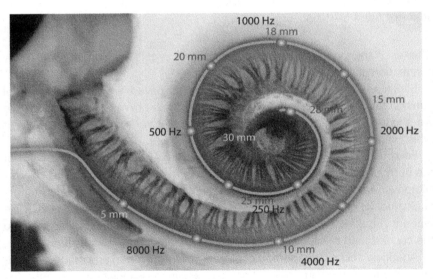

FIGURE 6.12 *Implanted twelve-channel, multielectrode device. (http://www.medel.com/uk/show2/index/id/1361/title/Complete-Cochlear-Coverage (accessed July 20, 2016).)*

Single channel   Multichannel

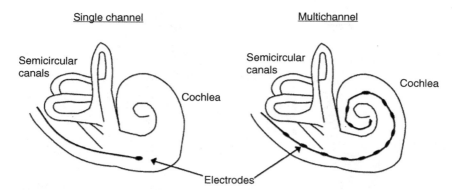

FIGURE 6.13 *Single-channel cochlear implant with single electrode. (Raghu Garud and Michael A. Rappa, "A Socio-Cognitive Model of Technology Evolution: The Case of Cochlear Implants,"* Organizational Science *5, no. 3 (1994): 350.)*

speech signal is filtered into a number of frequency bands, each corresponding to a given electrode in the electrode array. Thus, multichannel cochlear implant systems use place coding to transfer spectral information in the speech signal.[31]

In other words, the design of today's cochlear implant is based on Békésy's models, observations, and measurements from the late 1920s. "The pioneering work of Georg von Bekesy," Loizou concludes," showed that the basilar membrane in the inner ear is responsible for analyzing the input signal into different frequencies."[32] As such, his work became a critical part of science's program to mimic the human ear.

The first cochlear implants, however, were not multichannel. Dr. William House, for instance, outfitted his model from the early 1970s—the first aural prosthesis, in fact, to be approved by the FDA—with a single electrode. The House 3M, as it was called, filtered incoming sounds to a range of 340–2700 Hz and delivered the signal to only one place in the cochlea, near its base. Figure 6.13 is a basic illustration of a single-electrode, single-channel device.

Ensuing trials and research would show that single-channel implants were functionally inferior to their multichannel counterparts. However, they were budget friendlier and easier to use and maintain. What's more, most implantees did experience moderate benefits. They could, for instance, distinguish between speech and nonspeech sounds. But they weren't able to blindly understand entire sentences or pick out individual words. For the most part single-electrode devices made implantees defter lipreaders.[33] The multichannel, multielectrode design proved much more effective at regenerating an individual's ability to hear open-set words and phrases.[34] As a result, sales of

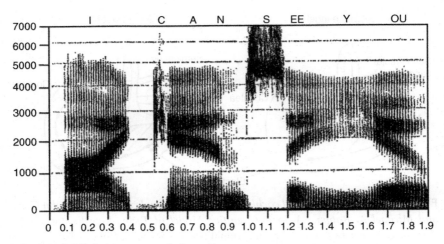

FIGURE 6.14 *Spectrogram of phrase* I can see you.

single-channel implants fell off fast when the multichannel technology made its debut in the mid-1980s.[35] And by the early 1990s production of single-channel devices was halted.

The problem, you've no doubt put together, was that single-channel implants didn't draw on Békésy's work. "It was not surprising," Loizou observes, "that relatively few patients could obtain open-set speech understanding with single-channel implants given the limited spectral information, [because] single-channel stimulation does not exploit the place code mechanism used by a normal cochlea for encoding frequencies." In other words, the single-electrode design completely ignored tonotopicity. (Imagine Békésy's horror!) So before we end this first half of our technolingual treatment of language-regenerating technology, let's take a closer look—with some helpful illustrations—at how multichannel implants are designed to handle the spectral character of speech, thus mirroring the cochlea's natural tonotopic configuration.

Figure 6.14 is a spectral readout, using the speech-analysis software Praat, of the phrase *I can see you*. You might recall, from our discussion in Chapter 5, that these visualizations of sound are called spectrograms. A spectrogram shows concentrations of acoustic energy according to frequency (indicated along the y-axis, in Hz) and time (along the x-axis, in seconds).

Notice that the vowels have clear bands of focused energy, and that these bands—called formants—are unique for each vowel. The vowel in *see*, for instance, has one peak stretch of energy between 50 and 700 Hz, a second between 2300 and 2900 Hz, and a third between 3100 and 3500 Hz. The vowel in *you* also displays a concentrated swath of sound waves between 50 and 700 Hz, but its second formant runs between 900 and 1200 Hz. Figure 6.15

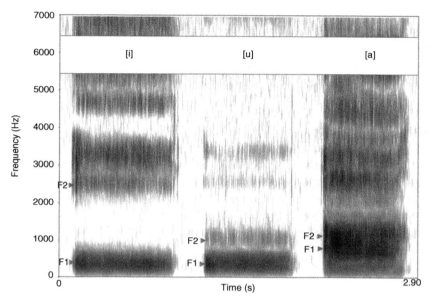

FIGURE 6.15 *Formant signatures of vowels in see and you. (https://commons. wikimedia.org/wiki/User:Ish_ishwar#/media/File:Spectrogram_-iua-.png (accessed July 24, 2016).)*

shows more clearly the distinct formant signatures of these vowels, as spoken in isolation.

As for the consonants, note in Figure 6.15 that, for starters, they don't have the same kind of formant structure. In place of focused, discernable bands, it looks more like a smearing of acoustic energy. The other thing you notice is that this energy occurs at different frequencies for each consonant. To wit, the first consonant in *can* produces energy from about 2000 to 5000 Hz, while the onset segment in *see* features a splotch of noise from 4200 all the way up to 7000 Hz.

What this means for the multichannel implant is that each electrode needs to be assigned a frequency range (or channel) that mirrors the formant signatures of vowels and the scattered acoustic patterns of consonants, that is, when the sound waves for *see* enter the implant's outer microphone and pass through the speech processor, the first electrodes to stimulate the cochlear nerve should be those electrodes located toward the base of the basilar membrane. Why the base? Because, remember, the *s* sound features high-frequency energy. And, as Békésy proved, the membrane is narrower and more rigid near the cochlea's base, and therefore more responsive to high-frequency waves.

Meanwhile, the other electrodes, situated farther down the implant's spiral array, closer to the cochlea's apex, don't need to fire— until, that is, the microphone picks up the vowel sound, whose spectral imprint includes a concentration of energy (i.e., formant) at lower frequencies. At this point, the electrodes at the base of the cochlea can cease firing, and the electrodes near the apex spring into action. Figure 6.16 is a simple illustration of how this works.

The little circles stand for the electrodes, and the lines represent electric stimulation. (Note that our illustration doesn't give exact time measurements of this stimulation, or the production of the sounds themselves.) Each electrode is assigned a frequency band (or channel), indicated—albeit roughly, as each implant is tailored to its wearer's cochlear condition—on the right. As you can see, because of the s sound's high-frequency profile, only the first five electrodes, situated closer to the cochlea's base, fire tiny jolts of electricity against the auditory nerve. For the vowel, though, these electrodes shut off, and nodes eight through ten, twenty, and twenty-one engage.

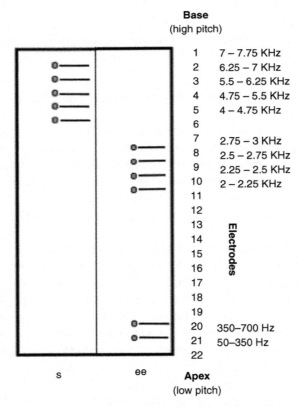

FIGURE 6.16 *Multielectrode firing in multichannel implant in response to see.*

This, then, is how language—in particular, the physiology behind our ear's processing of speech sounds—has shaped the cochlear implant. Our amazing, pea-sized bony spiral breaks down the complex sounds of vowels and consonants into smaller packets of information, by frequency, and assigns their processing to particular locations along the basilar membrane—the phenomenon of tonotopicity.

Georg von Békésy was the first scientist to physically observe, catalogue, and model this. After lackluster results, in the 1970s, with the single-electrode, single-channel design, inventors realized that the solution to constructing an effective auditory prosthesis lay in taking cues from the actual cochlea. In other words, they needed to make a device that imitates the inner ear's workings—processes that Békésy had demystified through decades of study. So engineers switched to a multielectrode, multichannel design platform, which has become the industry standard.

Welcome to the World of "Hearies":[36] How the Cochlear Implant Has Shaped Language and Identity

In this, the second half of our technolingual profile of the cochlear implant, we begin with the obvious: the cochlear implant shaped language by "restoring it" within a population of speakers. It enabled people to hear spoken language better, again, or for the first time. But to what extent, or degree of success, has the cochlear implant actually done this? We take on this question first.

Thereafter we turn our attention to matters of ideology and identity. Remember that our view of "language" encompasses more than just sounds, words, meanings, and grammatical rules. Throughout this book we've argued that "language" also comprises the ideas, attitudes, beliefs, and judgments with which speakers imbue their own language and/or which they project onto other speakers. Language is therefore as much about abstract ideologies as concrete structures. So when a technology succeeds in regenerating language, you can bet that this also bears consequences for speakers' ideas about said regenerated language and the speakers involved. F. G. Zang, respected professor of audiology at the University of California, Irvine, admits that there's more to cochlear implant research than membranes and electrode arrays:

As a typical scientific endeavor, we have solved many of the initial problems to make artificial hearing into a reality, but more problems have emerged to challenge us. There are cultural, educational, ethical, social, and economical issues that restrict the widespread application of the cochlear implant and demand our attention not only as scientists but also as human beings.[37]

The technological aspect of regenerating language, therefore, is really only half the story. And so, after we touch on patient outcomes and the physical restoration of language, we finish the chapter by considering how the cochlear implant has impacted identity and ideology within the Deaf community.

Part 1: Patient Outcomes

Let's lead off this section by dispatching two misconceptions about cochlear implants. First, some people might think that as soon as the audiologist out-fits the patient with the device and switches it on ... poof!—the patient can hear. However, as we limned in "Between Silence and Sound" (i.e., this chap-ter's opening narrative), it takes weeks, months, and sometimes years for the implant to reach its potential.

Most implantees' brains haven't received audio-neural information in a long time, if ever. And their besieged brains need time to neuronically regroup, as it were. (The medical terminology for this is *neural plasticity*.) In his fas-cinating autobiographical account of getting a cochlear implant, Michael Chorost details the extended—and often physically, mentally, and emotionally draining—adjustment his brain had to undergo to make sense of the new data it was suddenly inundated with:

> The neurons in my auditory cortex were slowly reorganizing themselves to handle the bewildering new input from the implant.... Over weeks and months my auditory cortex obediently refined its topography, making phys-ical divisions and auditory distinctions where none had existed before. The implant was literally reprogramming me.[38]

Moreover, even while all this cerebral reconfiguration is going on, the implantee is advised to undertake a welter of follow-ups.[39] There are map-ping sessions, during which the audiologist "tunes the levels and stimulation parameters of the speech processor so that sounds picked up by the micro-phone and processed are heard at the individual's ideal loudness level."[40] There are appointments with a speech pathologist, to work on articulation and voice modulation. And for many, there are also appointments with a psychologist, to help with the personal and/or social transition into the world of "hearies."

The takeaway here: although switch-on day is a life-shifting event for many implantees, allowing them to "hear" for the first time ever or the first time in a long time, the full effects of inner-cochlear electric stimulation come with time, patience, and work. As one authority puts it: "The process of learning to use information generated by a cochlear implant is typically lengthy, and focused practice and therapy are necessary."[41] Countless personal accounts—whether in blogs, books, academic journals, or popular magazines—attest to the therapeutic odyssey that follows the actual surgery.

The second popular myth we feel the need to upend: cochlear implants aren't "miracle ear replacements," that is, they don't outright make non- or hard-of-hearing people hear the same as those without auditory impairments. "Extensive clinical and research efforts indicate," says the Oxford Handbook of Deaf Studies, Language, and Education, "that although most users find them useful, cochlear implants do not change deaf people into hearing people," and that, furthermore, "information provided by implants is less specific and differentiated than that provided by a fully functioning cochlea, and their output is often described as 'course' or 'degraded' compared to the sounds received by hearing persons."[42]

Certainly, as we depicted in "Between Silence and Sound," once the electrodes are switched on patients can often hear environmental noises and speech sounds right away. (Indeed, this is what makes switch-on day such an emotional and exhilarating experience.) And after months of therapy and electrode mapping, many implantees develop auditory skills that were unthought of a few decades ago. "With current technology," Wilson and Dorman report, "the 'average' implant patient, when listening to predictable conversations in quiet, is able to communicate with relative ease."[43]

Still, it's important to keep this achievement, exciting and marvelous as it is, in perspective. A normally functioning cochlea has between 17,500 and 20,000 frequency-sensitive hair cells, with about 30,000 nerve fibers extending out of them and delivering auditory sensory information to the brain.[44] This anatomical arrangement allows for a lot of fine-grained, high-resolute frequency analysis. Today's cochlear implants, in comparison, have at most twenty-two electrodes that parse the frequency spectrum into channels of about 200–300 Hz. And the device can only deliver electrical stimulation to the cochlear nerve at twenty-two locations along the basilar membrane. All this goes to say that while cochlear implants are incredible language-regenerating implements, enabling recipients to reclaim or acquire exciting levels of sound perception, the technology is no match for the natural human ear.

And yet, it's incontrovertible that many of the (as of December 2012) 324,200 patients worldwide[45] who've been outfitted with a cochlear implant have had revolutionary aural experiences. Citing a number of studies, Paul and Whitelaw conclude:

> Despite controversy, current research highlights benefits based on carefully collected outcome data, much of which are longitudinal. Within 6 months of implantation of a multichannel monaural cochlear implantation in adults, significant increases in speech understanding ... are noted.[46]

According to Med-EI, one of the world's top-three makers of cochlear implants, users of its most advanced product, the Opus 2, are "able to still understand 50% of speech, even when the noise level [is] louder than the presented speech."[47] The leading developer of implants, Cochlear Limited, boasts on its website that it has "changed the lives of over 450,00 people," and offers dozens of video interviews with content patients praising the company's Nucleus 6 device.[48] We would note here, however, that the company's website doesn't post any statistical specifics or studies of the device's real performance.[49] Keep in mind, too, that these are companies whose financial well-being depends on selling cochlear implants; in other words, we should take their marketing material and performance claims with a grain of salt.

The most accurate answer to the question of how well cochlear implants regenerate hearing is less absolute. Fact is: results vary—sometimes greatly—by implantee.[50]

One important variable is when the deafness occurred, that is, how long ago, and at what age, the individual either begin to lose their hearing or lost it suddenly. Patients, for instance, who have already acquired language (referred to in the literature as "postlingual") and those who suffered sudden hearing loss less than a year prior to implantation—these patients generally experience the best and fastest effects. By comparison, a 40-year-old individual who was born deaf is likelier to show more modest auditory achievements. (Though we mustn't equate "modest" with "disappointing," from the recipient's perspective.)

Another crucial issue is how the deafness occurred, also called the "etiology." An individual whose hearing loss involved damage to the stereocilia or nerve cells, but whose auditory nerve wasn't damaged will respond well to the device's electrical stimulation. (Remember that the electrodes in a cochlear implant bypass the marred hair cells, and feed electric pulses directly to the auditory nerve.) But if the patient's hearing loss is due to damage of the auditory nerve, the benefits from the implant are more limited.

Other factors that influence how well the implant works have to do with the patient's involvement and response to the follow-up therapy, and the patient's overall personal situation, that is, their social, educational, psychological, and economic circumstances.[51]

Let's turn now to another phenomenon that's stemmed from the regeneration of language through cochlear implants, namely, the technology's impact on identity within the Deaf community. "An individual's choice of language," Barbara Kannapell writes, "and his or her expressed language attitudes serve to indicate, construct and maintain Deaf or hearing social identity during social interaction with others."[52] In the last segment of our chapter, we explore Kannapell's argument further. Ultimately, we see that when individuals experience, navigate, and think about *language* (in this case, spoken language and the auditory perception of it) in new and different ways, this inevitably feeds into the way that these individuals experience, navigate, and think about their *identity*, both with respect to others and to their own ideas of who they are.

Part 2: Identity and Ideologies

We'd like to begin by asking you to ponder this seemingly simple question: what makes you *you*? Take a minute and draw up a mental list.

We're going to guess that one or more of the following came to mind:

- The things you own and choose to show others

- The things you own but choose not to show others

- The familial, geographic, ethnic, and socioeconomic circumstances you were born into

- The choices you make or don't make

- The actions you take or don't take

- The way you think about yourself, others, and the world

- The way you think others and the world think about you

- The people you associate with and/or choose not to associate with

We're willing to bet, though, that language—the words and structures you use and/or avoid—didn't cross your mind. And we'd even double down and say that you didn't consider, as part of what makes you *you*, your emotional and attitudinal reactions to the words and structures you yourself use and/or avoid—let alone the words and structures that others use and/or avoid. Yet, as we've demonstrated throughout this book, language per se, and the notions we harbor about language and its users (aka language ideologies), interact in meaningful ways. In short, our linguistic persona is an intertwined, interrelating network of structures and ideas.

In this section we dilate this point further and connect language more directly with identity. Keeping our technolingual sights on the cochlear implant, particularly within a social context (i.e., among members of the Deaf community), we see that language and language ideologies also contribute to what makes us *us*.

We begin with the term *identity*. Our goal will be to provide a summary of how the scholarship has defined it, as well as our own—and perhaps more digestible—definition. Next we argue, in line with the scholarship of the past fifty years, that sign languages are bona fide, rule governed, and inexhaustibly expressive systems of communication. Finally, we connect these two topics to show how the cochlear implant has shaped and continues to shape ideas of language and identity within the Deaf community.

Defining Identity

In the *Handbook of Self and Identity*, the term is explained as follows:

> Identities are the traits and characteristics, social relations, roles, and social group memberships that define who one is. Identities can be focused on the past—what used to be true of one, the present—what is true of one now, or the future—the person one expects or wishes to become, the person one feels obligated to try to become, or the person one fears one may become.[53]

According to this interpretation, what makes you *you* is a combination of a) how you look/looked/will look; b) how you act/acted/will act; and c) the people you hang/hung/will hang out with. The authors go a step further, though, and conclude that, "together, identities make up one's *self-concept*—variously described as what comes to mind when one thinks of oneself."[54] How you think about yourself, then, is an extension of the dynamic and mutable pieces that make up your externally and/or internally perceived "identity."

This description also jibes with accounts concerning identity formation within and among the Deaf community. Irene Leigh, former professor of psychology at Gallaudet University and herself a member of the Deaf community, notes:

> Deaf identity, whatever its manifestation, evolves throughout life as a deaf person experiences specific family, school, and outside environments and develops specific linguistic communication capabilities in responding to these environments. These individualized experiences and capabilities work in tandem to create one's self-perception of deaf identity.[55]

At last—our linguist funny bone is tingling! Note that, unlike the explanation in the *Handbook of Self and Identity*, Leigh brings *language* into the mix.

As you might imagine, we align ourselves more with Leigh's take on identity. Everyone, we argue, constructs and has constructed their identity based—to varying extents—on language (as well as other variables, as we noted above). A few examples will suffice to buttress this argument:

- Example #1: The entertainer Madonna. From 2000 to 2008, the Michigan-born "Queen of Pop"[56] was married to British filmmaker Guy Ritchie. During those years the power couple raised a child together in England, where Madonna also reportedly "embraced British country living from riding horses to hanging out in pubs."[57] The natural next step in this evolution of persona was her language. It needed to match—and in so doing contribute to the formation of—the Material Girl's evolving identity. "She'd take the stage at an awards show," one reporter writes in the *New York Observer*, "and before the clapping even died down you could hear it: 'Thank kyeew. Thank kyeew.' Suddenly she wasn't some naughty Catholic girl from the Motor City. She sounded sort of ... continental. All proper, with flourishes thrown in, in unexpected places."[58] Her identity—look, life, and language—had come a long way from the Italian-American girl raised in a Detroit suburb, and who at 23 had made it big in the Big Apple.

- Example #2: Talia is a (fictional) 50-year-old Jewish woman from Brooklyn. While attending a professional conference in Madison, Wisconsin, she meets several new colleagues who invite her to join them later at the hotel bar for a drink. She cordially orders a bottle of wine for the group, but the bartender brings the wrong brand and she sends it back. Flustered, but wanting to mask it with some humor, she jokes, "A little *mishugga*, I guess." Her new acquaintances, however, only smile awkwardly; they have no clue what *mishugga* means. "You know," one of the new acquaintances attempts to dispel the awkwardness, "my husband is Jewish."

- Example #3: Heather is a (fictional) 16-year-old living in San Diego. On average she sends and receives more than 300 text messages a day, mostly to and from her peers. They write predominately in lowercase letters, and rarely use conventional punctuation. Moreover, her texts regularly contain clipped words like "whatev," "fantash" or—Heather's favorite—"totes fab." Such linguistic forms showcase and construct the teenagers' unique identity as nonconformist to all things "grown-up," "establishment," or what they think of as "has been."

These are three simple scenarios of how language interfaces with identity. More specifically, these scenarios illustrate how language serves—again, along with other factors—as a constructor and indexer of an individual's or group's identity.

Sign Languages Are Bona Fide

Now that we've established a little more clearly the link between language and identity, let's consider the dominant means that the Deaf community uses for communicating linguistically. Variously known as *manual, sign,* or *gesture language,* theirs is a strictly visual system of linguistic communication. And here we would like to dispel any possible misconceptions that you, Dear Reader, might have about sign languages: just because a system of linguistic communication is gestural, instead of oral, does not mean that said gestural language is in any way "inferior" or "less expressive" in terms of quality (i.e., how it can be expressed) and quantity (how much can be expressed).

Sign languages aren't just helter-skelter or makeshift flails of the extremities. Like their spoken cousins, gestural languages are rule governed, limitlessly creative systems for encoding and conveying information. "Despite the misconceptions," Carol A. Padden and Tom L. Humphries, who are both deaf and whose primary language is gestural, announce in *Deaf in America: Voices from a Culture,* "for Deaf people, their sign language is a creation of their history and is what allows them to fulfill the potential for which evolution has prepared them—to attain full human communication as makers and users of symbols."[59]

The first academic to deliver resounding evidence for the systematic structure of American Sign Language (ASL)—though native signers had already been aware of it for a long time—was William Stokoe. In more than three decades of work, beginning in the 1950s, Stokoe assembled a groundbreaking body of research. "Trained as a structural linguist," Paddy Ladd writes, "Stokoe made the all important breakthrough at Gallaudet University in the 1950s, and his assertion that sign languages were *bona fide* languages was confirmed by subsequent research."[60]

Stokoe's work centered mostly on ASL, although what he demonstrated applied to all manual languages, namely, that signers used patterned combinations of gestures to convey meaning through words (i.e., morphology) and utterances (syntax). Like oral languages, he argued, signed systems of communication are rule governed. The cognitively embedded blueprint that enables us to loop words into longer phrases and phrases into even longer sentences, a blueprint that is already present in our brains at birth though we remain largely unaware of it all our life—the theory of universal grammar, he argued, applies to *all* humans, verbal and nonverbal. As such, he believed that manual systems of communication (such as ASL) are also based on predictable and observable rules.

In order to prove this, he spent years observing, documenting, and analyzing ASL. And in a watershed monograph from 1960, with the telling title *Sign Language Structure*, he showed that signs are indeed complex, organized actions. Stokoe demonstrated, for example, that each sign is a coordination of three visual features: location or position (in relation to the signer's torso), configuration (i.e., shape of the hand), and movement. He writes:

> The sign clearly is, as the morpheme, the smallest unit of the language to which meaning attaches. That is, the significance [of each sign] resides, not in the configuration, the position, or the movement but in the unique combination of all three.[61]

Just as every spoken sound (or *phone*) is a composite of distinct *acoustic* features (e.g., voicing, lip rounding, aspiration), each sign is also made up of discrete *gestured* features. And the presence or absence of one or more of these gestured features will change the sign's meaning. Tables 6.1 and 6.2 show how this system of feature distinction works in both in oral and manual languages.

What these figures mean for actual communication, then, is that the difference between, say, "planned" and "bland" in spoken English, and between "think" and "disappointed" in ASL boils down to the presence or absence of

TABLE 6.1 Acoustic feature matrix of [p] and [b] sounds.

ACOUSTIC FEATURE	ORAL SOUND	
	[p] sound	[b] sound
stop	+	+
bilabial	+	+
nasalization	-	-
aspiration	-	-
frication	-	-
voicing	-	+

TABLE 6.2 Gestural feature matrix of signs for "to think" and "disappointed."

PARAMETER	GESTURAL FEATURE	VISUAL SIGN	
		'to think'	'disappointed'
hand shape	closed fist	+	+
	extended index finger	+	+
movement	unidirectional	+	+
	body contact	+	+
orientation	facing body	+	+
location	forehead	+	-
	chin	-	+

one feature: for the former, whether or not you engage your vocal chords and for the latter, whether you touch your forehead or chin.

As a matter of fact, linguists call sounds like *b* and *p* in spoken English *phonemes*. A phoneme is a "bare minimum" sound that speakers can use in systematic ways to create a difference in meaning in their language; to wit, in English we can use *b* and *p* to say either "planned" or "bland," "lap" or "lab," and so on. There are roughly forty such phonemes in standard American English, and upwards of forty-four in British Received Pronunciation.[64] Now, recall that Stokoe was educated in this kind of traditional linguistic thought. So when he observed in ASL what he took to be the same kind of systematic "bare minimum" sign differentiation he'd been schooled in for spoken languages, he introduced a new term: the chereme.[65] Cheremes are, essentially, "visual phonemes," and in his research Stokoe argued that there were nineteen cheremes in ASL.[66] Speakers use these cheremes to encode lexical (i.e., between words) and grammatical (i.e., between structures, like "occurring once" and "recurring") differences in their communications.

Stokoe's research, then, gave gesture-based systems of communication, like ASL, a linguistic vindication, as it were. "Through the publication of his work, he was instrumental in changing the perception of ASL from that of a broken or simplified version of English to that of a complex and thriving natural language in its own right with an independent syntax and grammar as functional and powerful as any found in the oral languages of the world."[67] And as we see below, this "complex and thriving natural language" has contributed heavily to the construction of identity in the American Deaf community. What's more, this identity—the product of linguistic, psychological, and sociocultural variables in constant interaction—has been challenged by the cochlear implant.

Connecting Sign Language, Ideologies, and Identity

As we make our way through this last section, we ask you to keep in mind the following premise: a crucial part of being human—hearie or non-hearie—is the ability to communicate. The need to convey our thoughts to others is as strong a biological imperative as eating, sleeping, or—dare we say it?—sex.

Most hearies meet this need by communicating with other hearies through a spoken medium (though there are many nonverbal cues involved, too). They encode their thoughts into sounds, assemble these into words, and string the words into sentences that ultimately deliver their message to other speakers. Moreover, as we've consistently argued throughout our exploration of techno-lingualism, this verbal medium of communication also contributes to who the speaker is (i.e., their identity). Spoken language shapes how speakers view themselves and others, and how speakers are viewed by others.

Most Deaf people communicate with other Deaf people through a signed medium. And this gestured linguistic medium of communication is just as integral to their conception of themselves and others as spoken language is to hearies. "One of the primary identifying characteristics of the Deaf community," University of California, San Diego, professors Carol Padden and Tom Humphries conclude in their book *Deaf in America: Voices from a Culture,* "is its language."[68] Just as speakers of English have interlayered their verbal language with social, cultural, and ideological values, so too have ASL users with their gestured language. This is what Kannapell, a deaf sociolinguist born to deaf parents, is getting at in her 1982 personal essay "Inside the Deaf Community," when she writes:

> ASL serves as a way for deaf people to communicate with each other, but there is much more to it than just a function of language. There is a symbolic function in relation to identity and power, and we often keep our use of ASL limited to ourselves to preserve these factors of identity and power.[69]

From this passage ones gets the idea that Deaf people take pride in their linguistic identity. What's more, Kannapell seems to be suggesting that the Deaf community operates with a sense of protectiveness and exclusiveness when it comes to their language. In other words, Deaf people feel a need to guard the integrity of their language, in part by excluding others from their linguistic community.

Harlan Lane, founder of the Center for Research in Hearing, Speech, and Language at the University of Massachusetts, has also written about this kind of "linguistic protectionism" within the Deaf community. Lane, however, frames his discussion in a way that smacks of antagonism toward hearies. In his controversial book, *The Mask of Benevolence: Disabling the Deaf Community*, he argues:

> Deaf identity itself is highly valued (within the deaf community); deaf people seem to agree that a hearing person can never fully acquire that identity and become a full-fledged member of the deaf community.... Speech and thinking like a hearing person are negatively viewed values in deaf culture. Deaf people who adopt hearing values and look down on other Deaf people are regarded as traitors.[70]

It's hard to know if such "anti-hearie" attitudes are (or were) as widespread among the Deaf as Lane suggests. Still, there's no better promoter of solidarity, or a sense of common identity, than the "us vs. them" paradigm.

And in fact the conflict that our imaginary heroine encounters in the cafeteria, in this chapter's opening vignette, gets at this us vs. them attitude. Emily, having received her implant, is vilified by some of the other Deaf students as a "traitor." They rebuke her as a "half hearie" who now thinks herself superior to the others in the community. Such attitudes, and especially the actions born out of them, serve as strong builders and performers of identity.

All this goes to say: signed languages are inextricably part and parcel of the identity of those who have acquired and/or use it as their primary means of communication. As with spoken languages, signed languages function as important personal and sociocultural markers. "ASL," Kannapell explains, "is the creation which grows out of the Deaf community. It is our language in every sense of the word. We create it, we keep it alive, and it keeps us and our traditions alive."[71] It's easy to see, then, why some within the Deaf community might regard the cochlear implant, with its implied "promises" of "curing" deafness or "fixing" the patient, not as a boon, but rather as a threat to their culture—first and foremost, to their language. And, in fact, this is precisely what has happened.

Soon after the medical community saw its first real success at regenerating language with multichannel implants—recall from earlier that this was in the 1980s—individuals with strong ties to Deaf culture, and who weren't part of the medical community, started to question the value of the "medical miracle."[72] More than anything, these individuals wondered what effects cochlear implants might have on language and identity. "As a growing number of deaf children receive cochlear implants," editors Kristin A. Lindgren, Doreen Deluca, and Donna Jo Napoli write in *Signs and Voices: Deaf Culture, Identity, Language, and Arts*, this "poses new challenges for defining both individual and collective identities."[73] Another example: in his *The Artificial Ear: Cochlear Implants and the Culture of Deafness*—a history/ethnography of what the author calls "the bionic ear"—Blume concludes that, by the late 1980s, when more and more devices were being developed and marketed and inserted, "Deaf people also felt that cochlear implantation threatened the Deaf community as a whole."[74] The cochlear implant, it seems safe to say, ignited a rethinking of "what it means to be Deaf" within many Deaf communities.

This reexamination of self and others extended to language, too. A general fear materialized that the cochlear implant would put pressure on signed languages—which, as we've seen, make up a major part of how the Deaf conceive of themselves as individuals and as a community. The concern was that if doctors continued to "cure" deafness, there would be no more need for gestured modes of communication; in other words, the medical world, despite its benevolent intentions, would cause a language death—and with it, a loss of identity and sense of belonging.

Two books on the sociocultural effects of cochlear implants within the Deaf community suggest that, for the last two decades in particular, this kind of linguistic worry (i.e., that cochlear implant technology could someday displace sign language and the identity ties associated with its use among members of the close-knit Deaf community) has been kicking around within the American Deaf community since multichannel devices grew in popularity in the 1990s.

In an alarmist tone that reflects the amount of emotion tied to the matter, Lane labels the cochlear implant "a biological means aimed at regulating and, ultimately, eliminating deaf culture, language, and community."[75] He's particularly vociferous when it comes to deaf children, whose parents make the decision to "fix" the children's deafness. In such cases, he decries the cochlear implant as "bio-power: a massive intervention in the life of a child in an attempt to impose the majority's language, culture, and values."[76] Note that by "majority" Lane means hearies. A similar tone traces through Paddy Ladd's *Understanding Deaf Culture*. For instance, he refers to the cochlear implant as another in a long line of weapons in "oralism's attack" on the Deaf community.[77] All this to say that Lane isn't alone with his bellicose, us vs. them rhetoric.

It goes without saying that these two authors' opinions are not representative of all members of the American Deaf community. We've noted them here as evidence that such sociolinguistic fears, though not universal, are in fact attestable.

The Regeneration of Language and Technolingualism

In this final chapter of our exploration of the reciprocal relationship between language and technology—aka technolingualism—we focused on a technology that, per our argument, amounts to a regeneration of language. The cochlear implant allows, to varying degrees, individuals with hearing loss to "hear," whether for the first time or once again. This miraculous device restores within these individuals the perception of spoken language (again, to varying degrees). Cochlear implants serve, in other words, as a patent example of technology developed for the regeneration of language.

Recall that we began by reviewing the physiology of the inner ear. We saw that an understanding of how the cochlea processes sound helps us pull back the curtain on how engineers created the cochlear implant. In particular, we pointed out the body's natural strategy of analyzing complex sound waves, namely, that the cochlea is outfitted with tens of thousands of tiny hairs nestled along a flexible membrane, whose surface responds differently according to frequency. Specifically, this membrane's thicker, less pliable portions register higher frequencies, while its thinner, more displaceable portions pick up lower frequencies. This multilocational processing of frequencies is called tonotopicity.

In step with our technolingual pursuit, we then explained the twofold question of how language both influenced and was influenced by the cochlear implant. For the former, we made the case that the inner ear's natural anatomy shaped the ultimate technological design of the modern-day multichannel device. Initial efforts to construct the "miracle ear" followed a single-electrode design scheme. However, this design scheme didn't take into account the cochlea's natural tonotopicity, which handles multiple channels, or frequencies, of incoming acoustic waves. As such, these single-electrode implants were less effective and were soon surpassed by multielectrode devices.

This multichannel technology, we showed, drew on the pioneering work of Georg von Békésy, a man who dedicated his life to observing and explaining the ear's wondrous physical and neuromechanical processes. Outfitted with upward of twenty-two electrodes, multichannel devices mimic the ear's natural tonotopic strategy for processing sound. Although this still doesn't match the cochlea's fine-tuned functionality—recall that the natural bony spiral is equipped with tens of thousands of hairs—multichannel devices nevertheless enable patients to hear many sounds, including spoken language.

As for the other side of our technolingual case, we laid out two compelling examples of how the cochlear implant has shaped language. First, we saw that, indeed, the technology has helped people with hearing loss, or those born without hearing, to "hear," that is, the technology has regenerated these individuals' ability to perceive spoken language. Clinical studies support this—though, as we discussed, the degree to which patients can "hear" depends on outside factors like clarity of the speech sound, noise environment, and the patient's social and medical history.

An even more compelling example of the technology's impact on language, we argued, is found when one looks past language structures per se and considers ideologies: the ideas, attitudes, and perceptions that interact with the formation of identity—whether within the individual, or the formation of a more communal identity, as with a group of speakers who share a cultural and sociolinguistic bond.

For members of the American Deaf community, we saw that a crucial aspect of Deaf identity is sign language. Put another way: to "be a Deaf person" in America means, in the minds of many Deaf Americans, that ASL is your natural language. It is your kneejerk, go-to linguistic means for communicating your thoughts and feelings with the world, though especially with other Deaf people. And, as with most hearing communities, this I-am-the-language-I-speak ideology is a powerful sociocultural force; oftentimes it's used to rationalize the acceptance, rejection, or questioning of an individual's allegiance to or membership in the community. Thus, when members of the American Deaf community began getting cochlear implants, other members of the community began to consider anew both their own communal identity (e.g., Does "being Deaf" mean that I accept my deafness and don't try to "be something I'm not, namely, a hearing person"?) and the identity of the individuals getting the implant (e.g., "Do they think that being deaf is something that should be cured?").

What's more, we saw that the arrival of the cochlear implant incited linguistic worry within the American Deaf community (and likely within many other Deaf communities worldwide). Some expressed concern that the technology could challenge, marginalize, or—taken to the extreme—lead to the demise of sign languages. Such concerns, we saw, have led at least one mainstream scholar to brand implant technology as a harmful "biopower" (i.e., a techno-biological means to diminish, or even eradicate, the languages and cultures of the Deaf). This sentiment applies especially to the outfitting of deaf babies or prelinguistic children with implants, a practice that another author has branded an "oralist attack" on Deaf language and culture.

In short, one can argue that the cochlear implant's impact on language attitudes—especially as these inform questions of cultural and linguistic belongingness within the Deaf community—rivals the technology's impact on language per se. Cochlear implants continue to change how members of the American Deaf community think about themselves, others, and even the language that unites them.

Conclusions, or

What We've Learned through Exploring the Relationship between Language and Technology

The last 200-odd pages have taken us on a journey—across times, places, languages, cultures, ideologies, and technologies. Our mission, you recall, was to explore the following pair of questions:

- How do language and technology interact?

- What happens, to either or both, as a result of this interaction?

Our journey led us through six stages of technolingual analysis. One by one we delved into, rummaged around in, and poked and prodded the *textualization, mechanization, abstraction, digitization, mobilization*, and *regeneration* of language. Moreover, throughout these six stages we considered eight different communication technologies: writing, the printing press, typewriter, telegraph, telephone, computer, mobile phone, and cochlear implant.

And all throughout our journey (read: at each stage) we turned out various answers to our overarching two-part question. Here, however, in this, the epilogue to our technolingual trek, we'd like to assemble these "answers from along the way" into a list of final, coherent thoughts.

In what follows we offer a countdown, as it were, of the "Top Five Things We've Learned from Exploring the Relationship between Language and Technology." And while we make no claims of the list's exhaustiveness, we nevertheless hope to summarize our discoveries in a manner justifiable—above all—to you, Dear Reader.

Thank you for accompanying us on this journey.

#5: Knowing about Language Leads to Better Technology

Again and again we've seen that when inventive minds, out-of-the-box think-ers, and ambitious engineers understand how human language works—whether the physiology of speech production, the acoustics of sound, the formal properties of grammar, or the anatomy of the inner ear—the better positioned they are to create superior communication technologies. Baldly put: knowing about language leads to better technology.

Korea's King Sejong applied what he knew about the role of the lips, tongue, and throat in speech production to formulate a unique writing system. Korean Hangul is an articulatorily iconic alphabet. The shapes of its symbols actually represent what the mouth, tongue, or throat does when a speaker articulates a sound in Korean. Alexander Graham Bell was born into a family that reveled in the study of language. This unique linguistic background aided him in early experiments—with a dead person's ear, even!—that ultimately led to the tel-ephone's diaphragm-membrane design, a breakthrough in the development of the technology. Early computer programmers, looking for ways to write more efficient and formalized languages for their machines to read, benefit-ted from Noam Chomsky's work in formal grammar theory. Engineers work-ing on speech-recognition software have only been able to make progress in recent decades through a better understanding of acoustic feature theory and the variability of speech. Finally, Georg von Békésy spent a lifetime observing and experimenting with the cochlea to learn how it processes sound. Early developers of the cochlear implant didn't integrate Békésy's key discovery—tonotopicity—into their design; consequently, the single-channel coch-lear implant was less effective and ultimately discontinued. Multielectrode devices, however, which capitalize on Békésy's findings in cochlear mechan-ics, are more effective and have become the industry standard.

#4: Technology-inspired Linguistic Paranoia Is Old News and Unfounded

The concerns that we hear or read about technology's harmful influence on language—often directed at mobile phones, text messaging, computers, and social media—are not unique to our day and age. Socrates saw writing as a devolvement of spoken rhetoric. To him it was dehumanized language: you can't question or converse with it, and it's stripped from its original context. Writing, in his opinion, would only lead to mental laziness. The printing press spawned concern over authorial exclusivity; to wit, that the ability to mass produce copies of a text would mean the end of an author's exclusive owner-ship of their words and ideas. In this vein, Johann Fichte wrote a passionate essay about what he considered the "illegality" of printing. And there were those who prophesized the death of handwriting on account of the typewriter, or claimed that it "mechanized" our linguistic thoughts.

Speakers have been decrying for a long time language's certain and immi-nent "destruction" or "degradation" at the hands of technology. But this has yet to actually happen. Instead, as we've seen, language adapts to the new communicative venues and circumstances created by the technology. Speakers come up with new structures and practices. Linguistic repertoires expand. In the end, language becomes richer, more dynamic and expressive, on account of new technologies.

#3: There Is an Observable "Alphabet Effect"

The invention of writing followed three basic linguistic paths; symbols were created to stand for 1) words, 2) syllables, or 3) sounds. All are equally expres-sive and adequate as systems for representing spoken language. And when written by hand, there's nothing that suggests that one or the other is more efficient or practical. In other words, an Italian using the alphabet for a hand-written diary entry wouldn't be any more or less challenged or advantaged than a Japanese using kanji to do the same thing.

The invention of the printing press, however, disrupted this parity. It quickly became apparent that a logographic writing system, with its cache of thou-sands of dissimilar characters, presented certain logistical challenges as com-pared to an alphabet, with its smaller number of combinable letters. Early Chinese printers had to make and store a lot of material to accommodate their logographic system. German printers needed for their alphabet just a few dozen different movable types, stored in a single box. The alphabet, in other words, gave printers an advantage in terms of ease and speed (though by no means in terms of expressiveness).

The alphabet effect (i.e., the technological benefit that came from having an alphabet) played a similar role in the development of the typewriter, tele-graph, and digital word processor. Early typewriters for Japanese kanji, for instance, were large, complicated, and expensive. Sholes's Remington had only forty-six keys and fit atop a desk. Chinese telegraphic code assigned a distinct four-digit number (0000–9999) for each character. Operators had to either memorize thousands of these twice-coded codes (i.e., coded once into a sequence of circuit on-offs, and coded again as a number), or they had to look them up in a catalog. Samuel Morse only had to come up with twenty-six different dot-and-dash combinations for English. Non-alphabet writing systems posed a burden to digital word processing, too. Logographic systems required longer bit-coding schemes, and either larger keyboards or more complicated sequences of input with the keys. The ASCII coding system for digit word processing with the Roman alphabet, developed in the 1960s, required only a seven-bit coding platform, and its keyboard remained much the same as Sholes's typewriter a century before.

To be sure: none of this should be interpreted to mean that alphabets are inherently "better" or "more linguistically expressive" than non-alphabets. You can convey just as much information, in just as "good" a way, with kanji (i.e., logographic script for Japanese) as with Cyrillic (i.e., the alphabetic script for Russian) or Coptic (i.e., the alphabetic script for Coptic Egyptian). Our argument here is that inventors working on technologies that used an alphabetic writing system had a logistic advantage due to their writing system's smaller unit inventory, and the combinability of these units.

#2: Language Ideologies Abound

Many times along our journey through technolingualism we both insisted and illustrated that "language" is more than the sounds, words, and phrases that flow out of our mouths and fingers. There is also, built into our personal linguistic repertoire, a battery of abstract and powerful judgments, values, opinions, perceptions, etc. *about* language—the way we think and feel about structures, practices, and especially speakers of language. Language ideologies, we've seen, play a meaningful role in the language-technology dynamic.

The invention of writing led to new ideas of linguistic "validity" and "goodness." When a language was textualized, this now-visible version of the language often became the "standard" for education and societal administration too. Written language took on a perceived aura of prestige. Speakers came to view speech as less "bona fide" and "correct," while its written counterpart was deemed as the "better" or "actual" instantiation. The printing press carried on and deepened this ideological trend. Geographically large-scale language standardization, we saw, was an epiphenomenon of the printing press. The abstraction and mobilization of language also spawned new language ideologies. Each technology, from the telegraph and telephone to the mobile phone, sparked an emergence of opinions as to: 1) how you should and shouldn't use language while using the technology; 2) which forms of language you should and shouldn't use while using the technology; and 3) the character of the speaker who does or does not use the technology. Often these ideologies were documented and promoted by etiquette manuals. Finally, we saw that cochlear implant technology, while constituting an amazing medical achievement in the regeneration of language, brought with it whole new conceptions of what it means to be "Deaf."

The novelties of words and sounds that cropped up on account of technological advancements is only part of the story. A full picture comes into view when you bring language ideologies into the fray.

#1: Language and Technology: The Effect Is Mutual

Most importantly, our six chapters uncovered compelling evidence in favor of the proposition that language both influences and is influenced by technology—a sociolinguistic state of affairs we've christened *technolingualism*. The cornerstone of technolingualism, we've held, is that the influence is a two-way street.

The natural discreteness of language and the articulatory features of speech informed the creation of writing systems. Conversely, writing prompted new lexical and syntactic forms, new communicative practices, and new language ideologies.

A language's writing system influenced the physical configurations and mechanics of the printing press and typewriter, and the digital coding schemes of digital word processing. And these technologies returned the favor. The printing press, among other things, contributed to the standardization of language and new conceptions of ownership of written language. The typewriter made writing faster, and imparted a mechanical, staccato-ish flavor to (some) users' writing; it also spawned new opinions of who should or shouldn't use the typewriter and what you should or shouldn't use it for. Digital word processing—in particular, email—also inspired new forms, practices, and ideologies associated with linguistic communication.

The sound and spelling patterns of English informed the layout of the typewriter's keyboard, and the dot-and-dash arrangement of the telegraph's code. Equally, the telegraph gave rise to Morse Speak and Morse Jargon, innovative stylistic trends in journalistic writing, and a new conceptualization of what it means to "communicate."

Formal grammar theory, a branch of linguistics that sought to describe and formalize the abstract rules and generative processes of our language grammar—the insights from this obscure field gave the first generation of computer programmers the methodological and theoretical baseline for writing "languages" that computers could understand. Computers, on the other hand, engendered fresh varieties of communication, new research areas in the field of linguistics, new venues and potentialities for studying language, and—of course—oodles of beliefs and judgments as to what constitutes the "proper" etiquette for language usage via computer.

The acoustic properties and inherent variability of speech guided the development of speech-recognition technology. Computer scientists drew on what linguists had uncovered—using new instruments like the spectrograph—about the physical characteristics of speech sounds. They (computer scientists) then parlayed this knowledge into the development of mathematic modeling schemes that allowed speech-recognition hardware to process and manage acoustic variation.

Finally, the anatomy that underlies the production and perception of speech (i.e. the human vocal tract and ear) inspired crucial innovation in the development of the telephone and cochlear implant. Bell reassembled a dead person's middle ear, observed how the tiny bones transduced sound waves absorbed by a thin membrane, and used this insight to devise his telephone's unique magneto-diaphragm feature. The multichannel implant drew on the work of Georg von Békésy, who spent a lifetime observing how the cochlea processes sounds. Alternatively, we saw that the telephone brought with it new linguistic forms, practices, and language ideologies, and that the cochlear implant altered the ideological and sociolinguistic landscape within the Deaf community, leading to new conceptions and perceptions of what it means to be "Deaf."

*

You, me, everyone who can read this final sentence—we are all technolinguals.

Notes

Chapter 1

1 See Maryanne Wolf's *Proust and the Squid: The Story and Science of the Reading Brain* (New York: HarperCollins, 2008).

2 Hesse, Hermann, *My Belief: Essays on Life and Art* (New York: Farrar, Straus, and Giroux, 1974), 153.

3 Christian Vandendorpe, *From Papyrus to Hypertext: Toward the Universal Digital Library* (Champaign: University of Illinois Press, 2009), 9.

4 http://www.english.illinois.edu/-people-/faculty/debaron/482/482readings/phaedrus.html (accessed January 20, 2017).

5 Ibid., 216.

6 Jack Goody and Ian Watt, "The Consequences of Literacy," in *Comparative Studies in Society and History*, vol. 5, no. 3 (1963): 304–45.

7 Logan Robert, *The Alphabet Effect: The Impact of the Phonetic Alphabet on the Development of Western Civilization* (New York: St. Martin's Press, 1987), 17–18.

8 Laura Ahearn's *Living Language: An Introduction to Linguistic Anthropology* (Hoboken, NY: Wiley-Blackwell, 2011), ch. 7, offers a good primer on how anthropologists study the interplay between writing and societies.

9 Steven Roger Fischer has written, in my opinion, one of the most comprehensive and accessible introductions to this topic: *A History of Writing* (London: Reaktion Books, 2001).

10 The alphabet I'm using right now to type this book in English, for instance, was borrowed from a writing system that Romans used more than 2,000 years ago. But the Romans didn't invent it; they got their writing system from the Etruscans who got it from the Greeks who copied it from the Phoneticians.

11 Note the spelling of discrete with one *e*; language can certainly be *discreet*—but that's a different, socially charged matter.

12 Note that, despite the spelling, we pronounce the *-ed* suffix as a voiceless *t* without a preceding vowel, and most of us don't pronounce the *l* after the *a*.

13 Strictly speaking, Chinese *pinyin* is a logosyllabic system, meaning that there is a one-to-one relationship between character and syllable. However, since the vast majority of Chinese words are monosyllabic, it's accurate enough for our purposes to call Chinese logographic. Moreover, many characters comprise smaller graphic pieces that indicate semantic and syntactic categories (so-called classifiers) and even pronunciation.

14 Dr. Sheila Blumstein has done some impressive work on this at Brown University. I recommend her chapter "Reflections on the Cognitive Neuroscience of Language," in *The Cognitive Neurosciences*, ed. Michael S. Gazzaniga (Cambridge, MA: MIT Press, 2009).

15 The glottal stop sound is written in other languages, however. In Hawaiian the sound is indicated with an apostrophe: *'a'a* is a type of jagged lava rock; *O'ahu*, meaning "the gathering place," is the third largest of the Hawaiian islands.

16 As illustrated in Figure 1.7, English has aspirated sounds, too. But we don't use them to change a word's meaning. Hold a sheet of paper up to your mouth and say the word *pot*; the leaf should flutter when you pronounce the *p*. Now say *pot* again and do your best to suppress the extra puff of air. It might sound a little strange when you say it—perhaps close to a *b*, as in *bot*—but there is no difference in meaning between *pot*-with-an-aspirated-*p* and *pot*-with-an-<u>un</u>aspirated-*p*.

17 Amalia Gnanadesikan, *The Writing Revolution: Cuneiform to the Internet* (Hoboken, NJ: Wiley-Blackwell, 2008), 201.

18 "be, v." OED Online. http://www.oed.com.ezproxy.ithaca.edu:2048/view/Entry/16441?rskey=9V8wxi&result=1&isAdvanced=false (accessed January 22, 2017).

19 Regrettably, the sociohistorical reasons for the stigmatization of *ain't* are too lengthy to cover here. For that I recommend David Skinner's charming and informative *The Story of Ain't*, where he couches the narrative of *ain't* in the larger context of the controversy over the third edition of *Webster's New International Dictionary. The Story of Ain't: America, Its Language, and the Most Controversial Dictionary Ever Published* (New York: HarperCollins, 2012).

20 https://www.ethnologue.com/enterprise-faq/how-many-languages-world-are-unwritten-0 (accesses August 26, 2017).

21 "cordwainer, n." OED Online. http://www.oed.com.ezproxy.ithaca.edu:2048/view/Entry/41483?redirectedFrom=cordwainer (accessed January 22, 2017).

22 "cruse, n." OED Online. http://www.oed.com.ezproxy.ithaca.edu:2048/view/Entry/45265?redirectedFrom=cruse (accessed January 22, 2017).

23 Scores of fun books, quirky desktop paraphernalia, and trivia material are based on "arch"-words. Just to name a few: Mark Forsyth's *Horologicon: A Day's Jaunt through the Lost Words of the English Language* (New York: Berkley, 2013); Simon Hertnon's *Endangered Words: A Collection of Rare Gems for Book Lovers* (New York: Skyhorse, 2009); and Jeffrey Kacirk's yearly release *Forgotten English Page-a-Day Calendar* (South Portland, ME: Sellers, 2016).

24 www.oxforddictionaries.com (accessed March 22, 2015).

25 In fact, today ongoing missionary efforts are bringing writing to strictly oral language communities. In 2008, Wycliffe USA launched the Last Languages Campaign, which endeavors to "start a Bible translation program in every language still needing one by the year 2025" (https://www.wycliffe.org/about, accessed January 26, 2017). While some of these languages may already be written and just in need of a Bible translation, many others are not. The missionaries will need to devise an orthographic system.

26 Browsing the Ethnologue website (www.ethnologue.com) can be both exciting and unsettling; it's unnerving to see so many of the world's languages listed as "threatened," "moribund," "nearly extinct," "dormant," or "extinct."

27 Although written documentation is a tremendous help in reconstructing older forms of languages and classifying languages into families, a seasoned historical linguist will tell you that it's not always necessary. Many Native American languages of North America, for instance, have been reconstructed and classified without archaic texts as guides.

28 Something similar is happening with cell phones and "textspeak." We discuss this in Chapter 5, "Mobilization of Language: The Cell Phone."

First interlude

1 For more comprehensive treatments of language change, see Rudi Keller's *On Language Change: The Invisible Hand in Language* (New York: Routledge, 1994), and Joseph Salmons's *A History of German: What the Past Reveals about Today's Language* (Oxford: Oxford University Press, 2012).

2 William C. Hannas, *The Writing on the Wall: How Asian Orthography Curbs Creativity* (Philadelphia: University of Pennsylvania Press, 2003), 171–2.

3 Ibid., 173.

Chapter 2

1 Friedrich Kittler, *Gramophone, Film, Typewriter* (Stanford: Stanford University Press, 1999), 191.

2 Amalia Gnanadesikan, *The Writing Revolution: Cuneiform to the Internet* (Hoboken, NJ: Wiley-Blackwell, 2008), 252.

3 Elizabeth Eisenstein, *The Printing Press as an Agent of Change: Communications and Cultural Transformations in Early Modern Europe* (Cambridge: Cambridge University Press, 1979).

4 Ibid., xvi.

5 Eisenstein also refers to Marshall McLuhan's *The Gutenberg Galaxy: The Making of Typographic Man* (Toronto: University of Toronto Press, 1962), as a source of inspiration.

6 McLuhan, *The Gutenberg Galaxy*, 124.

7 The Kangxi Dictionary from the eighteenth century, for example, contained nearly 50,000 characters.

8 Naomi Baron, *Alphabet to Email: How Written English Evolved and Where It's Heading* (London: Routledge, 2000), 83.

9 Ibid., 84.

10 http://www.hrc.utexas.edu/educator/modules/gutenberg/books/legacy/
    (accessed December 17, 2014).

11 Elizabeth Eisenstein, *The Printing Revolution in Early Modern Europe*
    (Cambridge: Cambridge University Press, 1983), 81.

12 Steven R. Fischer, *A History of Writing* (London: Reaktion Books, 2001), 272.

13 Baron, *Alphabet to Email*, 97.

14 "busy, adj." OED Online (accessed July 31, 2014).

15 Baron, *Alphabet to Email*, 56–7.

16 Eisenstein, *The Printing Revolution in Early Modern Europe*, 50.

17 Fisher, *A History of Writing*, 265.

18 Robert C. Allen, *Global Economic History: A Very Short Introduction*
    (Oxford: Oxford University Press, 2011), 25.

19 McLuhan, *The Gutenberg Galaxy*, 145.

20 Ibid.

21 Eisenstein, *The Printing Revolution in Early Modern Europe*, 42.

22 Baron, *Alphabet to Email*, 54.

23 Ibid., 53.

24 Michael B. Klein, *Rabelais and the Age of Printing* (Geneva: Librairie Droz,
    1963), 54.

25 Eisenstein, *The Printing Revolution in Early Modern Europe*, 84.

26 Watson, George, *The New Cambridge Bibliography of English
    Literature: Volume 1, 600–1600* (Cambridge: Cambridge University Press,
    1974), 973.

27 http://www.copyrighthistory.com/anne.html (Accessed December 17, 2014).

28 Martha Woodmansee, "The Genius and the Copyright: Economic and
    Legal Conditions of the Emergence of the 'Author,'" in *The Printed Word
    in the Eighteenth Century* (Baltimore: Johns Hopkins University Press,
    1984), 426.

29 Ibid., 427.

30 Baron, *Alphabet to Email*, 69.

31 Joan Acocella, "The Typing Life: How Writers Used to Write," *New Yorker*,
    April 9, 2007.

32 An extensive telling of this history can be found in Current, Richard Nelson.
    The Typewriter and the Men Who Made It (Champaign: University of Illinois
    Press, 1954).

33 Be it noted, however, that Sholes was the *fifty-second* person to "invent"
    the typewriter; his apparatus was just the first commercial success.

34 If the term QWERTY is new for you, just take a look at the top row of letters
    on the nearest keyboard, even the one on your mobile phone.

35 http://www.jpo.go.jp/seido_e/rekishi_e/kyota_sugimoto.htm (accessed
    December 22, 2014).

36 Richard Sproat, *Language, Society, and Technology* (New York: Oxford University Press, 2010), 169–70.

37 Sproat, *Language, Society, and Technology*, 159.

38 Front-strike "visible" typewriters weren't made until the 1890s.

39 Sproat, *Language, Society, and Technology*, 158.

40 Ibid.

41 http://norvig.com/mayzner.html (accessed June 21, 2015).

42 Sproat, *Language, Society, and Technology*, 158.

43 Ibid., 157.

44 Martin Heidegger, *Parmenides*. Trans. André Shuwer and Richard Rojcewicz (Bloomington: Indiana University Press, 1992), 81.

45 Ibid., 80.

46 Ibid., 85.

47 Darren Wershler-Henry, *The Iron Whim: A Fragmented History of Typewriting* (Ithaca, NY: Cornell University Press, 2005), 51.

48 Kittler, *Gramophone, Film, Typewriter*, 203.

49 Ibid., 203.

50 Baron, *Alphabet to Email*, 53.

51 Matthew Schillemann, "Typewriter Psyche: Henry James's Mechanical Mind," *Journal of Modern Literature* 36, no. 3 (Spring 2013): 14–30.

52 Theodora Bosanquet, *Henry James at Work*, ed. Lyall H. Powers (Ann Arbor: University of Michigan Press, 2006), 35.

53 Kittler, *Gramophone, Film, Typewriter*, 191.

54 Current, *The Typewriter and the Men Who Made It*, 116.

55 Matthew Solan, "Tracking Down Typewriters," *Poets & Writers*, September/October (2009): 33. http://site.xavier.edu/polt/typewriters/solan.pdf (accessed June 27, 2015).

56 Readings, "The Typing Life," *New Yorker*, April 9, 2007. http://www.newyorker.com/magazine/2007/04/09/the-typing-life (accessed June 27, 2015).

57 Baron, *Alphabet to Email*, 201.

58 Bruce Bliven Jr., *The Wonderful Writing Machine* (New York: Random House, 1954), 134.

59 Bosanquet, *Henry James at Work*, 34.

60 Baron, *Alphabet to Email*, 211.

61 Ibid.

62 Bliven, *The Wonderful Writing Machine*, 134.

63 Baron, *Alphabet to Email*, 210.

64 Margery Davies, *Woman's Place Is at the Typewriter: Office Work and Office Workers 1870–1930* (Philadelphia: Temple University Press, 2010), 30.

65 Edward Tenner, *Our Own Devices: How Technology Remakes Humanity* (New York: Vintage, 2004), 240.

66 Ibid., 240.

67 Baron, *Alphabet to Email* 203.

68 Twain notes, for instance, in his autobiography that "that early machine was full of caprices, full of defects—devilish ones." https://americanliterature. com/author/mark-twain/short-story/the-first-writing-machines (accessed February 2, 2017).

69 Ibid.

70 Ibid.

71 Michael B. Frank and Harriet Elinor Smith, eds. *Mark Twain's Letters, 1874–1875* (Berkeley: University of California Press, 2002), 308.

72 Bliven, *The Wonderful Writing Machine*, 61.

73 Rose-Marie Dechaine, Strang Burton, and Eric Vatikiotis-Bateson. *Linguistics for Dummies* (Hoboken, NY: John Wiley & Sons, 2012), 308.

74 http://en.wikipedia.org/wiki/Words_per_minute (accessed July 2, 2015).

75 Dave Bledsoe Jr., "Handwriting Speed in an Adult Population," *Advance: Occupational Therapy Practitioners* 27, no. 22 (October 2011): 10.

76 http://en.wikipedia.org/wiki/Words_per_minute (accessed July 2, 2015).

Chapter 3

1 Bernard W. Carlson and Michael E. Gorman, "A Cognitive Framework to Understand Technological Creativity," in *Inventive Minds: Creativity in Technology*, ed. Robert John Weber and David N. Perkins (New York: Oxford University Press, 1992), 58.

2 Ibid.

3 Countless sources on the history of the telegraph include this account. Perhaps the earliest of these is Samuel I. Prime's biography of Morse, *Samuel F. B. Morse: Inventor of the Electro-Magnetic Recording Telegraph* (New York: Appleton, 1875). Additionally, one finds the same anecdote and quotation in Edward L. Morse's *Samuel F. B. Morse: His Letters and Journals* (Boston/New York: Houghton Mifflin, 1914). http://archive.org/stream/ samuelfbmorsehis11018gut/11018.txt (accessed February 13, 2017).

4 James W. Carey first elaborated on this idea in *Communication as Culture: Essays on Media and Society* (London: Routledge, 1989), 201–30.

5 Lewis Coe, *The Telegraph: A History of Morse's Invention and Its Predecessors in the United States* (Jefferson, NC: McFarland, 1993), 77.

6 For example, on pp. 23–6 of *The Story of Telecommunications* (Macon, GA: Mercer University Press, 1992), author G. P. Olsin presents Alfred Vail as the creator of the dot-and-dash code. Coe, on the other hand, notes on p. 9 in *The Telegraph* that "the legend has persisted that it was Vail and not Morse who invented the telegraphic alphabet."

7   In fact, European scientists devised at least two other alphabetic codes
    for sending information electronically. In 1820 the Estonian diplomat Pavel
    Schilling came up with a code based on the left or right movement of a
    magnetized needle: one movement to the right signified the letter E; one
    movement to the left was a T; a single left movement followed by one right
    denoted the letter A; and so on. And in the 1830s the German polymath
    and inventor Carl Steinheil created a code based on dots—printed higher
    or lower relative to each other—marked onto a moving piece of paper and
    operated through the making and breaking of an electric current.

8   Morse, *Samuel F. B. Morse*, 65.

9   W. Baxter, "The Real Birth of the Electric Telegraph" (Morristown,
    NJ: Historic Speedwell, 1880/1981). As cited by Alexander Pope in "The
    American Inventors of the Telegraph, with Special References to the
    Services of Alfred Vail," in *The Century: Illustrated Monthly Magazine*,
    April 1888.

10 http://en.wikipedia.org/wiki/Chinese_telegraph_code (accessed February
    21, 2015).

11 David Crystal, *Internet Linguistics* (New York: Routledge, 2011), 76.

12 Note than an en-dash (–) indicates an intra-character gap, also called a
    "standard" gap. It was equal in duration to a normal dot and was inserted
    between dots and dashes within a single character. An *e*, for example, was
    a single dot (·) and spoken as *dit*. An *i* comprised two standard dots (· ·)
    pronounced as *di-dit*. But an *o* was a dot followed by a standard gap followed
    by another dot (· ·) and was spoken as *dit–dit*. Also note the long dash for
    l. Intra-character gaps and the long dash were unique to American Morse
    code, used only in the United States and South America. Neither the intra-
    character gaps nor the long dash was carried over into international Morse
    code, which was created in 1848 and eventually became the universal
    standard. So American Morse code *dit–dit* for *o* and *daah* for *l* became
    dah-dah-dah (———) and *di-dah-di-dit* (· – · ·), respectively, in international
    Morse code.

13 Here's a transcription and translation of the fictionalized dialogue:
    Operator 1: R U BUYN (Are you buying?)
    Operator 2: N U R (No, you are.)
    Operator 1: OK (Okay.)
    Operator 2: THK. 92. PLS. (Thanks. 92 [= Deliver promptly] please.)
    The "joke" between the operators is that the number 92 was common
    wire service jargon for "deliver promptly" and was used by Western Union
    Telegraph's most frequent customers (who often had the reputation of being
    difficult to work with): newspapermen.

14 David Hochfelder, *The Telegraph in America, 1832–1920* (Baltimore: Johns
    Hopkins University Press, 2012), 75.

15 Richard Harnett, *Wirespeak: Codes and Jargon of the News Business* (San
    Mateo, CA: Shorebird Press, 1997), 53.

16 Ibid., 7.

17 Ibid, 123–9.

18 Hochfelder, *The Telegraph in America*, 78–9.

19 Harnett, *Wirespeak*, 129.

20 Tom Standage, *The Victorian Internet: The Remarkable Story of the Telegraph and the Nineteenth Century's On-Line Pioneers* (New York: Walker, 2007), 110.

21 http://www.encyclopedia.com/topic/telegraph.aspx (accessed February 27, 2015).

22 US Bureau of the Census, Department of Commerce. *Historical Statistics of the US: Colonial Times to 1970* (Washington, DC: Government Printing Office, 1971), 188. https://fraser.stlouisfed.org/files/docs/publications/histstatus/hstat1970_cen_1975_v2.pdf (accessed February 13, 2017).

23 http://www.davemanuel.com/inflation-calculator.php (accessed February 27, 2015).

24 Hochfelder, *The Telegraph in America*, 74.

25 Naomi S. Baron, *Alphabet to Email: How Written English Evolved and Where It's Heading* (London: Routledge, 2000), 218.

26 Ibid., 218.

27 Menahem Blondheim, *News Over the Wires: The Telegraph and the Flow of Public Information in America, 1844–1897* (Boston: Harvard University Press, 1994), 34.

28 Hochfelder, *The Telegraph in America,* 77.

29 Blondheim, *News Over the Wires*, 35.

30 Ansgard, Heinrich, *Network Journalism: Journalistic Practice in Interactive Spheres* (New York/Abingdon, Oxon: Routledge, 2011), 48.

31 Baron, *Alphabet to Email*, 245.

32 Blondheim, *News Over the Wires*, gives an outstanding historical account of the AP and its connection to the telegraph. See especially chapter 2, "Time Past to Time Present: Linking the Telegraph and the Press," and chapter 3, "A Better-Organized System: Establishing the New York Associated Press."

33 Blondheim, *News Over the Wire*, 196.

34 Ibid.

35 James W. Care, *Communication as Culture, Revised Edition: Essays on Media and Society* (New York/London: Routledge, 2009), 163.

36 Blondheim, *News Over the Wire*, viii.

37 Herbert Mitgang, "George Seldes: Author and Thought Collector," *New York Times*, May 26, 1985.

38 Baron, *From Alphabet to Email*, 246.

39 Hochfelder, *The Telegraph in America*, 81–2.

40 Ibid., 83.

41 Ibid., 74.

42 Carey, *Communication as Culture*, 157.

43 Ibid.

44 Anthony Enns, "The Human Telephone: Physiology, Neurology, and Sound Technologies," in *Sounds of Modern History: Auditory Cultures in 19th- and 20th-Century Europe*, ed. Daniel Morat (New York: Berghahn Books, 2014), 52.

45 http://en.wikipedia.org/wiki/Alexander_Melville_Bell (accessed March 1, 2015).

46 Charles Snyder, "Clarence John Baker and Alexander Graham Bell: Otology and the Telephone," *The Annals of Otology, Rhinology, & Laryngology* 83, no. 4 (1974): 7.

47 Ibid., 6

48 Note that Deaf is written with a capital. Wikipedia explains: "When used as a cultural label especially within the culture, the word deaf is often written with a capital D and referred to as 'big D Deaf' in speech and sign. When used as a label for the audiological condition, it is written with a lower case d." https://en.wikipedia.org/wiki/Deaf_culture (accessed July 26, 2016).

49 Alexander Graham Bell. "Prehistoric Telephone Days," *The National Geographic Magazine* 41, no. 3 (March 1922): 228–9.

50 Snyder, "Clarence John Baker and Alexander Graham Bell," 12.

51 Ibid.

52 Bell and Blake preserved the blackened glass plates, and the wavy lines that the stylus had traced on them, by covering them with varnish. Moreover, if they couldn't share in person, they took photographs of the plates and sent them to each other.

53 Enns, "The Human Telephone," 59.

54 Alexander G. Bell, *The Bell Telephone: The Deposition of Alexander Graham Bell, in the Suit Brought by the United States to Annul the Bell Patents* (Boston: American Bell Telephone Company, 1908), 39.

55 Clarence J. Blake, "Sound in Relation to the Telephone," *Journal of the Society of Telegraph Engineers* 8 (1879): 252.

56 Robert Hopper, *Telephone Conversation* (Bloomington: Indiana University Press, 1992), 27.

57 Among other inventors, John Phillips Reis, Elisha Gray, and Antonio Meucci took a crack at the telephone. http://en.wikipedia.org/wiki/Invention_of_the_telephone (accessed March 10, 2015).

58 Todd Timmons, *Science and Technology in Nineteenth-Century America* (Westport, CT: Greenwood Press, 2005), 53.

59 Romana LeFevre, *Rude Hand Gestures of the World: A Guide to Offending Without Words* (San Francisco: Chronicle Books, 2011), 110.

60 Henry Boettinger, "Our Sixth-and-a-Half Sense," in *The Social Impact of the Telephone*, ed. Itheil de Sola Pool (Cambridge, MA: MIT Press, 1977), 205.

61 This is a central question investigated in discourse analysis and conversation analysis, cousin academic fields to linguistics.

62 Hopper, *Telephone Conversation*, 34.

63 Ibid., 41.

64 Naomi S. Baron, *Always On: Language in an Online and Mobile World* (New York: Oxford University Press, 2008), 173.

65 Paul Ten Have, "Comparing Telephone Call Openings: Theoretical and Methodological Reflections," in *Telephone Calls: Unity and Diversity in Conversational Structure across Languages and Cultures*, ed. Kang Kwong Luke and Theodossia-Soula Pavlidou (Amsterdam/Philadelphia: John Benjamins, 2002), 234–48.

66 William Grimes, "Great 'Hello' Mystery Is Solved," *New York Times*, March 5, 1992. http://www.nytimes.com/1992/03/05/garden/great-hello-mystery-is-solved.html (accessed February 14, 2017).

67 Baron, *Always On*, 173.

68 Maria Sifianou, "On the Telephone Again! Telephone Conversation Openings in Greek," in *Telephone Calls*, 49–85.

69 Yong-Yae Park, "Recognition and Identification in Japanese and Korean Telephone Conversation Openings," in *Telephone Calls*, 25–47.

70 Allen Koenigsburg, "The First 'Hello!': Thomas Edison, the Phonograph, and the Telephone," *Antique Phonograph Monthly* 8, no. 6 (1987).

71 Ibid.

72 For the history buffs out there: *The United States Telegraph* was a propaganda paper for Andrew Jackson. It served as Jackson's political mouthpiece during his time as gung-ho aspirant to the Oval Office and even into the first year of his presidency.

73 http://www.oed.com.ezproxy.ithaca.edu:2048/view/Entry/85687 (accessed March 13, 2015).

74 Ibid.

75 http://en.wikipedia.org/wiki/Hello (accessed March 13, 2015).

76 Emanuel A. Schegloff. "Identification and Recognition in Interactional Openings," in *The Social Impact of the Telephone*, 416.

77 This last construct, you might have already surmised, also covers the long-standing and puerile institution known as the prank call. Indeed, this qualifies as one of the telephone's most unique contributions to our technolingual world. Bart Simpson is perhaps the most well-known telephonic practical joker of modern American pop culture, particularly for his clever prank calls to the eponymous owner of Moe's Tavern. Wikiquote.org has them all catalogued according to season and episode: http://en.wikiquote.org/wiki/List_of_Simpsons_Prank_Calls (accessed March 13, 2017). The 2014 book, *Bart Simpson's Manual of Mischief (The Vault of Simpsonology)*, even contains an extra booklet on "the art of the prank call."

78 Adapted from Schegloff, "Identification and Recognition in Interactional Openings," in *The Social Impact of the Telephone*, 418–21.

79 Hopper, *Telephone Conversation*, 218

80 Sidney Aronson, "The Sociology of the Telephone," *International Journal of Comparative Sociology* 12 (1971): 165.

81 Claude Fischer, *America Calling: A Social History of the Telephone to 1940* (Berkeley and Los Angeles: University of California Press, 1992), 69.

82 Fischer, *America Calling*, 70.

83 Ibid.

84 We weren't able to find original publication details for the booklet. Stamped on the back cover, however, is the third iteration of Bell System's logo, used between 1921 and 1939.

85 Fischer, *America Calling*, 183–7.

86 Annie Randall White, 1901. *Twentieth Century Etiquette: An Up-to-date Book for Polite Society* (1901), 146. https://books.google.com/books/about/Twentieth_Century_Etiquette.html?id=Tc46AQAAMAAJ (accessed February 14, 2017).

87 Emily Post, *Etiquette* (New York: Funk & Wagnalls, 1923), 128. https://books.google.com/books?id=HhAYAAAAIAAJ (accessed February 14, 2017).

88 Fischer, *America Calling*, 184.

89 Ellen Weiss, *Telephone Time: A First Book of Do's and Don't's* (New York: Random House, 1986), 10.

90 Weiss, *Telephone Time*, 16.

91 Carrie Finn, *Manners on the Telephone* (Minneapolis: Picture Window Books, 2007), 3.

92 Ibid., 7.

93 Ibid., 5.

94 Hiroko Tabuchi, "Japan's Top Voice: High, Polite, and on the Phone" *New York Times*, December 14, 2013. http://www.nytimes.com/2013/12/15/business/international/japans-top-voice-high-polite-and-on-the-phone.html (accessed February 12, 2017).

95 http://www.jtua.or.jp/education/concours (accessed March 25, 2015).

96 http://www.jtua.or.jp/education/concours/kekka_new.html (accessed March 25, 2015).

97 Tabuchi, "Japan's Top Voice." http://www.nytimes.com/2013/12/15/business/international/japans-top-voice-high-polite-and-on-the-phone.html (accessed February 14, 2017).

98 Ibid.

99 Ibid.

Chapter 4

1 Note that our discussion will focus only on digital computers. There were also analog computers. These machines "used the continuously changeable aspects of physical phenomena such as electrical, mechanical, or hydraulic quantities to model the problem being solved, in contrast to digital computers that represented varying quantities symbolically, as their numerical values change." By the 1960s, however, pure analog computers had been replaced by their digital counterparts. https://en.wikipedia.org/wiki/Analog_computer (accessed June 17, 2015).

2   Thomas Haigh, "Remembering the Office of the Future: The Origins of Word Processing and Office Automation," *IEE Annals of the History of Computer* 28, no. 4 (2006): 6.

3   Charles Petzold, *Code: The Hidden Language of Computer Hardware and Software* (Redmond, WA: Microsoft Press, 2000), 286.

4   For a comprehensive and readable treatment of how the human brain processes language, see Matthew Traxler's *Introduction to Psycholinguistics: Understanding Language Science* (Hoboken, NY: Wiley-Blackwell, 2011). As for how a computer's CPU handles input, Roger Young's *How Computers Work: Processor And Main Memory* (CreateSpace Independent Publishing Platform, 2009) offers an adequate and easy-to-follow explanation.

5   https://en.wikipedia.org/wiki/Rotokas_alphabet (accessed June 19, 2015).

6   Richard Sproat, *Language, Technology, and Society* (New York: Oxford University Press, 2010), 174.

7   http://www.ethnologue.com/enterprise-faq/how-many-languages-world-are-unwritten (accessed June 22, 2015).

8   http://www.omniglot.com/writing/alphabets.htm (accessed June 22, 2015).

9   For a superb description of how early phonetic conversion software handled Japanese writing, see Joseph Becker's "Multilingual Word Processing," *Scientific American* 251, no. 1 (1984): 96–107.

10 William C. Hannas, *The Writing on the Wall: How Asian Orthography Curbs Creativity* (Philadelphia: University of Pennsylvania Press, 2003), 250.

11 Ibid.

12 Ibid., 251.

13 Ibid.

14 Ibid., 252.

15 Ibid., 253.

16 https://en.wikipedia.org/wiki/Programming_language_theory (accessed July 10, 2015).

17 https://en.wikipedia.org/wiki/Software (accessed July 10, 2015).

18 https://en.wikipedia.org/wiki/Assembly_language (accessed July 13, 2015).

19 "The word 'low' refers to the small or nonexistent amount of abstraction between the language and machine language; because of this, low-level languages are sometimes described as being 'close to the hardware.'" https://en.wikipedia.org/wiki/Low-level_programming_language (accessed July 13, 2015).

20 Noam Chomsky, "On Certain Formal Properties of Grammars," *Information and Control* 2, no. 2 (1959): 137.

21 Simply put, a rewrite rule is a mechanism that replaces one thing with another in a systematic way. For example, in any language you have the abstract notion of a "sentence," which can be replaced by a string of concrete words. In formal linguistic theory, a rewrite rule is conventionally indicated by a ➔. Thus, if "S" stands for the abstract notion of any potential

sentence in a language, and "P" stands for the actually produced string of words, we could describe this process with the rewrite rule S ➔ P. An example of an English grammar rewrite rule is S ➔ NP VP. This means that the abstract idea of a sentence in English can be replaced by a concrete noun phrase (e.g., "the dog") and verb phrase (e.g., "barks").

22 Noam Chomsky, "Three Models for the Description of Language," *IRE Transactions on Information Theory* 2 (1956): 113.

23 Chomsky, "On Certain Formal Properties of Grammars," 141.

24 Noam Chomsky, *Syntactic Structures* (The Hague/Paris: Mouton, 1957), 5.

25 In a personal communiqué from May 29, 2015, for instance, Richard Sproat notes: "Concerning Chomsky's influence on programming languages: Well of course the influence is indirect in that Chomsky himself never had any direct input (AFAIK [As far as I know] he was never interested in such things). However inasmuch as he is usually credited with the invention of Context Free Grammars, I guess one could start by looking at early books on compiles such as Aho, Sethi and Ullman, which discuss CFG's and efficient ways of dealing with them."

26 Note that modern-day computer-programming theory recognizes syntax *and* semantics as foundational. The two are also independent of each other; a sentence's syntax can be grammatical without making any semantic sense. This notion also applies to natural language, the classic example coming from Chomsky: "Colorless green ideas sleep furiously."

27 Tao Jiang, Li, Ming, Bala Ravikumar, and Kenneth Regan, "Formal Grammars and Languages," in *Algorithms and Theory of Computation Handbook*, ed. Mikhail J. Atallah and Marina Blanton (Boca Raton: CRC Press, 2009), 20–1.

28 Donald, Knuth, *Selected Papers on Computer Languages* (Stanford: Center for the Study of Language and Information, 2003), x.

29 Ibid.

30 Moreover, one needs a thorough background in logic and computability theory in order to understand each Chomsky grammar type.

31 Margaret A. Boden, *Mind as Machine: A History of Cognitive Science* (Oxford: Oxford University Press, 2006), 628.

32 Gerhard Jäger and James Rogers, "Formal Language Theory: Refining the Chomsky Hierarchy," *Philosophical Transactions of the Royal Society B*, 367 (2012): 1956.

33 John Cocke, and J. T. Schwartz, *Programming Languages and Their Compilers* (New York: Courant Institute of Mathematical Sciences, 1970), 8.

34 See, for instance, https://en.wikipedia.org/wiki/Internet_linguistics (accessed November 11, 2015), and David Crystal's *Internet Linguistics* (New York: Routledge, 2011).

35 As promised, here's our CMC Hall of Fame lineup: Susan C. Herring, ed. *Computer-Mediated Communication: Linguistic, Social and Cross-Cultural Perspectives* (Amsterdam/Philadelphia: John Benjamin's, 1996); David Crystal's *Language and the Internet* (Cambridge: Cambridge University Press, 2006); Naomi Baron's *Always On: Language in an Online and Mobile*

World. (New York: Oxford University Press, 2010); Bodomo B. Adams's *Computer-Mediated Communication for Linguistics and Literacy: Technology and Natural Language Education* (Hershey, PA: IGI Global, 2010); and Carmen Frehner's *Email—SMS—MMS: The Linguistic Creativity of Asynchronous Discourse in the New Media Age* (Bern: Peter Lang, 2008).

36 Unfortunately, after its seventh annual conference the International Pragmatics Association discontinued its tradition of publishing proceedings. Thus, at the time of this writing we aren't able to report the attendees' consensus answer to the workshop's stated query.

37 Michael Beißwenger and Angelika Storrer, "Corpora of Computer-Mediated Communication," in *Corpus Linguistics: An International Handbook*, ed. Anke Lüdeling and Merja Kytö (Berlin: Walter de Gruyter, 2008), 293.

38 Naomi Baron, "Computer Mediated Communication as a Force in Language Change," *Visible Language XVII2*, no. 2 (1984): 118.

39 Ibid., 119.

40 Ibid., 120.

41 Milena Collot and Nancy Belmore, "Electronic Language: A New Variety of Language," in *Computer-Mediated Communication*, 13–28.

42 Ibid., 28.

43 Baron, *Always On*, 29.

44 Crystal, *Internet Linguistics*, 16.

45 Ibid., 32.

46 Ibid., 21.

47 Jan Blommaert, "Supervernaculars and Their Dialects," *Dutch Journal of Applied Linguistics* 11 (2012), 2.

48 Ibid., 3.

49 A perspectivistic approach, according to Nietzsche, posits that all ideations arise from particular perspectives. Or, as Wikipedia puts is: "There are many possible conceptual schemes, or perspectives in which judgment of truth or value can be made." https://en.wikipedia.org/wiki/Perspectivism (accessed October 22, 2015).

50 Baron, "Computer Mediated Communication as a Force in Language Change," 120.

51 Crystal, *Internet Linguistics*, 19.

52 Ibid., 127.

53 https://en.wikipedia.org/wiki/ARPANET (accessed November 23, 2015).

54 "The Man Who Made You Put Away Your Pen," *NPR*, November 15, 2009. http://www.npr.org/templates/story/story.php?storyId=120364591 (accessed November 23, 2015).

55 Ian Peter, *History of the Internet*. http://www.nethistory.info/History%20 of%20the%20Internet/email.html (accessed November 23, 2015).

56 http://www.radicati.com/wp/wp-content/uploads/2015/02/Email-Statistics-Report-2015-2019-Executive-Summary.pdf (accessed November 23, 2015).

57 Ibid.

58 Baron, *Alphabet to Email*, 252.

59 Crystal, *Language and the Internet*, 17.

60 Ibid., 130.

61 Naomi Baron, "Why Email Looks Like Speech: Proofreading, Pedagogy and Public Face," *New Media Language*, ed. Jean Aitchison and Diana Lewis (London: Routledge, 2003), 86.

62 Baron, *Alphabet to Email*, 188–9.

63 Naomi Baron, "Put On a Public Face," *New York Times*, April 11, 2001. http://www.nytimes.com/2001/04/11/opinion/put-on-a-public-face.html (accessed November, 28 2015).

64 Baron, "Why Email Looks Like Speech, 87–8.

65 Susan Adams, "57 Ways to Sign Off on an Email," *Forbes*, September 27, 2013. http://www.forbes.com/sites/susanadams/2013/09/27/57-ways-to-sign-off-on-an-email (accessed November 28, 2015).

66 http://www.enron-mail.com/email/skilling-j (accessed December 1, 2015).

67 Joan Waldvogel, "Greetings and Closings in Workplace Email," *Journal of Computer-Mediated Communication* 12 (2007), 471.

68 Crystal, *Language and the Internet*, 127.

69 Carmen K. M. Lee, "Linguistic Features of Email and ICQ Instant Messaging in Hong Kong," in *The Multilingual Internet: Language, Culture, and Communication Online*, ed. Brenda Danet and Susan C. Herring (New York: Oxford University Press, 2007), 195.

70 Mark Warschauer, Ghada R. El Said, and Ayman G. Zohry, "Language Choice Online: Globalization and Identity in Egypt," in *The Multilingual Internet: Language, Culture, and Communication Online*, 303–18.

71 Ibid., 308–9.

72 Note, however, that *Wired Style* goes with the unhyphenated form *email*. The authors explain on pages 13–14 that, "*E-mail* looked odd ... the hyphen looked more and more anachronistic, ... so we spell *email* solid."

73 Lisa A. Smith, *Business E-Mail: How to Make It Professional and Effective* (San Anselmo, CA: Writing & Editing at Work, 2002), 2.

74 Jeanne M. Fraser, *Email Etiquette for Business Success: Use Emotional Intelligence to Communicate Effectively in the Business World* (CreateSpace Independent Publishing Platform, 2011), 1.

75 David Shipley and Will Schwalbe, *SEND: Why People Email So Badly and How to Do It Better*, Revised Edition (New York: Alfred A. Knopf, 2010), 4.

76 Ibid., 1.

77 Judith Kallos, *Email Etiquette Made Easy* (Raleigh, NC: Lulu, 2007), 3.

78 http://www.netmanners.com/email-etiquette-expert (accessed December 12, 2015).

79 Virginia Shea, *Netiquette* (San Francisco: Albion Books, 1994), 41.

80 Take, for instance, Kawasaki's definition of "electronic mail": "A method for receiving messages you cannot understand, from people you don't know, concerning things you don't care about." Guy Kawasaki, *The Guy Kawasaki Computer Curmudgeon* (Carmel, IN: Hayden Books, 1992), 46.

81 Ibid., 52.

82 Constance Hale and Jessie Scanlon, *Wired Style: Principles of English Usage in the Digital Age* (New York: Broadway Books, 1999), 3.

83 Ibid., 12.

84 David Angell and Brent Heslop, *The Elements of E-Mail Style* (Reading, MA: Addison-Wesley, 1994), xi.

85 Ibid., 56.

86 Ibid., 83–98.

87 Ibid., 3.

88 National League of Cotillions, *E-Etiquette: The Definitive Guide to Proper Manners in Today's Digital World.* (New York: Skyhorse, 2010), 54.

89 Ibid.

90 Crystal, *Internet Linguistics*, 1.

91 Ibid., 77.

92 Beißwenger and Storrer, "Corpora of Computer-Mediated Communication," 296.

93 http://genius.com/Genius-about-genius-annotated (accessed January 16, 2016).

94 Charley Locke, "Young Thug Isn't Rapping Gibberish, He's Evolving Language," *Wired*, October 10, 2015. http://www.wired.com/2015/10/young-thug-evolution-of-language (accessed January 17, 2016).

95 http://www.ucalgary.ca/dflynn/rap (accessed January 17, 2016).

96 Locke, "Young Thug Isn't Rapping Gibberish, He's Evolving Language."

97 Ibid., 10.

98 Adam Kilgarriff and Gregory Grefenstette, "Introduction to the Special Issue on the Web as Corpus," *Computational Linguistics* 29, no. 3 (2003): 334.

99 Sue Atkins, Jeremy Clear, and Nicholas Oster, "Corpus Design Criteria," *Literary & Linguistic Computing* 7, no. 1 (1992): 1.

100 Gunnar Bergh, Aimo Seppänen, and Joe Trotta, "Language Corpora and the Internet: A Joint Linguistic Resource," in *Explorations in Corpus Linguistics*, ed. Antoinette Renouf (Amsterdam/Atlanta: Rodopi, 1998), 41.

101 http://www.uow.edu.au/~dlee/CBLLinks.htm (accessed January 10, 2016).

102 http://corpus.byu.edu/corpora.asp (accessed January 10, 2016).

103 Marianne Hundt, Nadja Nesselhauf, and Carolin Biewer, *Corpus Linguistics and the Web* (Amsterdam/New York: Rodopi, 2007).

104 Gunnar Bergh, "Review of *Corpus Linguistics and the Web*," *ICAME Journal* 23 (2008: 260).

105 Crystal, *Internet Linguistics*, 7.

106 http://www.sms4science.org (accessed January 15, 2016).

107 http://www.natcorp.ox.ac.uk (accessed January 12, 2016).

108 http://corpus.byu.edu/coca (accessed January 12, 2016).

109 http://secrets.rutgers.edu/dai/queryPages/querySelection.php (accessed January 15, 2016).

110 http://www.webclark.org (accessed January 16, 2016).

111 Ibid.

112 Ibid.

113 https://www.uni-marburg.de/fb10/studium/studiengaenge/malingwebtech (accessed January 16, 2016).

114 https://www.uni-marburg.de/studium/studienangebot/ki/ki10lingwebtech-m.pdf (accessed January 16, 2016).

115 https://www.newschallenge.org/challenge/data/entries/mapping-english-with-wordnik (accessed January 16, 2016).

116 https://en.wikipedia.org/wiki/Wordnik (accessed January 16, 2016).

117 https://www.wordnik.com/faq (accessed January 16, 2016).

118 http://www.ethnologue.com/language/eng (accessed January 16, 2016).

119 https://www.kickstarter.com/projects/1574790974/lets-add-a-million-missing-words-to-the-dictionary (accessed January 16, 2016).

120 Jean-Baptiste Michel, Yuan Kui Shen, Aviva Presser Aiden, et al., "Quantitative Analysis of Culture Using Millions of Digitized Books," *Science* 331 (January 14, 2011): 177.

121 https://www.kickstarter.com/projects/1574790974/lets-add-a-million-missing-words-to-the-dictionary/posts/1444209 (accessed January 16, 2016).

Second interlude

1 Note, for instance, Crispin Thurlow's criticism: "[It] is by no means only lay writers who are responsible for some of the exaggerated rhetoric about CMD, as evidenced by [comments] by renowned linguist David Crystal in his widely cited book *Language and the Internet*." Thurlow, Crispin. "From Statistical Panic to Moral Panic: The Metadiscursive Construction and Popular Exaggeration of New Media Language in the Print Media," *Journal of Computer-Mediated Communication* 11 (2006): 687–8.

2 Charley Rowe and Eva L. Wyss, eds., *Language and New Media: Linguistic, Cultural, and Technological Evolutions* (Creskill, NJ: Hampton Press, 2009), 1.

3 Bodomo Adams, *Computer-Mediated Communication for Linguistics and Literature: Technology and Natural Language Education* (Hershey, PA: IGI Global, 2009), 37.

4 Baron, *Always On*, 29.

5 Ibid., 163.

6   Ibid., 183–4.

7   David Crystal, *Language and the Internet*, 2nd edition
    (Cambridge: Cambridge University Press: 2006), xxviii.

8   Ibid., 75.

9   Ibid.

10 Anne Clune, "Text-Messages and Language," *Irish Times*, August 6, 2001.
    http://www.irishtimes.com/opinion/letters/text-messages-and-language-
    1.321334 (accessed February 18, 2017).

11 Auslan Cramb, "Girl Writes English Essay in Phone Text Shorthand,"
    Telegraph, March 3, 2003. http://www.telegraph.co.uk/news/uknews/
    1423572/Girl-writes-English-essay-in-phone-text-shorthand.html (accessed
    February 18, 2017).

12 Ibid.

13 "My summer holidays were a complete waste of time. Before, we used to
    go to New York to see my brother, his girlfriend, and their three screaming
    kids face to face. I love New York, it's a great place."

14 "The Decline and Fall of Spellin' & Writin'," *Vancouver Sun*, November
    3, 2001.

15 John Humphrys, "I h8 txt msgs: How Texting Is Wrecking Our Language,"
    Daily Mail, September 24, 2007.

16 Thurlow, "From Statistical Panic to Moral Panic," 667.

17 Ibid., 695–701.

18 "Language and Electronics: The Coming Global Tongue," *The Economist*,
    December 21, 1996. https://www.highbeam.com/doc/1G1-18975943.html
    (accessed February 18, 2017).

19 Sven Berkert, "Into the Electronic Millennium," *Boston Review*,
    October 1991.

20 David Rothenberg, "How the Web Destroys the Quality of Students'
    Research Papers," *Chronicle of Higher Education*, August 15, 1997.

21 See, for instance, the views presented in Neil Selwyn. *Digital Technology
    and the Contemporary University: Degrees of Digitization* (New York/
    Abingdon: Routledge, 2014).

22 Thurlow, "From Statistical Panic to Moral Panic," 677.

23 Ibid., 682.

24 http://www.kulturinstitut.org/fileadmin/user_upload/SPRACHSTELLE/
    Nachlese/Interview_Peter_Schlobinski.pdf (accessed November 17, 2015).

25 Frehner, *Email—SMS—MMS*.

26 Crystal, *Language and the Internet*, 276.

27 Eiaja-Liisa Kasesniemi and Pirjo Rautiainen, "Mobile Culture of Children
    and Teenagers in Finland," in *Perpetual Contact: Mobile Communication,
    Private Talk, Public Performance*, ed. James E. Katz and Mark Aakhus
    (Cambridge: Cambridge University Press: 2002), 184.

28 Beverly Plester, Clare Wood, and Puja Joshi, "Exploring the Relationship
    between Children's Knowledge of Text Message Abbreviations and School

Literacy Outcomes," *British Journal of Developmental Psychology* 27, no. 1 (2009): 158.

29 Ibid., 151.

30 Ibid., 149.

31 Michelle Drouin and Claire Davis, "R u txting? Is the Use of Text Speak Hurting Your Language?" *Journal of Literacy Research* 41 (2009): 47–67.

32 Abbie Grace and Nenagh Kemp, "Undergraduates' Attitudes to Text Messaging Language Use and Intrusions of Textisms into Formal Writing," *New Media & Sociology* 17, no. 5 (2013): 792–809.

33 Crystal, *Language and the Internet*, 16.

Chapter 5

1 At Apple's 2015 Worldwide Developers conference in San Francisco, Craig Federighi, Apple's senior vice president of software engineering, stated that Siri's speech-recognition capability now has a 5 percent word-error rate. http://www.cbsnews.com/news/apple-wwdc-2015-iphone-ipad-apple-watch-music-streaming accessed July 27, 2015).

2 B.-H. Juang and L. R. Rabiner, "Automatic Speech Recognition: A Brief History of the Technology Development," in *Encyclopedia of Language and Linguistics*, ed. K. Brown (Amsterdam: Elsevier Science, 2005), 810.

3 Daniel Jurafsky and James H. Martin, *Speech and Language Processing: An Introduction to Natural Language Processing, Computational Linguistics, and Speech Recognition*, 2nd edition (Upper Saddle River, NJ: Prentice Hall, 2009), 228.

4 Allard Jongman, *Oxford Bibliographies: Acoustic Phonetics*. http://www.oxfordbibliographies.com/view/document/obo-9780199772810/obo-9780199772810-0047.xml (accessed July 17, 2015).

5 Juang and Rabiner, "Automatic Speech Recognition," 811.

6 K. H. Davis, R. Biddulph, and S. Balashek, "Automatic Recognition of Spoken Digits," *Journal of Acoustic Society of America* 24, no. 6 (1952): 627–42.

7 Jongman, *Oxford Bibliographies: Acoustic Phonetics*.

8 Jarsky and Martin, *Speech and Language Processing*, 238–9.

9 Michael Studdert-Kennedy and D. H. Whalen, "A Brief History of Speech Perception Research in the United States," in *A Guide to the History of the Phonetic Sciences in the United States* (Berkeley: University of California, 2009), 21.

10 Ralph K. Kimball, George A. Kopp, and Harriett Green Kopp, *Visible Speech* (New York: D. Van Nostrand, 1947). Note that there's no relation to Alexander M. Bell's *Visible Speech: The Science of Universal Alphabetics* from 1867.

11 Jongman, *Oxford Bibliographies: Acoustic Phonetics*.

12 Richard S. Hill, "*Visible Speech*: A Review," *Notes, Second Series* 4, no. 4 (September 1947): 468.

13   Sara Solomon, "Phonetics and Phonology: 1949–1989," in *North American Contributions to the History of Linguistics*, ed. Francis P. Dinneen and E. F. K. Koerner (Philadelphia: John Benjamins Publishing, 1990), 213.

14   Ignatius G. Mattingly, "A Short History of Acoustic Phonetics in the U.S.," in *A Guide to the History of the Phonetic Sciences in the United States* (Berkeley: University of California, 2009), 2.

15   Nikolai Trubetzkoy, *Principles of Phonology* (*Grundzüge der Phonologie*) (Prague: Travaux du cercle linguistique de Prague 7), 1939. Translated by Christiane Baltaxe (Berkeley: University of California Press), 1969.

16   Note that it would take a background in math and computer science, and a lot more than one paragraph, to cover the technical details involved in each process of computerized speech recognition. Our explanation, therefore, will leave much of this out. For a more elaborate description see Richard Sproat, *Language, Technology, and Society* (New York: Oxford University Press, 2010), 188–205.

17   Ibid., 190.

18   For a mind-bending discussion of how even nonhuman (i.e., alien) anatomical features would affect the acoustics of speech, see David J. Peterson, *The Art of Language Invention: From Horse-Lords to Dark Elves, the Words Behind World-Building* (New York: Penguin Books, 2015), 82–7.

19   Ibid., 191.

20   Ibid., 193.

21   Juang and Rabiner, "Automatic Speech Recognition," 815.

22   Ibid.

23   Zoubin Ghahramani, "An Introduction to Hidden Markov Models and Bayesian Networks," *International Journal of Pattern Recognition and Artificial Intelligence* 15, no. 1 (2001): 10.

24   Juang and Rabiner, "Automatic Speech Recognition," 816.

25   Sproat, *Language, Technology, and Society*, 198.

26   Juang and Rabiner, "Automatic Speech Recognition," 817.

27   Certainly, cell phones have affected spoken forms and practices of language. For information on this important aspect, the reader is directed to the following sources: Anandam P. Kavoori and Noah Arceneaux, eds., *The Cell Phone Reader: Essays in Social Transformation* (New York: Peter Lang Publishing, 2006), and Rich Ling, *The Mobile Connection: The Cell Phone's Impact on Society* (San Francisco: Morgan Kaufmann Publishers, 2004).

28   Gordon Janey, "The Cell Phone: An Artifact of Popular Culture and a Tool of the Public Sphere," in *The Cell Phone Reader*, 51.

29   David Crystal, *A Glossary of Netspeak and Textspeak* (Edinburgh: Edinburgh University Press, 2004), 139–76.

30   In 2000 there was as yet only one mobile phone with an alphanumeric keypad on the market. Nokia released the 9000 Communicator in the United States in 1997; however, at $800 per unit, "it drew a dedicated following among certain business users, but never commanded a mass

audience." Anton Toianovski and Sven Grundberg, "Nokia's Bad Call on Smartphones," *Wall Street Journal*, July 18, 2012. http://www.wsj.com/articles/SB10001424052702304388004577531002591315494 (accessed December 16, 2015).

31   David Crystal, *Txtng: The Gr8 Db8* (Oxford: Oxford University Press, 2008), 45–6.

32   http://transl8it.com (accessed December 17, 2015).

33   Crispin Thurlow and Michele Poff, "Text Messaging," in *Pragmatics of Computer-Mediated Communication*, ed. Susan C. Herring, Dieter Stein, and Tuija Virtanen (Boston: Mouton de Gruyter, 2013), 175.

34   Naomi Baron and Rich Ling, "Necessary Smileys & Useless Periods: Redefining Punctuation in Electronically Mediated Communication," *Visible Language* 45, nos. 1/2 (2011): 57.

35   The decision to describe smileys as "necessary" in the title was motivated by qualitative data that the authors collected for their study. In focus groups conducted with seventy-five texters, several participants mentioned that they often include smileys at the end of a message in order to soften their tone, which might otherwise be perceived as terse. For instance, the SMS *no meet me there* and—especially—*no meet me there.* carry stringent undertones, whereas *no meet me there:)* comes across more neutral.

36   David Crystal, "Texting," *ELT Journal* 62, no. 1 (2008): 77.

37   Gabrielle Mander, *Wan2tlk?: Ltl Bk of Txt Msgs* (London: Michael O'Mara Books, 2000).

38   Gabrielle Mander, *IH8U: Ltl Bk of Txt Abuse* (London: Michael O'Mara Books, 2001).

39   Elspaß, Stephan Elspaß, "Alter Wein und neue Schläuche? Briefe der Wende zum 20. Jahrhundert und Texte der neuen Medien—ein Vergleich," in *Breifkommunikation im 20. Jahrhundert* (Duisburg: Gilles & Franke, 2002), 7–32.

40   Jacques Anis, "Neography: Unconventional Spelling in French SMS Text Messages," in *The Multilingual Internet: Language, Culture, and Communication Online*, ed. Brenda Danet and Susan C. Herring (New York: Oxford University Press, 2007), 110.

41   Ibid., 97.

42   Crystal, *Txtng: The Gr8 Db8*, 132.

43   http://www.statista.com/statistics/276494/number-of-sms-and-mms-sent-in-china (accessed December 18, 2015).

44   http://www.statista.com/statistics/215776/mobile-messaging-volumes-in-the-us (accessed December 18, 2015).

45   Collette Snowden, "Casting A pwr4l spL.L: D EvOLshn f SMS," in *The Cell Phone Reader*, 116.

46   Rich Ling, "The Sociolinguistics of SMS: An Analysis of SMS Use by a Random Sample of Norwegians," in *Mobile Communications: Renegotiation of the Social Sphere,* ed. Rich Ling and Per E. Pedersen (New York: Springer, 2005), 338–40.

47 Naomi S. Baron, *Always On: Language in an Online and Mobile World* (New York: Oxford University Press, 2010), 144–6.

48 http://www.sms4science.uzh.ch (accessed on December 19, 2015).

49 Simone Ueberwasser, "Non-standard Data in Swiss Text Messages with a Special Focus on Dialectal Forms," in *Non-standard Data Sources in Corpus-Based Research*, ed. Marcos Zampieri and Sascha Diwersy (Aachen: Shaker, 2008), 7–24.

50 https://en.wikipedia.org/wiki/Cell_phone_novel (accessed December 22, 2015).

51 Dana Goodyear, "I ♥ Novels: Young Women Develop a Genre for the Cellular Age," *New Yorker*, December 22, 2008. http://www.newyorker.com/magazine/2008/12/22/i-%E2%99%A5-novels (accessed December 22, 2015).

52 http://www.textnovel.com/keitai.php (accessed December 22, 2015).

53 Yukiko Nishimura, "Japanese *Keitai* Novels and Ideologies of Literacy," in *Digital Discourse: Language in the New Media*, ed. Crispin Thurlow and Kristine Mroczek (New York: Oxford University Press, 2011), 91.

54 Ibid., 89.

55 Ibid., 92–100.

56 Olivia Solon, "Movellas Democratises Ebook Publishing," *Wired UK*, August 16, 2011. http://www.wired.co.uk/news/archive/2011-08/16/movellas-europe (accessed December 22, 2015).

57 Goodyear, "I ♥ Novels."

58 Norman Silver, *Age, Sex, Location: Poems from the TXT Café* (Text Café, 2006). http://www.txtcafe.net/index.php?view=txtpoems&poem=flirt_lines (accessed December 22, 2015).

59 Victor Keegan, "The Message Is the Medium," *Guardian*, May 3, 2001. http://www.theguardian.com/technology/2001/may/03/internet.poetry (accessed December 23, 2015).

60 Ibid.

61 Snowden, "Cstng A pwr4l spLL," 116.

62 https://en.wikipedia.org/wiki/Emoticon (accessed December 23, 2015).

63 Anne Casselman, "The Emoticon Turns 25," *Discover Magazine*, October 2007. http://discovermagazine.com/2007/oct/the-emoticon-turns-25 (accessed December 23, 2015).

64 "Smile! A History of Emoticons," *Wall Street Journal*, September 27, 2013. http://www.wsj.com/articles/SB10001424052702304213904579093661814158946 (accessed December 24, 2015).

65 Paul Bignell, "Happy 30th Birthday Emotion!:-)," *Independent*, September 8, 2012. http://www.independent.co.uk/life-style/gadgets-and-tech/news/happy-30th-birthday-emoticon-8120158.html (accessed December 24, 2015).

66 David W. Sanderson, *Smileys* (Sebastopol, CA: O'Reilly Media, Inc., 1993).

67 Casselman, "The Emoticon Turns 25."

68 Nick Stockton, "Emoji—Trendy Slang or a Whole New Language?" *Wired*, June 24, 2015. http://www.wired.com/2015/06/emojitrendy-slang-whole-new-language (accessed December 26, 2015).

69 http://emojipedia.org/faq (accessed December 26, 2015).

70 http://narrativesinemoji.tumblr.com (accessed December 26, 2015).

71 Jenna Wortham, "Emoji: The Very Bearable Lightness of Meaning," *Womanzine*, March 21, 2014. http://issuu.com/lindseyweber5/docs/emoji_by_womanzine/18 (accessed December 27, 2015).

72 Caitlin Dewey, "Meet the Guy Trying to Turn Emoji into a Legitimate, Usable Language," *Washington Post*, April 30, 2015. https://www.washingtonpost.com/news/the-intersect/wp/2015/04/30/meet-the-guy-trying-to-turn-emoji-into-a-legitimate-usable-language (accessed December 26, 2015).

73 Abbie Grace and Nenagh Kemp, "Text Messaging Language: A Comparison of Undergraduates' Naturalistic Textism Use in Four Consecutive Cohorts," *Writing Systems Research* 7, no. 2 (2015): 220.

74 Crystal, *Txtng*, 20.

75 https://www.smartphowned.com_388331_1381172264 (accessed December 29, 2015).

76 https://en.wikipedia.org/wiki/Cupertino_effect (accessed December 29, 2015).

77 Perhaps the most notable site for autocorrect gaffes is damnyouautocorrect.com. It offers countless examples of autocorrect-instigated blunders and is updated daily.

78 Gloria Jacobs, "Complicating Contexts: Issues of Methodology in Researching the Language and Literacies of Instant Messaging," *Reading Research Quarterly* 39, no. 4 (2004): 394–406.

79 Ibid., 402.

80 Ibid.

81 Kris M. Markman, "Learning to Work Virtually: Conversational Repair as a Resource for Norm Development in Computer-Mediated Team Meetings," in *Interpersonal Relations and Social Patterns in Communication Technologies: Discourse Norms, Language Structures and Cultural Variables*, ed. Jung-ran Park and Eileen Abels (Hershey, PA: IGI Global, 2010), 225.

82 However, if you're looking for tips on how to use texting to negotiate corporal success with the opposite sex, our Amazon search turned up several guidebooks.

83 Calandra Izquierdo and Lazarus Potter, *Textiquette: The Do's and Don'ts of Texting* (CreateSpace Independent Publishing Platform, 2013), 67.

84 Ibid., 3.

85 Ibid.

86 Ibid., 23.

87 Ibid., 65.

88 Ibid., 41.

89 Ibid., 29.

90 Ibid., 7.

91 Ibid., 25.

92 Jessica Bennett, "When Your Punctuation Says It All," *New York Times*, February 27, 2015. https://www.nytimes.com/2015/03/01/style/when-your-punctuation-says-it-all.html (Accessed February 18, 2017).

93 Ibid.

94 Ibid.

95 http://www.huffingtonpost.com/news/texting (accessed January 5, 2016).

96 http://www.huffingtonpost.com/dana-holmes/text-etiquette-guide_b_2474980.html (accessed January 5, 2016).

97 Ibid.

98 http://www.huffingtonpost.com/lisa-mirza-grotts (accessed January 5, 2016).

99 http://www.huffingtonpost.com/lisa-mirza-grotts/textiquette-good-bad-and_b_5050687.html (accessed January 5, 2016).

100 http://www.huffingtonpost.com/julie-dobrow/cell-phone-etiquette_b_4073806.html (accessed January 5, 2016).

101 Ibid.

102 http://emilypost.com/about (accessed January 5, 2016).

103 http://emilypost.com/advice/texting-manners (accessed January 5, 2016).

104 Ibid.

105 Ibid.

106 Juang and Rabiner, "Automatic Speech Recognition," 825.

Chapter 6

1 http://www.utdallas.edu/news/2012/7/25-18951_Cochlear-Implant-Pioneer-Professor-Lost-to-Cancer_article.html (accessed June 21, 2016).

2 Philipos C. Loizou, "Mimicking the Human Ear," *IEEE Signal Processing Magazine* 15, no. 5 (1998): 102.

3 Bernard W. Carlson and Michael E. Gorman, "A Cognitive Framework to Understand Technological Creativity," in *Inventive Minds: Creativity in Technology*, ed. Robert John Weber and David N. Perkins (New York: Oxford University Press, 1992), 58.

4 http://slideplayer.com/slide/4280354 (accessed June 30, 2016).

5 Loizou, "Mimicking the Human Ear," 103.

6 Bernard W. Blume, *The Artificial Ear: Cochlear Implants and the Culture of Deafness* (Piscataway, NJ: Rutgers University Press, 2010), 31.

7 Blake S. Wilson, "Engineering Design of Cochlear Implants," in *Cochlear Implants: Auditory Prostheses and Electric Hearing*, ed. Fan-Gang S. Zeng, Arthur N. Popper, and Richard R. Fay (New York: Springer-Verlag, 2004), 14.

8 Elizabeth S. Olson, Hendrikus Duifhuis, and Charles R. Steele, "Von Bekesy and Cochlear Mechanics," *Hearing Research* 293, vol. 1 (2012): 31.

9 Douglas Mook, *Classic Experiments in Psychology* (Westport, CT: Greenwood Press, 2004), 285.

10 Floyd Ratliff, *Georg von Békésy: A Biographical Memoir* (Washington, DC: National Academy of Sciences, 1976), 25. http://www.nasonline.org/publications/biographical-memoirs/memoir-pdfs/von-bekesy-georg.pdf (accessed July 10, 2016).

11 Georg Békésy, "My Experiences in Different Laboratories," *Fizikai Szemle*, no. 5 (1995). http://fizikaiszemle.hu/archivum/fsz9905/bekesy.html (accessed July 10, 2016).

12 Carl Gustaf Berhard, "Presentation Speech for Nobel Prize in Physiology or Medicine 1961," in *Nobel Lectures in Physiology or Medicine 1942–1962* (Singapore/NJ/London/Hong Kong: World Scientific, 1999), 720.

13 Daniel C. Geisler, "Electrical Characteristics of Cochlear Tissues," in *Cochlear Implants: Models of the Electrically Stimulated Ear*, ed. Joseph M. Miller and Francis Spelman (New York: Springer-Verlag, 2004), 7–8.

14 Loizou, "Mimicking the Human Ear," 105.

15 https://en.wikipedia.org/wiki/Basilar_membrane (accessed July 14, 2016).

16 Ratliff, *Georg von Békésy*, 36. http://www.nasonline.org/publications/biographical-memoirs/memoir-pdfs/von-bekesy-georg.pdf (accessed July 14, 2016)

17 Berhard, "Presentation Speech for Nobel Prize in Physiology or Medicine 1961," 721.

18 Georg Békésy, *Experiments in Hearing* (New York/Toronto/London: McGraw-Hill, 1960), 11–12.

19 Ibid, 404.

20 Remember that the cochlea is about the size of a pea, and the bone itself one of the hardest in the human body. So you can't just poke or saw at it with any tool and expect it to crack open. Moreover, recall that it's filled with liquid. So the moment you extract it from the cadaver and lay it open, you lose the ear's medium for conveying the sound waves, and the precious membranes within start drying out. In order to observe how the cochlea works, special equipment and techniques were needed. Unfortunately for Helmholtz, the technology that would allow for such real-time observations wasn't yet available.

21 Békésy, *Experiments in Hearing*, 404.

22 Georg Békés,. "Concerning the Pleasures of Observing, and the Mechanics of the Inner Ear," Nobel Lecture, December 11, 1961. http://www.nobelprize.org/nobel_prizes/medicine/laureates/1961/bekesy-lecture.pdf (accessed July 17, 2016).

23 Ratliff, *Georg von Békésy*, 36.

24 S. S. Stevens, "Georg von Békésy," *Physics Today* 25, no. 9 (1972): 78–9.

25 Ibid, 408.

26 Békésy, "Concerning the Pleasures of Observing, and the Mechanics of the Inner Ear."

27 Békésy, "My Experiences in Different Laboratories." http://fizikaiszemle.hu/archivum/fsz9905/bekesy.html (accessed July 19, 2016).

28 Ratliff, *Georg von Békésy*, 35.

29 Mook, *Classic Experiments in Psychology*, 287.

30 Ratliff, *Georg von Békésy*, 35.

31 American Speech-Language-Hearing Association. *ASHA Technical Report on Cochlear Implants*, March 2003. http://www.asha.org/policy/TR2004-00041 (accessed July 20, 2016).

32 Loizou, "Mimicking the Human Ear," 103.

33 Fang-Gang Zeng, "Auditor Prostheses: Past, Present, and Future," in *Cochlear Implants: Auditory Prostheses and Electric Hearing*, 3–4.

34 *ASHA Technical Report on Cochlear Implants*.

35 Garud and Rappa, "A Socio-Cognitive Model of Technology Evolution," 349.

36 The term "hearie" is a colloquial expression used within the Deaf community to refer to people with unimpaired hearing. Though not without its critics (generally within the hearing community), "hearie" is not intended to be offensive; rather, it's a jocular, inner-group term.

37 Zeng, "Auditor Prostheses," 8.

38 Michael Chorost, *Rebuilt: How Becoming Part Computer Made Me More Human* (Boston/New York: Houghton Mifflin, 2005), 87.

39 Peter V. Paul and Gail M. Whitelaw, *Hearing and Deafness: An Introduction for Health and Education Professionals* (Sudbury, MA: Jones and Bartlett, 2011), 118.

40 *Alexander Graham Bell Association for the Deaf and Hard of Hearing* http://www.agbell.org/Document.aspx?id=1836 (accessed July 29, 2016).

41 Patricia Elizabeth Spencer and Marc Marshark, "Cochlear Implants: Issues and Complications," in *Oxford Handbook of Deaf Studies, Language, and Education*, ed. Marc Marshark and Patricia Elizabeth Spencer (New York: Oxford University Press, 2001), 443.

42 Ibid, 435.

43 Blake S. Wilson and Michael F. Dorman, "Cochlear Implants: A Remarkable Past and a Brilliant Future," *Hear Res* 242 (2008): 3.

44 http://neuronbank.org/wiki/index.php/Cochlea_hair_cell (accessed July 31, 2016).

45 https://www.nidcd.nih.gov/health/cochlear-implants (accessed July 31, 2016).

46 Paul and Whitelaw, *Hearing and Deafness*, 120.

47 http://www.medel.com/us/performance (accessed August 8, 2016).

48 http://www.cochlear.com/wps/wcm/connect/us/home/stories-and-community/watch-recipient-videos (accessed August 8, 2016).

49 At the time of this writing, on its subsite for "professionals," the company only offers two announcements from researchers "seeking participants" for

clinical studies not funded by Cochlear Limited. http://www.cochlear.com/wps/wcm/connect/us/for-professionals/research-and-clinical-studies/clinical-studies (accessed August 8, 2016).

50 For a list of variables that determine the success of a cochlear implant, see Federal Drug Administration, "What Is a Cochlear Implant?" 2014. http://www.fda.gov/MedicalDevices/ProductsandMedicalProcedures/ImplantsandProsthetics/CochlearImplants/ucm062823.htm (accessed August 1, 2016).

51 In fact, these psychosocial factors are sometimes more influential on an implantee's progress than physical conditions.

52 Barbara Kannapell, *Language Choice, Language Identity: A Sociolinguistic Study of Deaf College Students* (Burtonsville, MD: Linstok Press, 1993), 29.

53 Daphna Oyserman, Kristen Elmore, and George Smith, "Self, Self-Concept, and Identity," in *Handbook of Self and Identity*, 2nd edition, ed. Mark R. Leary and June Price Tangney (New York: Guilford Press, 2012), 69.

54 Ibid.

55 Irene W. Leigh, "Who Am I? Deaf Identity Issues," in *Signs and Voices: Deaf Culture, Identity, Language, and Arts*, ed. Kristin A. Lindgren, Doreen Deluca, and Donna Jo Napoli (Washington, DC: Gallaudet University Press, 2008), 27.

56 https://en.wikipedia.org/wiki/Madonna (accessed August 22, 2016).

57 Karen Butler, "Madonna Admits She Felt Like an Outsider in England," United Press International, February 5, 2011. http://www.upi.com/Madonna-admits-she-felt-like-an-outsider-in-England/26011328478351/ (accessed August 22, 2016).

58 Amy Lorocca, "Thank Kyeew! Madonna's Phony Accent Is the Latest Fashionable Thing," *New York Observer*, January 17, 2000. http://observer.com/2000/01/thank-kyeew-madonnas-phony-accent-is-the-latest-fashionable-thing (accessed August 22, 2016).

59 Carol A. Padden and Tom Humphries, *Deaf in America: Voices from a Culture* (Cambridge, MA: Harvard University Press, 1988), 9.

60 Paddy Ladd, *Understanding Deaf Culture: In Search of Deafhood* (Clevedon: Multilingual Matters, 2003), 150.

61 William C. Stokoe, *Sign Language Structure: An Outline of the Visual Communication Systems of the American Deaf* (Buffalo, NY: University of Buffalo Press, 1960), 39.

62 http://www.lifeprint.com/asl101/pages-signs/t/think.htm (accessed September 29, 2016).

63 http://www.wikihow.com/Sign-Feelings-and-Emotions-in-American-Sign-Language (accessed September 29, 2016).

64 https://en.wikipedia.org/wiki/English_phonology (accessed September 29, 2016).

65 Stokoe, *Sign Language Structure*, 30.

66 Ibid., 34.

67 https://en.wikipedia.org/wiki/William_Stokoe (accessed September 20, 2016).

68 Padden and Humphries, *Deaf in America*, 6.

69 Barbara Kannapell, "Inside the Deaf Community," *Deaf American* 26 (1982): 25.

70 Harlan Lane, *The Mask of Benevolence: Disabling the Deaf Community* (New York: Knopf, 1992), 17.

71 Kannapell, "Inside the Deaf Community," 26–7.

72 One internationally renowned medical center writes, for instance: "A cochlear implant is defined in many cases as a 'medical miracle' because it enables individuals with severe to profound hearing loss to hear." http://www.assafh.org/sites/en/Pages/Cochlear.aspx (accessed October 13, 2016).

73 Kristin A. Lindgren, Doreen Deluca, and Donna Jo Napoli, eds., *Signs and Voices: Deaf Culture, Identity, Language, and Arts* (Washington, DC: Gallaudet University Press, 2008), xiii.

74 Stuart Blume, *The Artificial Ear: Cochlear Implants and the Culture of Deafness* (New Brunswick/New Jersey/London: Rutgers University, 2010), 78.

75 Lane, *The Mask of Benevolence*, 216.

76 Ibid., 206.

77 Ladd, *Understanding Deaf Culture*, 208.

Bibliography

Adams, Bodomo B. *Computer-Mediated Communication for Linguistics and Literacy: Technology and Natural Language Education* (Hershey, PA: IGI Global, 2010).

Adams, Mark. "Ephemera: Remington Notes," 2, no. 11 (1912). http://type-writer.org/wp-content/uploads/2014/03/Tolstoy-and-his-typewriter.jpg (accessed June 28, 2015).

Adams, Susan. "57 Ways to Sign Off on an Email," *Forbes*, September 27, 2013.

Ahearn, Laura. *Living Language: An Introduction to Linguistic Anthropology* (Hoboken, NY: Wiley-Blackwell, 2011).

Allen, Robert C. *Global Economic History: A Very Short Introduction* (Oxford: Oxford University Press, 2011).

American Speech-Language-Hearing Association. *ASHA Technical Report on Cochlear Implants*, March 2003.

Angell, David and Brent Heslop. *The Elements of E-mail Style* (Reading, MA: Addison-Wesley, 1994).

Anis, Jacques. "Neography: Unconventional Spelling in French SMS Text Messages," in *The Multilingual Internet: Language, Culture, and Communication Online*, edited by Brenda Danet and Susan C. Herring (New York: Oxford University Press, 2007).Ansgard, Heinrich. *Network Journalism: Journalistic Practice in Interactive Spheres* (New York/Abingdon, Oxon: Routledge, 2011).

Aronson, Sidney. "The Sociology of the Telephone," *International Journal of Comparative Sociology* 12 (1971).

Atkins, Sue, Jeremy Clear, and Nicholas Oster. "Corpus Design Criteria," *Literary & Linguistic Computing* 7, no. 1 (1992).

Baron, Naomi. "Computer Mediated Communication as a Force in Language Change," *Visible Language* XVII2, no. 2 (1984).

Baron, Naomi. *Alphabet to Email: How Written English Evolved and Where It's Heading* (London: Routledge, 2000).

Baron, Naomi. "Put On a Public Face," *New York Times*, April 11, 2001.

Baron, Naomi. "Why Email Looks Like Speech: Proofreading, Pedagogy and Public Face," in *New Media Language,* edited by Jean Aitchison and Diana Lewis (London: Routledge, 2003).

Baron, Naomi S. *Always On: Language in an Online and Mobile World* (New York: Oxford University Press, 2008).

Baron, Naomi and Rich Ling. "Necessary Smileys & Useless Periods: Redefining Punctuation in Electronically Mediated Communication," *Visible Language* 45, nos. 1/2 (2011).

Baxter, William. *The Real Birth of the Electric Telegraph* (Morristown, NJ: Historic Speedwell, 1880/1981).

Becker, Joseph. "Multilingual Word Processing," *Scientific American* 251, no. 1 (1984).

Beißwenger, Michael and Angelika Storrer. "Corpora of Computer-Mediated Communication," in *Corpus Linguistics: An International Handbook*, edited by Anke Lüdeling and Merja Kytö (Berlin: Mouton de Gruyter, 2008).

Békésy, Georg. *Experiments in Hearing* (New York/Toronto/London: McGraw-Hill, 1960).

Békésy, Georg. "Concerning the Pleasures of Observing, and the Mechanics of the Inner Ear," Nobel Lecture (December 11, 1961).

Békésy, Georg. "My Experiences in Different Laboratories," *Fizikai Szemle*, no. 5 (1995).

Bell, Alexander G. *Visible Speech: The Science of Universal Alphabetics* (London: Simpkin, Marshall, 1867).

Bell, Alexander G. *The Bell Telephone: The Deposition of Alexander Graham Bell, in the Suit Brought by the United States to Annul the Bell Patents* (Boston: American Bell Telephone Company, 1908).

Bell, Alexander G. "Prehistoric Telephone Days," *National Geographic Magazine* 41, no. 3 (March 1922).

Bennett, Jessica. "When Your Punctuation Says It All," *New York Times* (February 27, 2015).

Bergh, Gunnar, Aimo Seppänen, and Joe Trotta. "Language Corpora and the Internet: A Joint Linguistic Resource," in *Explorations in Corpus Linguistics*, edited by Antoinette Renouf (Amsterdam/Atlanta: Rodopi, 1998).

Bergh, Gunnar. "Review of *Corpus Linguistics and the Web*," *ICAME Journal* 23 (2008).

Berhard, Carl Gustaf. "Presentation Speech for Nobel Prize in Physiology or Medicine 1961," in *Nobel Lectures in Physiology or Medicine 1942–1962* (Singapore/NJ/London/Hong Kong: World Scientific, 1999).

Bignell, Paul. "Happy 30th Birthday Emotion!:-)," *Independent* (September 8, 2012).

Blake, Clarence J. "Sound in Relation to the Telephone," *Journal of the Society of Telegraph Engineers* 8 (1879).

Bledsoe, Dave Jr. "Handwriting Speed in an Adult Population," *Advance: Occupational Therapy Practitioners* 27, no. 22 (October 2011).

Bliven, Bruce Jr. *The Wonderful Writing Machine* (New York: Random House, 1954).

Blommaert, Jan. "Supervernaculars and Their Dialects," *Dutch Journal of Applied Linguistics* 11 (2012).

Blondheim, Menahem. *News Over the Wires: The Telegraph and the Flow of Public Information in America, 1844–1897* (Boston: Harvard University Press, 1994).Blume, Stuart. *The Artificial Ear: Cochlear Implants and the Culture of Deafness* (Piscataway, NJ: Rutgers University Press, 2009).

Blumstein, Sheila. "Reflections on the Cognitive Neuroscience of Language," in *The Cognitive Neurosciences*, edited by Michael S. Gazzaniga (Cambridge, MA: MIT Press, 2009).

Boden, Margaret A. *Mind as Machine: A History of Cognitive Science* (Oxford: Oxford University Press, 2006).

Boettinger, Henry. "Our Sixth-and-a-Half Sense," in *The Social Impact of the Telephone*, edited by Itheil de Sola Pool (Cambridge, MA: MIT Press, 1977).

Bosanquet, Theodora. *Henry James at Work*, ed. Lyall H. Powers (Ann Arbor: University of Michigan Press, 2006).

Butler, Karen. "Madonna Admits She Felt Like an Outsider in England," United Press International (February 5, 2011).

Carey, James W. *Communication as Culture, Revised Edition: Essays on Media and Society* (New York/London: Routledge, 2009).

Carlson, Bernard W. and Michael E. Gorman. "A Cognitive Framework to Understand Technological Creativity," in *Inventive Minds: Creativity in Technology*, edited by Robert John Weber and David N. Perkins (New York: Oxford University Press, 1992).

Casselman, Anne. "The Emoticon Turns 25," *Discover Magazine* (October 2007).

Chomsky, Noam. "Three Models for the Description of Language," *IRE Transactions on Information Theory* 2 (1956).

Chomsky, Noam. *Syntactic Structures* (The Hague/Paris: Mouton, 1957).

Chomsky, Noam. "On Certain Formal Properties of Grammars," in *Information and Control* 2, no. 2 (1959).

Chorost, Michael. *Rebuilt: How Becoming Part Computer Made Me More Human* (Boston/New York: Houghton Mifflin, 2005).

Clune, Anne. "Text-Messages and Language," *Irish Times* (August 6, 2001).

Cocke, John and J. T. Schwartz. *Programming Languages and Their Compilers* (New York: Courant Institute of Mathematical Sciences, 1970).

Coe, Lewis. *The Telegraph: A History of Morse's Invention and Its Predecessors in the United States* (Jefferson, NC: McFarland, 1993).

Collot, Milena and Nancy Belmore. "Electronic Language: A New Variety of Language," in *Computer-Mediated Communication: Linguistic, Social and Cross-Cultural Perspectives*, edited by Susan C. Herring (Amsterdam, NL: John Benjamins, 1996).

Cramb, Auslan. "Girl Writes English Essay in Phone Text Shorthand," *Telegraph* (March 3, 2003).

Crystal, David. *A Glossary of Netspeak and Textspeak* (Edinburgh: Edinburgh University Press, 2004).

Crystal, David. *Language and the Internet* (Cambridge: Cambridge University Press, 2006).

Crystal, David. *Txtng: The Gr8 Db8* (Oxford: Oxford University Press, 2008).

Crystal, David. *Internet Linguistics* (New York: Routledge, 2011).

Current, Richard Nelson. *The Typewriter and the Men Who Made It* (Champaign: University of Illinois Press, 1954).

Davies, Margery. *Woman's Place Is at the Typewriter: Office Work and Office Workers 1870–1930* (Philadelphia: Temple University Press, 2010).

Davis, K. H., R. Biddulph, and S. Balashek. "Automatic Recognition of Spoken Digits," *Journal of Acoustic Society of America* 24, no. 6 (1952).

Dechaine, Rose-Marie, Strang Burton, and Eric Vatikiotis-Bateson. *Linguistics for Dummies* (Hoboken, NY: John Wiley, 2012).

Dewey, Caitlin. "Meet the Guy Trying to Turn Emoji into a Legitimate, Usable Language," *Washington Post* (April 30, 2015).

Drouin, Michelle and Claire Davis. "R u txting? Is the Use of Text Speak Hurting Your Language?" *Journal of Literacy Research* 41 (2009).

Dürscheid, Christa. *Einführung in die Schriftlinguistik* (Göttingen, DE: Vandenhoeck & Ruprecht, 2006).

Eisenstein, Elizabeth. *The Printing Press as an Agent of Change: Communications and Cultural Transformations in Early Modern Europe* (Cambridge: Cambridge University Press, 1979).

Eisenstein, Elizabeth. *The Printing Revolution in Early Modern Europe* (Cambridge: Cambridge University Press, 1983).

Elspaß, Stephan. "Alter Wein und neue Schläuche? Briefe der Wende zum 20. Jahrhundert und Texte der neuen Medien—ein Vergleich," in *Breifkommunikation im 20. Jahrhundert* (Duisburg: Gilles & Franke, 2002).

Enns, Anthony. "The Human Telephone: Physiology, Neurology, and Sound Technologies," in *Sounds of Modern History: Auditory Cultures in 19th- and 20th-Century Europe*, edited by Daniel Morat (New York: Berghahn Books, 2014).

Finn, Carrie. *Manners on the Telephone* (Minneapolis: Picture Window Books, 2007).

Fischer, Claude. *America Calling: A Social History of the Telephone to 1940* (Berkeley and Los Angeles: University of California Press, 1992).

Fisher, Steven Roger. *A History of Writing* (London: Reaktion Books, 2001).

Forsyth, Mark. *Horologicon: A Day's Jaunt through the Lost Words of the English Language* (New York: Berkley Books, 2013)

Frank, Michael B. and Harriet Elinor Smith, eds. *Mark Twain's Letters, 1874–1875* (Berkeley: University of California Press, 2002).

Fraser, Jeanne M. *Email Etiquette for Business Success: Use Emotional Intelligence to Communicate Effectively in the Business World* (CreateSpace Independent Publishing Platform, 2011).

Frehner, Carmen. *Email—SMS—MMS: The Linguistic Creativity of Asynchronous Discourse in the New Media Age* (Bern: Peter Lang, 2008).

Garud, Raghu and Michael A. Rappa. "A Socio-Cognitive Model of Technology Evolution: The Case of Cochlear Implants," *Organizational Science* 5, no. 3 (1994).

Ghahramani, Zoubin. "An Introduction to Hidden Markov Models and Bayesian Networks," *International Journal of Pattern Recognition and Artificial Intelligence* 15, no. 1 (2001).

Gnanadesikan, Amalia. *The Writing Revolution: Cuneiform to the Internet* (Hoboken, NJ: Wiley-Blackwell, 2008)

Goody, Jack and Ian Watt. "The Consequences of Literacy," *Comparative Studies in Society and History* 5, no. 3 (Cambridge: Cambridge University Press, 1963).

Goodyear, Dana. "I ♥ Novels: Young Women Develop a Genre for the Cellular Age," *New Yorker* (December 22, 2008).

Grace, Abbie and Nenagh Kemp. "Undergraduates' Attitudes to Text Messaging Language Use and Intrusions of Textisms into Formal Writing," *New Media & Sociology* 17, no. 5 (2013).

Grace, Abbie and Nenagh Kemp. "Text Messaging Language: A Comparison of Undergraduates' Naturalistic Textism Use in Four Consecutive Cohorts," *Writing Systems Research* 7, no. 2 (2015).

Grimes, William. "Great 'Hello' Mystery Is Solved," *New York Times*, March 5, 1992.

Haigh, Thomas. "Remembering the Office of the Future: The Origins of Word Processing and Office Automation," *IEE Annals of the History of Computer* 28, no. 4 (2006).

Hale, Constance and Jessie Scanlon. *Wired Style: Principles of English Usage in the Digital Age* (New York: Broadway Books, 1999).

Hannas, William. *The Writing on the Wall: How Asian Orthography Curbs Creativity* (Philadelphia: University of Pennsylvania Press, 2003).

Harnett, Richard. *Wirespeak: Codes and Jargon of the News Business* (San Mateo, CA: Shorebird Press, 1997).

Heidegger, Martin. *Parmenides.* Translated by André Shuwer and Richard Rojcewicz (Bloomington: Indiana University Press, 1992).

Herring, Susan C., ed. *Computer-Mediated Communication: Linguistic, Social and Cross-Cultural Perspectives* (Amsterdam/Philadelphia: John Benjamins, 1996).

Hertnon, Simon. *Endangered Words: A Collection of Rare Gems for Book Lovers* (New York: Skyhorse, 2009).

Hill, Richard S. *"Visible Speech*: A Review," *Notes, Second Series* 4, no. 4 (September 1947).

Hochfelder, David. *The Telegraph in America, 1832–1920* (Baltimore, MD: Johns Hopkins University Press, 2012).

Hopper, Robert. *Telephone Conversation* (Bloomington: Indiana University Press, 1992).

Houston, Keith. "Smile! A History of Emoticons," in *Wall Street Journal*, September 27, 2013.

Humphrys, John. "I h8 txt msgs: How Texting Is Wrecking Our Language," *Daily Mail* (September 24, 2007).

Hundt, Marianne, Nadja Nesselhauf, and Carolin Biewer. *Corpus Linguistics and the Web* (Amsterdam/New York: Rodopi, 2007).

Izquierdo, Calandra and Lazarus Potter. *Textiquette: The Do's and Don'ts of Texting* (CreateSpace Independent Publishing Platform, 2013).

Jacobs, Gloria. "Complicating Contexts: Issues of Methodology in Researching the Language and Literacies of Instant Messaging," *Reading Research Quarterly* 39, no. 4 (2004).

Jäger, Gerhard and James Rogers. "Formal Language Theory: Refining the Chomsky Hierarchy," *Philosophical Transactions of the Royal Society B*, 367 (2012).

Janey, Gordon. "The Cell Phone: An Artifact of Popular Culture and a Tool of the Public Sphere," in *The Cell Phone Reader: Essays in Social Transformation*, edited by Anandam P. Kavoori and Noah Arceneaux (New York: Peter Lang, 2006).

Jiang, Tao, Ming Li, Bala Ravikumar, and Kenneth W. Regan. "Formal Grammars and Languages," in *Algorithms and Theory of Computation Handbook*, edited by Mikhail J. Atallah and Marina Blanton (Boca Raton: CRC Press, 2009).

Jongman, Allard. *Oxford Bibliographies: Acoustic Phonetics* (March 2013).

Juang, B.-H. and L. R. Rabiner. "Automatic Speech Recognition: A Brief History of the Technology Sevelopment," in *Encyclopedia of Language and Linguistics*, edited by K. Brown (Amsterdam: Elsevier Science, 2005).

Jurafsky, Daniel and James H. Martin. *Speech and Language Processing: An Introduction to natural Language Processing, Computational Linguistics, and Speech Recognition*, 2nd edition (Upper Saddle River, NJ: Prentice Hall, 2009).

Kacirk, Jeffrey. *Forgotten English Page-a-DayCalendar* (South Portland, ME: Sellers, 2016).

Kallos, Judith. *Email Etiquette Made Easy* (Raleigh, NC: Lulu, 2007).

Kannapell, Barbara. *Language Choice, Language Identity: A Sociolinguistic Study of Deaf College Students* (Burtonsville, MD: Linstok Press, 1993).

Kasesniemi, Eiaja-Liisa and Pirjo Rautiainen. "Mobile Culture of Children and Teenagers in Finland," in *Perpetual Contact: Mobile Communication, Private Talk, Public Performance*, edited by James E. Katz and Mark Aakhus (Cambridge: Cambridge University Press: 2002).

Kavoori, Anandam P. and Noah Arceneaux, eds. *The Cell Phone Reader: Essays in Social Transformation* (New York: Peter Lang, 2006)

Kawasaki, Guy. *The Guy Kawasaki Computer Curmudgeon* (Carmel, IN: Hayden Books, 1992).

Keegan, Victor. "The Message Is the Medium," *Guardian* (May 3, 2001).

Keller, Rudi. *On Language Change: The Invisible Hand in Language* (New York: Routledge, 1994).

Kilgarriff, Adam and Gregory Grefenstette. "Introduction to the Special Issue on the Web as Corpus," *Computational Linguistics* 29, no. 3 (2003).

Kimball, Ralph K., George A. Kopp, and Harriett Green Kopp. *Visible Speech* (New York: D. Van Nostrand, 1947).

Kittler, Friedrich. *Gramophone, Film, Typewriter* (Stanford, CA: Stanford University Press, 1999).

Klein, Michael B. *Rabelais and the Age of Printing* (Geneva, Switzerland: Librairie Droz, 1963).

Knuth, Donald. *Selected Papers on Computer Languages* (Stanford: Center for the Study of Language and Information, 2003).

Koenigsburg, Allen. "The First 'Hello!': Thomas Edison, the Phonograph, and the Telephone," *Antique Phonograph Monthly* 8, no. 6 (1987).

Ladd, Paddy. *Understanding Deaf Culture: In Search of Deafhood* (Clevedon: Multilingual Matters, 2003).

Lane, Harlan. *The Mask of Benevolence: Disabling the Deaf Community* (New York: Knopf, 1992).

Lee, Carmen K. M. "Linguistic Features of Email and ICQ Instant Messaging in Hong Kong," in *The Multilingual Internet: Language, Culture, and Communication Online*, edited by Brenda Danet and Susan C. Herring (New York: Oxford University Press, 2007).

LeFevre, Romana. *Rude Hand Gestures of the World: A Guide to Offending Without Words* (San Francisco: Chronicle Books, 2011).

Leigh, Irene W. "Who Am I? Deaf Identity Issues," in *Signs and Voices: Deaf Culture, Identity, Language, and Arts*, edited by Kristin A. Lindgren, Doreen Deluca, and Donna Jo Napoli (Washington, DC: Gallaudet University Press, 2008).Lindgren, Kristin A., Doreen Deluca, and Donna Jo Napoli, eds. *Signs and Voices: Deaf Culture, Identity, Language, and Arts* (Washington, DC: Gallaudet University Press, 2008).

Ling, Rich. *The Mobile Connection: The Cell Phone's Impact on Society* (San Francisco: Morgan Kaufmann Publishers, 2004).

Ling, Rich. "The Sociolinguistics of SMS: An Analysis of SMS Use by a Random Sample of Norwegians," in *Mobile Communications: Renegotiation*

of the Social Sphere, edited by Rich Ling and Per E. Pedersen
(New York: Springer, 2005).

Locke, Charley. "Young Thug Isn't Rapping Gibberish, He's Evolving Language,"
Wired, October 10, 2015.

Loizou, Philipos C. "Mimicking the Human Ear," *IEEE Signal Processing Magazine*
15, no. 5 (1998).

Logan, Robert. *The Alphabet Effect: The Impact of the Phonetic Alphabet on the
Development of Western Civilization* (New York: St. Martin's Press, 1987).

Lorocca, Amy. "Thank Kyeew! Madonna's Phony Accent Is the Latest
Fashionable Thing," *New York Observer,* January 17, 2000.

Mander, Gabrielle. *Wan2tlk?: Ltl Bk of Txt Msgs* (London: Michael O'Mara
Books, 2000).

Mander, Gabrielle. *IH8U: Ltl Bk of Txt Abuse* (London: Michael O'Mara
Books, 2001).

Markman, Kris M. "Learning to Work Virtually: Conversational Repair as a
Resource for Norm Development in Computer-Mediated Team Meetings,"
in *Interpersonal Relations and Social Patterns in Communication
Technologies: Discourse Norms, Language Structures and Cultural Variables,*
edited by Jung-ran Park and Eileen Abels (Hershey, PA: IGI Global, 2010).

Marsico, Katie. *Good Manners on the Phone* (North Mankato, MN: Magic
Wagon, 2009).

Mattingly, Ignatius G. "A Short History of Acoustic Phonetics in the U.S.,"
in *A Guide to the History of the Phonetic Sciences in the United States*
(Berkeley: University of California, 2009).

McLuhan, Marshall. *The Gutenberg Galaxy: The Making of Typographic Man*
(Toronto: University of Toronto Press, 1962).

Michel, Jean-Baptiste, Yuan Kui Shen, Aviva Presser Aiden, et al. "Quantitative
Analysis of Culture Using Millions of Digitized Books," *Science* 331 (January
14, 2011).

Mitgang, Herbert. "George Seldes: Author and Thought Collector," *New York
Times,* May 26, 1985.

Moncel, Count Du. *The Telephone, the Microphone and the Phonograph*
(New York: Harper & Brothers, 1879).

Mook, Douglas. *Classic Experiments in Psychology* (Westport, CT: Greenwood
Press, 2004).

Morse, Edward L. "The Dot and Dash Alphabet," *Century Illustrated Monthly
Magazine,* 83, 1912.

Morse, Edward L. *Samuel F. B. Morse: His Letters and Journals* (Boston/
New York: Houghton Mifflin Company, 1914).

National League of Cotillions. *E-Etiquette: The Definitive Guide to Proper
Manners in Today's Digital World* (New York: Skyhorse, 2010).

Nishimura, Yukiko. "Japanese *Keitai* Novels and Ideologies of Literacy," in *Digital
Discourse: Language in the New Media,* edited by Crispin Thurlow and
Kristine Mroczek (New York: Oxford University Press, 2011).

Olsin, G. P. *The Story of Telecommunications* (Macon, GA: Mercer University
Press, 1992).

Olson, Elizabeth S., Hendrikus Duifhuis, and Charles R. Steele. "Von Bekesy and
Cochlear Mechanics," *Hearing Research* 293, vol. 1 (2012).

Oyserman, Daphna, Kristen Elmore, and George Smith. "Self, Self-Concept, and
    Identity," in *Handbook of Self and Identity*, 2nd edition, edited by Mark R.
    Leary and June Price Tangney (New York: Guilford Press, 2012).
Padden, Carol A. and Tom Humphries. *Deaf in America: Voices from a Culture*
    (Cambridge, MA: Harvard University Press, 1988).Park, Yong-Yae. "Recognition
    and Identification in Japanese and Korean Telephone Conversation Openings,"
    in *Telephone Calls: Unity and Diversity in Conversational Structure across
    Languages and Cultures*, edited by Kang Kwong Luke and Theodossia-Soula
    Pavlidou (Amsterdam/Philadelphia: John Benjamins, 2002).
Paul, Peter V. and Gail M. Whitelaw. *Hearing and Deafness: An Introduction for
    Health and Education Professionals* (Sudbury, MA: Jones and Bartlett, 2011).
Peterson, David J. *The Art of Language Invention: From Horse-Lords to Dark
    Elves, the Words Behind World-Building* (New York: Penguin Books, 2015).
Petzold, Charles. *Code: The Hidden Language of Computer Hardware and
    Software* (Redmond, WA: Microsoft Press, 2000). Plester, Beverly, Clare
    Wood, and Puja Joshi. "Exploring the Relationship between Children's
    Knowledge of Text Message Abbreviations and School Literacy Outcomes,"
    British Journal of Developmental Psychology 27, no. 1 (2009).
Pope, Alexander. "The American Inventors of the Telegraph, with Special
    References to the Services of Alfred Vail," *The Century: Illustrated Monthly
    Magazine*, April 1888.
Prime, Samuel I. *Samuel F. B. Morse: Inventor of the Electro-Magnetic Recording
    Telegraph* (New York: Appleton, 1875).
Ratliff, Floyd. *Georg von Békésy: A Biographical Memoir* (Washington,
    DC: National Academy of Sciences, 1976).
Readings, "The Typing Life," *New Yorker*, April 9, 2007.
Rowe, Charley and Eva L. Wyss, eds. *Language and New Media: Linguistic,
    Cultural, and Technological Evolutions* (Creskill, NJ: Hampton Press, 2009).
Salmons, Joseph. *A History of German: What the Past Reveals about Today's
    Language* (Oxford: Oxford University Press, 2012).
Sanderson, David W. *Smileys* (Sebastopol, CA: O'Reilly Media, 1993).
Schegloff, Emanuel A. "Identification and Recognition in Interactional Openings,"
    in *The Social Impact of the Telephone*, ed. Ithiel de Sola Pool (Cambridge,
    MA: MIT Press, 1977).
Schillemann, Matthew. "Typewriter Psyche: Henry James's Mechanical Mind,"
    Journal of Modern Literature 36, no. 3 (Spring 2013).Shea, Virginia. *Netiquette*
    (San Francisco: Albion Books, 1994).
Shipley, David and Will Schwalbe. *SEND: Why People Email So Badly and How to
    Do It Better, Revised Edition* (New York: Alfred A. Knopf, 2010).
Sifianou, Maria. "On the Telephone Again! Telephone Conversation Openings in
    Greek," in *Telephone Calls: Unity and Diversity in Conversational Structure
    across Languages and Cultures*, edited by Kang Kwong Luke and Theodossia-
    Soula Pavlidou (Amsterdam/Philadelphia: John Benjamins, 2002).
Silver, Norman. *Age, Sex, Location: Poems from the TXT Café* (Text Café, 2006).
Skinner, David. *The Story of Ain't: America, Its Language, and the Most
    Controversial Dictionary Ever Published* (New York: HarperCollins, 2012).
Smith, Lisa A. *Business E-Mail: How to Make It Professional and Effective* (San
    Anselmo, CA: Writing & Editing at Work, 2002).

Snowden, Collette. "Casting A pwr4l spL.L: D EvOLshn f SMS," in *The Cell Phone Reader: Essays in Social Transformation*, edited by Anandam Kavoori and Noah Arceneaux (New York: Peter Lang, 2006).

Snyder, Charles. "Clarence John Baker and Alexander Graham Bell: Otology and the Telephone," *The Annals of Otology, Rhinology, & Laryngology* 83, no. 4 (1974).

Solomon, Sara. "Phonetics and Phonology: 1949–1989," in *North American Contributions to the History of Linguistics*, edited by Francis P. Dinneen and E. F. K. Koerner (Philadelphia: John Benjamins, 1990).

Solon, Olivia. "Movellas Democratises Ebook Publishing," *Wired UK* (August 16, 2011).

Spencer, Patricia Elizabeth and Marc Marshark, "Cochlear Implants: Issues and Complications," in *Oxford Handbook of Deaf Studies, Language, and Education*, edited by Marc Marshark and Patricia Elizabeth Spencer (New York: Oxford University Press, 2001)

Sproat, Richard. *Language, Society, and Technology* (New York: Oxford University Press, 2010).

Standage, Tom. *The Victorian Internet: The Remarkable Story of the Telegraph and the Nineteenth Century's On-line Pioneers* (New York: Walker, 2007).

Stevens, S. S. "Georg von Békésy," *Physics Today* 25, no. 9 (1972).

Stockton, Nick. "Emoji—Trendy Slang or a Whole New Language?" *Wired* (June 24, 2015).

Stokoe, William C. *Sign Language Structure: An Outline of the Visual Communication Systems of the American Deaf* (Buffalo, NY: University of Buffalo Press, 1960).

Studdert-Kennedy, Michael and D. H. Whalen. "A Brief History of Speech Perception Research in the United States," in *A Guide to the History of the Phonetic Sciences in the United States* (Berkeley: University of California, 2009).

Tabuchi, Hiroko. "Japan's Top Voice: High, Polite, and on the Phone" *New York Times*, December 14, 2013.

Ten Have, Paul. "Comparing Telephone Call Openings: Theoretical and Methodological Reflections," in *Telephone Calls: Unity and Diversity in Conversational Structure across Languages and Cultures*, edited by Kang Kwong Luke and Theodossia-Soula Pavlidou (Amsterdam/Philadelphia: John Benjamins, 2002).

Tenner, Edward. *Our Own Devices: How Technology Remakes Humanity* (New York: Vintage, 2004).

Thurlow, Crispin. "From Statistical Panic to Moral Panic: The Metadiscursive Construction and Popular Exaggeration of New Media Language in the Print Media," *Journal of Computer-Mediated Communication* 11 (2006).

Thurlow, Crispin and Michele Poff. "Text Messaging," in *Pragmatics of Computer-Mediated Communication*, edited by Susan C. Herring, Dieter Stein, and Tuija Virtanen (Boston: Mouton de Gruyter, 2013).

Timmons, Todd. *Science and Technology in Nineteenth-Century America* (Westport, CT: Greenwood Press, 2005).

Toianovski, Anton and Sven Grundberg, "Nokia's Bad Call on Smartphones," *Wall Street Journal*, July 18, 2012.

Traxler, Matthew. *Introduction to Psycholinguistics: Understanding Language Science* (Hoboken, NY: Wiley-Blackwell, 2011)

Trubetzkoy's, Nikolai. *Grundzüge der Phonologie* (Prague: Travaux du cercle linguistique de Prague 7, 1939).

Ueberwasser, Simone. "Non-standard Data in Swiss Text Messages with a Special Focus on Dialectal Forms," in *Non-standard Data Sources in Corpus-based Research*, edited by Marcos Zampieri and Sascha Diwersy (Aachen: Shaker, 2008).

Vandendorpe, Christian. *From Papyrus to Hypertext: Toward the Universal Digital Library* (Champaign: University of Illinois Press, 2009).

Waldvogel, Joan. "Greetings and Closings in Workplace Email," *Journal of Computer-Mediated Communication* 12 (2007).

Warschauer, Mark, Ghada R. El Said, and Ayman G. Zohry. "Language Choice Online: Globalization and Identity in Egypt," in *The Multilingual Internet: Language, Culture, and Communication Online*, edited by Brenda Danet and Susan C. Herring (New York: Oxford University Press, 2007).

Watson, George. *The New Cambridge Bibliography of English Literature: Volume 1, 600–1600* (Cambridge: Cambridge University Press, 1974).

Weiss, Ellen. *Telephone Time: A First Book of Do's and Don't's* (New York: Random House, 1986).

Wershler-Henry, Darren. *The Iron Whim: A Fragmented History of Typewriting* (Ithaca, NY: Cornell University Press, 2005).

White, Annie Randall. *Twentieth Century Etiquette: An Up-to-Date Book for Polite Society* (1901).

Wilson, Blake S. "Engineering Design of Cochlear Implants," in *Cochlear Implants: Auditory Prostheses and Electric Hearing*, edited by Fan-Gang S. Zeng, Arthur N. Popper, and Richard R. Fay (New York: Springer-Verlag, 2004).

Wilson, Blake S. and Michael F. Dorman, "Cochlear Implants: A Remarkable Past and a Brilliant Future," *Hear Res* 242 (2008).

Wolf, Maryanne. *Proust and the Squid: The Story and Science of the Reading Brain* (New York: HarperCollins, 2008).

Woodmansee, Martha. "The Genius and the Copyright: Economic and Legal Conditions of the Emergence of the 'Author,'" in *The Printed Word in the Eighteenth Century*, edited by Raymond Birn (Baltimore, MD: Johns Hopkins University Press, 1984).

Wortham, Jenna. "Emoji: The Very Bearable Lightness of Meaning," *Womanzine* (March 21, 2014).

Young, Roger. *How Computers Work: Processor and Main Memory* (CreateSpace Independent Publishing Platform, 2009).

Zeng, Fan-Gang. "Auditor Prostheses: Past, Present, and Future," in *Cochlear Implants: Auditory Prostheses and Electric Hearing*, edited by Fan-Gang Zeng and Richard R. Fay (New York: Springer Science and Business Media, 2013).

Index